AN INQUIRY CONCERNING
THE PRINCIPLES
OF MORALS

The Library of Liberal Arts

OSKAR PIEST, FOUNDER

AN INQUIRY
CONCERNING THE
PRINCIPLES
OF MORALS

With a Supplement: A DIALOGUE

DAVID HUME

Edited, with an introduction, by
CHARLES W. HENDEL

· ·

The Library of Liberal Arts

Macmillan Publishing Company
New York
Collier Macmillan Publishers
London

David Hume: 1711-1776

AN INQUIRY CONCERNING THE PRINCIPLES OF MORALS
was originally published in 1751

. . . .

Macmillan Publishing Company
866 Third Avenue
New York, New York 10022

First Edition
Nineteenth Printing — 1987

Library of Congress Catalog Card Number: 57-1076
ISBN 0-02-353130-4

CONTENTS

AN INQUIRY CONCERNING THE PRINCIPLES OF MORALS

INTRODUCTION

I. THE IMPORTANCE OF THE INQUIRY IN HUME'S LIFE

In 1752 "was published in London my *Inquiry Concerning Human Morals* which, in my own opinion (who ought not to judge on that subject), is of all my writings, historical, philosophical, or literary, incomparably the best. It came unnoticed and unobserved into the world." These statements were made by Hume in *My Own Life,* dated April 18, 1776.[1]

In that very short work of autobiography written only a few months before the end of his life, Hume was passing in review his entire literary career: "This narrative," he said, "shall contain little more than the history of my writings, as, indeed, almost all my life has been spent in literary pursuits and occupations." [2]

The story tells again and again of experiences similar to that here cited, that writings highly valued by the author himself were scarcely regarded at all by the reading public, sometimes not even noticed. It began with the two books, published in 1739, of the *Treatise of Human Nature,* which were far from having the success Hume had expected. The same fate awaited the third book of the *Treatise,* though Hume had tried to forestall the failure by publishing *An Abstract of a Treatise of Human Nature* which was an anonymous book review written by himself—he sought therein to draw attention to very significant "novelties" in philosophy disclosed in the first book, *On Human Understanding,* and at the same time to whet the appetite of the reader for the book that was forthcoming, treating of *Morals.* That desperate device of the youthful author (who

[1] See *My Own Life,* published with Hume's *Inquiry Concerning Human Understanding,* Liberal Arts Press edition, p. 6.
[2] *Ibid.,* p. 3.

of course does not confess in *My Own Life* to having resorted to it [3]) proving unsuccessful, Hume in his disappointment over the reception of his philosophical treatises turned to publishing volumes of short essays on morals, politics, and criticism, and these, indeed, had some effect, over the course of several years, in attracting readers to his work. Then he hopefully recast in essay form the materials of his first book of the Treatise, imparting to them the quality of literary elegance he had learned to produce in his other essays. The *Philosophical Essays Concerning Human Understanding* were then advertised as "by the author of the *Essays, Moral and Political.*" This work came out in 1748 and received scant attention.[4]

Still Hume was resolved to save from oblivion whatever he could from the youthful masterpiece and proceeded to extract from his voluminous third book the essentials of his study of morals, and this became his *Inquiry Concerning the Principles of Morals*—"unnoticed."

Hume's preoccupation with success may seem a very unphilosophical concern of a philosopher. He frankly confessed, indeed, that "love of literary fame" had been a "ruling passion." [5] But this "passion" does not seem to have affected his calm, rational judgment or to have made him trim his sails to the winds of opinion. It is apparent from his conduct that he knew the value and the originality of his philosophy and resolutely held to his objective of convincing the learned world of what he regarded

[3] See the story of the identification of Hume as the author of *An Abstract* in the Introduction to the edition by J. M. Keynes and S. Sraffa. Also Introduction to Hume's *Inquiry Concerning Human Understanding,* Liberal Arts Press edition, pp. xviiff., and the reprinting of the *Abstract* itself in that edition.

[4] On the attention paid to it by contemporaries and later posterity see Introduction, Liberal Arts Press edition, pp. xi-xvii. To avoid confusion, the *Philosophical Essays,* etc., will always be cited in the references to the book on *Human Understanding,* not using the term *Inquiry* (a later change in the title), but reserving *Inquiry* for the work we are here [that is, in the *present* work] concerned with.

[5] *My Own Life,* p. 10.

as truth and genuine discoveries. He made accommodations to the public taste in his manner of presentation, but "the arguments" which he wanted the public "to attend to" remained unimpaired, and indeed they were in some instances perfected in the rewriting, for, as stated in the *Philosophical Essays,* he sought to combine "profound inquiry with clearness, and truth with novelty." It is equally characteristic of him therefore not only to have told that the *Inquiry* was unnoticed but also to have declared his own unshaken opinion that it was incomparably the best of all his writings philosophical, historical or literary.[6]

Let us examine that judgment of the author. First, such an extremely high opinion invites, if not a comparison, at least taking note of those other writings with respect to which it was, according to Hume, beyond comparison.

Other Works and their Importance

What were those "historical, philosophical or literary works"? We have already mentioned the various essays preceding the publication of the *Inquiry,* but we should now give consideration to the other writings on which Hume reports in *My Own Life,* and incidentally reporting, too, a turn for the better in his fortunes. The *Political Discourses* came out the very year in which the *Inquiry* appeared and became his first outstanding success in the world of letters. The same year saw his appointment as Librarian of the Faculty of Advocates in Edinburgh, which afforded him the opportunity to write his *History of England,* the four volumes of which appeared from 1754 to 1761 —and this, too, brought him fame though seasoned with the notoriety of being treated as a Tory because he challenged the prevalent Whig view of the seventeenth-century revolution. It

---

[6] See Norman Kemp Smith's tribute to Hume's philosophic spirit: "The manner in which Hume reacted to his disappointment has every claim upon our respect. . . . It was himself he blamed, not the public," etc. *The Philosophy of David Hume* (London, 1941), pp. 523ff.

was, in large part, these political and historical writings that gave Hume his great reputation on the continent, and generally in the learned world of the eighteenth century.[7]

At the time of the writing of the *Inquiry* and the *Political Discourses* Hume was also engaged upon a statement of his own intellectual struggles with the question of religious belief. He had been quite concerned in his youth with the arguments for the existence and nature of God, and he had included in the *Philosophical Essays* (1748) an essay on "A Particular Providence and a Future State," but he had very much more to offer in discussion of the whole subject.[8] Nothing about this is mentioned in the autobiography, but the reason may have been the fact that in May, 1776, when he wrote his publisher William Strahan telling of "a very inoffensive piece, called *My Own Life* . . . ," the publication of the *Dialogues Concerning Natural Religion* was still in doubt.[9] The only work on the subject of religion about which Hume could then speak was the *Natural History of Religion* that came out in 1757 and was a companion piece to the strictly philosophical *Dialogues,* both of which had been written in part in 1751, at the very time when Hume was preparing his *Inquiry* and the *Political Discourses* for the press. Hume was much concerned in the very last days of his life about the unpublished *Dialogues* and desired to make certain of their posthumous publication. To that end he had entered into negotiations, first, with Adam Smith and, then, with William Strahan, a publisher, but he finally stipulated in his will that

[7] See *Hume's Political Essays,* Liberal Arts Press edition, Introduction, treating of the significance of Hume's work for Europe and America, pp. xli-lx.

[8] See *Inquiry Concerning Human Understanding,* Liberal Arts Press edition, Introduction, pp. xlvi-l, and Sect. XI, pp. 142-157. See also C. W. Hendel, *Studies in the Philosophy of Hume* (Princeton, 1925), pp. 13-19, and Chapters XI-XIII; Norman Kemp Smith, *Hume's Dialogues Concerning Natural Religion* (Oxford, 1935), especially Appendix C, pp. 110f.

[9] See Hendel, *op. cit.,* pp. 2f., and letter to William Strahan, May 3, 1776, *The Letters of David Hume,* edited by J. Y. T. Greig, II, 317f.

his nephew David Hume should see to the matter.[10] Of these *Dialogues* he wrote to Adam Smith, Aug. 15, 1776: "On revising them (which I have not done these fifteen years) I find that nothing can be more cautiously and more artfully written." It would seem from Hume's letters, too, that he counted upon the *Dialogues* eventually to serve as the answer to the common sense critics, like James Beattie, who had with so much acclaim belabored his skeptical philosophy, the philosophy of the first book of the *Treatise*. With the *Dialogues* available, posterity might render a better verdict on his philosophy than those contemporaries who had been so disturbed by his various inquiries.

What Hume himself would have said about the relative merits of the *Inquiry Concerning the Principles of Morals* and the *Dialogues Concerning Natural Religion* one can hardly gather from the record. The two works do seem comparable in this respect, however, that Hume evidently depended upon the *Dialogues* to enlighten the world as to the meaning of his philosophical skepticism, and upon the *Inquiry,* on the other hand, to reveal the positive principles of his moral philosophy.

Why Hume favored the Inquiry

One thing is clear from the story: that the years around 1752, when the *Inquiry* appeared, were Hume's *floruit*. It was a time of great productivity when Hume was at the peak of achievement. He produced within a short period those divers philosophical, historical, and literary works which he had in mind in expressing that evaluation of the *Inquiry*. Besides it he had written the *Political Discourses,* the *Dialogues* and the *Natural History of Religion,* and his *History of England.* Thereafter he devoted his time to emendations of these writings in the interest of accuracy and nicety and preparing them for the definitive edition of his collected works. In retrospect, twenty-four years

[10] See the letters to Adam Smith of May 3, Aug. 15, and Aug. 23, 1776, and to William Strahan, June 8 and June 12, 1776. Greig, *op. cit.,* II, 316-319; 323; 325f.; 334f.; Norman Kemp Smith, *op. cit.,* pp. 116f.

later, Hume seems to have envisaged 1752 as a fortunately crucial year.

The *Inquiry* was part of that whole experience of consummate achievement, and Hume thought well of all that had come to birth in that period; yet of the published works in his lifetime the *Inquiry* was singularly neglected by the public. It seems, then, as if he were the more disposed to favor this child above the others that so much enjoyed the general attention. Thus he wrote in 1753 to Sir David Dalrymple, "I must confess that I have a partiality for that work, and esteem it the most tolerable of anything that I have composed." [11] He may have been so partial, too, for another reason which Norman Kemp Smith has stressed, that Hume's first adventures in philosophy were in the moral philosophy of Francis Hutcheson. If Hume had been diverted by the skeptical discoveries concerning reasoning from his *original* interest in "moral subjects," it is understandable that when he was able to return to his first love he should have devoted the greatest care to the effective presentation of his own "principles of morals." [12]

The positive sense of that phrase in the title is significant. Hume was inquiring concerning *principles*—and the finding of them was the objective of his work. He believed, therefore, in the possibility of reaching principles in ethics as well as in

[11] *Letters*, May 3, 1753. This was written on the occasion of the second edition of the *Inquiry* which was being included with various other pieces in an edition of *Essays and Treatises*. Another letter reveals how long-enduring that "partiality" was. Writing to Abbé Le Blanc, translator of his *Political Discourses*, Nov. 5, 1755, Hume said, "I have never in my life received greater satisfaction than by the passage of M. Maupertuis' letters which you have been so good as to transmit to me. . . . I have long been a great admirer of M. Maupertuis." The passage was the report of a conversation in which a Mr. Grierson, an Irish man of letters, "tells me [Maupertuis] that there is a work of Hume even superior [to the *Discourses*] on the Principles of Morals." Greig, *op. cit.*, II, p. 226 and note.

[12] See Norman Kemp Smith, *The Philosophy of Hume*, Chap. II, "Hutcheson's Teaching and its Influence on Hume"; Chap. XXIV, "Summary and Conclusions," especially pp. 537-9; and Chap. XXV, "Concluding Comments," the final sentence p. 566: "Hume's ethics is integral to his general philosophical outlook, and stands or falls together with it."

economics and politics. Witness his words in a letter to his friend Baron Mure, to whom he declared on the eve of the American Revolution: "I am American in my principles." [13] Of course a public avowal of such convictions on that political question would not have helped many of Hume's contemporaries toward an appreciation of the constructive character of his philosophy. But a generation bred in the new British tradition and reading the works of Shaftesbury, Bishop Butler, and Hutcheson might properly be expected to discern the positive merits of this *Inquiry Concerning the Principles of Morals,* and this unhappily they had not yet done.

II. TOWARD AN UNDERSTANDING OF HUME'S MORAL PHILOSOPHY

Americans especially might take their cue today from their own forebears in the eighteenth century in making an approach to Hume's philosophy. For in 1787, when the statesmen of the new American republic were discussing for many arduous months their design of a new constitution for the United States, they alluded almost daily to various writings of Hume as well as to the monumental masterpiece of Montesquieu, the *Spirit of the Laws.* In their minds the constructive lessons and the meaning of both philosophers were much the same. From Hume's *History of England* and his "moral and political essays" (which included essays in economics) they learned about the struggles of a previous revolution in England, and how the problem of reconciling liberty and authority must be solved afresh in every generation—and they were impressed, too, by his constant emphasis on balance and limitation of power. On this latter score Montesquieu's lessons were exactly the same, and he too celebrated English liberty and institutions and customs.

---

[13] See letter to Baron Mure, Oct. 27, 1775, in Greig, *op. cit.,* II, 303: quoted in *Hume's Political Essays,* Liberal Arts Press edition, Introduction, p. lx.

Montesquieu adduced a great body of historical material from the European past and from the records of peoples all over the globe to demonstrate that there are many other factors besides the laws of the State that "govern" human affairs, and that out of these many ruling principles in the life of man in society, a "spirit of the laws," indeed, a "spirit of the nation" emerges which exercises a real, though often invisible, control over political power and thus effectively limits its authority.[1]

An Instructive Affinity of Hume and Montesquieu

When the *Spirit of the Laws* came out, Hume welcomed it and congratulated Montesquieu. The year of its appearance happened to be 1748, the very year when Hume's first rewriting of the *Treatise* was published, the *Philosophical Essays Concerning Human Understanding,* and Hume had the gratification of receiving a witty letter of appreciation of his own work. The two authors thus exchanged mutual compliments on their respective performances—and this occurred, be it noted, before Hume's *Political Discourses* which were to win such acclaim in France four years later. Such instant sympathy and mutual understanding between them testify to an affinity and a deep-lying agreement in the trend of their thinking. We might, therefore, reasonably expect to derive some light on Hume's moral philosophy from his perceptive and congenial contemporary.

The Scope of the Subject of Morals

Montesquieu had, of course, made his laudatory comments in 1748 only on the *Philosophical Essays*. But even those essays concerning understanding contained hints of the subsequent study of morals. Indeed, the opening discussion in the earlier

[1] See *Hume's Political Essays,* Liberal Arts Press edition, Introduction, especially pp. xii-xxvii, xli-l, and Sect. V, pp. l-lx; also the essay in English "To Montesquieu: Acknowledgment and Appreciation" by C. W. Hendel for the bicentenary issue, devoted to Montesquieu, of the *Revue internationale de philosophie* (Brussels, October 1955), pp. 1-20, especially pp. 11-14; 16-18.

work seems now much more appropriate to the later one. "Moral Philosophy, or the Science of Man" is divided into "two species" according to the two chief aspects of human nature. "Man is a reasonable being; and as such, receives from science his proper food and nourishment. . . . Man is a sociable, no less than a reasonable being. . . . Man is also an active being." Man as sociable and active is the special concern of "moralists" who "search for some common principle to explain the diversity of our moral sentiments and who have, indeed, every right to expect" to find some general principles. All the social and active phenomena of human nature which are the concern at once of the moralist and of the moral philosopher are covered by the blanket term "morals."

The first step, then, toward understanding Hume's *Inquiry* is to gain an adequate idea of the meaning of "morals" as he used the term, and as it was used and understood by thinkers like Montesquieu who were also concerning themselves with humanistic science.

Montesquieu's View of the Role of Morals in Society

In a chapter of the *Spirit of the Laws* which is devoted to the topic of "the corruption of the principles of all governments" Montesquieu was making some animadversions regarding the parlous state of European society when he pointed out this ray of hope, saying: "By and large, the peoples of Europe are still governed by morals." [2] In general he held that the ultimate governance in the life of any people is that of "the spirit of the laws" which is at the same time "the spirit of the nation." The laws are but one of a number of other regulative factors; and these other factors may be physical causes as well as moral ones, climate as well as religion and morality and the examples of greatness or merit from the past that continue to sway the minds and hearts of a later generation. Though Montesquieu's attention to such things as climate often misled readers into thinking that he made physical causes the *determining* ones—as Marx

[2] *Spirit of the Laws,* Book VIII, Chap. 8.

and his followers were later to do—Montesquieu himself insisted that the moral factors were often the most potent, and in the passage quoted he was saying that what was saving Europe from corruption was the general morality of the peoples of the continent. Here, then, was a most important subject of study for a philosopher concerned with human nature and society in that day and age. Montesquieu had already produced his great work concerning the "principles of government" and on the whole complex of institutions that constituted a nation's system of life; but there was this other work still to be accomplished—begun by Hume as a part of his *Treatise* and to be done over again as an inquiry "concerning the principles of morals."

Hume's Particular Conviction Regarding Human Nature as an Appropriate Object of a Humanistic Science

After thus linking Hume's inquiry with the work of Montesquieu as a companion enterprise, we must note, however, an important difference of interest between the two philosophers even though they were so congenial in their way of thinking. Montesquieu's investigations ranged over the whole globe and the field of history with a view to the aspect of diversity—"infinite diversity," he called it—of the forms of government, the customs, the manners, the morals, the traditions, etc.   Montesquieu took pains to delineate the individual national "spirit" for each society in the light of the historical evidence available. Hume himself was not without this interest and he had produced independently, and the very year of the appearance of the *Spirit of the Laws*, a striking essay, "Of National Characters." [3] Hume also appreciated the important fact of variety in the ways of human life. But Hume also had that philosophical penchant described by himself, of searching for *common principles*. In fact, he declares himself very strongly in the *Inquiry*, for he calls them "universal principles." Underlying such an expectation was his conviction that there is a "human nature" which is

[3] Published first in the 1748 edition of the *Essays Moral and Political*. See *Essays*, Green and Grose edition, I, 244ff.

fundamentally one and the same in all people. The diversities are granted but they are viewed as the resultant of the conjunction of the nature of man with the different circumstances in which men happen to live and act.[4]

What the Concept of Morals Comprises for Hume in this Inquiry

Morals are phenomena of the life of man as a "sociable" and "active" being. They are the morals of the society or nation and of the members thereof individually, as "persons." They are regulative of the life in society, but they do not govern as law and government do, for they are internal powers or "virtues" which work from within. Under "morals," too, must be classed any esteemed qualities which are treasured from the past of a people and which are regarded as forming a part of "personal merit." It may even be that there are meritorious qualities which are distinct from those regarded as "virtues." Thus morals comprise much more than merely rules of social behavior, for they include virtues and valuable dispositions *in the persons themselves,* in their minds and characters. And always one must remember that morals involve distinctions between virtue and vice, right and wrong, merit and, on the other hand, that which we regard with "contempt" (to use Hume's own strong term). The subject of "morals" contains all these things, moral distinctions, virtues and vices, valued qualities of persons, and other qualities negatively regarded, and rules or standards of conduct. This whole complex of things needs to be analyzed and investigated so that we may "reach the foundation of ethics and find . . . universal principles . . ." (Section I).

---

[4] See *A Dialogue,* which was published with the *Inquiry.* In it Hume follows the style of the famous *Persian Letters* of Montesquieu, and, while paying attention to the "national character," affirmed his conviction regarding "first principles" underlying all diversities. The *Dialogue* is reprinted in the present edition, pp. 141ff.

Hume's Conception of Ethics Similar to that of Ancient Ethics

A certain affinity is to be noted between Hume's view of both the nature of morality and ethics and classical views. Selby-Bigge, who edited Hume's *Treatise* and the *Inquiries,* paid a tribute in his Introduction to *The British Moralists* which applies more significantly to Hume than to any other British writer on moral philosophy of that period. He is describing—

> the chief characteristic of the British school of moralists . . . . They concentrate their attention on the phenomena of the normal moral consciousness in a cool and impartial manner which reminds us of Aristotle . . . . It is generally said that British ethics are psychological, and though that epithet is to be avoided on account of the controversies with which it is associated, it may fairly be said that the chief achievements of the eighteenth-century moralists were in the psychology of ethics. They thought seriously about the content . . . of plain men's moral judgments and their natural and legitimate implications, and there is perhaps no body of ethical writing which within its own sphere can compare for originality and sincerity with the work of this period.[5]

Selby-Bigge's reference to Aristotle is worth heeding, with a little further explanation. It is no accidental coincidence that Hume should recall the "cool and impartial manner" of Aristotle. *My Own Life* tells how versed he was in classical literature. There is other evidence of it from the quotations he readily introduces in his personal letters as well as throughout his writings. In telling, for instance, about his reading for the essay "Of the Populousness of Ancient Nations," he claims to have studied all the Greek and Latin authors for his data. But there are passages where Hume expressly identifies his own philosophy with "the principles of the ancients" (Section I). It is very interesting to see, moreover, that in the *Abstract of a Treatise of Human Nature* (1740) Hume, after summing up the part on Understanding already published, goes on to indicate the

5 *The British Moralists* (Oxford, 1897), I, xviif.

subject matter of the forthcoming work on *Morals* when he declares that "morals and criticism regard our tastes and sentiments." [6] The same phrase recurs early in Section I of the *Inquiry:* "the ancient philosophers, though they often affirm that virtue is nothing but conformity to reason, yet, in general, seem to consider morals as deriving their existence from taste and sentiment."

This view could with some plausibility be attributed to Aristotle. For him virtue certainly depended upon reason but it does not originate from reason. Virtue is a habit of man's nature, a habit or disposition to action "in the mean." The genesis of virtue, as described in the *Nicomachean Ethics*, is from social custom in the community. This was partly in criticism of the Socrates of Plato's account who had so much disparaged sophistic convention and custom and insisted upon reason and nature. And likewise in criticism of the *Republic* and too much planning of ideal states by philosophers. Aristotle stressed this point about law, for instance, that "a law derives all its strength from custom and this requires a long time to establish." [7] In both cases, in morals and in politics, Aristotle placed first the established ways of life in society that channel the impulses and feelings of the members of the society and thus set their primary goals of action and their preferences and values. The function of reason is not originative, though we must recognize that for Aristotle reason had a "crowning," supervening role in the end.

So the story of morals in the ancient manner might read as follows: Human beings grow up in a society that has established ways which introduce them to the virtues they should practice and deter them from the faults or the excesses they should avoid. The norms of human behavior are thus not reached by each individual alone simply following the guidance of his own nature and his reason. Men learn to know by doing and by the

[6] See the *Abstract* in the Liberal Arts Press edition of *An Inquiry Concerning Human Understanding*, p. 184.

[7] *Politics*, Bk. II 1269a; translation by William Ellis ("Everyman's Library").

practice of a morality that is the established outcome of social experience and evaluations. Thus ethics is properly a study of the valued "characters" of human excellence, the virtues or the habits and dispositions to action. And Aristotle himself classifies them under two general rubrics, "justice and nobility."

We are not drawing an exact parallel between Hume and Aristotle, but cannot fail to note certain affinities of thought and sometimes even of language. The first thing Hume insists upon against any skepticism in morality is "the reality of moral distinctions." They are real and they are important. They are not merely matters of convention or products of education. They originate naturally in the life of man in society. It is not accidental or arbitrary that men find certain qualities in themselves and other persons "estimable" and certain others "odious." And it is significant that they evaluate not only particular acts but also the character of the men themselves who perform them. Moral distinctions have reference ultimately to "personal merit" and both the interest in the merit or quality of excellence in man and the sources of such judgments regarding "character and action," or "the origin of morals," are the subject of investigation in this study of morals.

The Concern with Personal Merit

Throughout all his philosophical writings Hume was concerned with human nature. In this *Inquiry* he envisaged the nature of man in the aspect of moral character. He preferred to use the term "personal merit." This is a "complication of qualities," no simple entity. The qualities are "mental qualities" in the form of an "attitude" or a "habit, or sentiment, or faculty" of the person (Section I).

The following observation of Rachel Kydd in *Reason and Conduct in Hume's Treatise* is pertinent and instructive: "Frequently, in the *Treatise* and even more often in the *Inquiry*, Hume advances the argument that it is not, strictly speaking, actions that we approve of but the character-dispositions which give rise to them" (Appendix p. 190).

On Language and Ethics

Other writers on ethics today who have more or less affiliated themselves with Hume have seen fit to restrict the proper study of ethics as a philosophical discipline to investigation in the language and logic of statements about moral phenomena. Hume himself does treat of language, but it is instrumental, as a means of diagnosis. It is used in order to detect those *moral qualities* marked "in common life" as possessing merit or otherwise. "The very nature of language guides us almost infallibly in forming a judgment of this nature. . . ." Expressions of "esteem and affection or of hatred and contempt" or "of praise or blame" are found in all languages and they pertain to qualities of persons, that is, qualities of "habit or sentiment or faculty." But lest his concern with language here and elsewhere in the *Inquiry* be misunderstood, Hume discusses "verbal disputes" in his fourth and final *Appendix* where he begins: "Nothing is more usual than for philosophers to encroach upon the province of grammarians, and to engage in disputes of words, while they imagine that they are handling controversies of the deepest importance and concern." Then, explaining his own procedure or "very simple method," "I . . . proposed simply to collect a list of those mental qualities which are the object of love or esteem, and form a part of personal merit, and on the other hand a catalogue of those qualities which are the object of censure or reproach, and which detract from the character of the person possessed of them." Hume thus dealt with language only in the primary stage of his research, as a means by which to identify those particular qualities that have a moral character. His inquiry proceeds then beyond that stage to the analysis of the nature and ground of the moral judgments recorded in language.

Hume dismisses the subject of language with this declaration: "A moral, philosophical discourse needs not enter into all these caprices of language." This need not, however, abash the present-day student of ethics, for one might contend that the preoccupation with language nowadays is precisely intended to avoid disputes over these "caprices" and instead to find the common sense of language. It may be further asserted that more may be discoverable today in the light of our techniques of analysis than Hume could anticipate with all the acuteness of his genius; and surely that philosopher who was professing to be guided by experience would be the last to deny the possibility of novel insights and therefore the need of further inquiry into the usage of language. Nevertheless, as *students of Hume,* we are under the scholar's obligation not to attribute to him interests and theories of ethics which he manifestly did not have. Hume has his eye on the *phenomenon of character and personal merit,* and how men actually *judge* of these things. The main part of his investigation advances far beyond any study of language and usage. He would not be content as a philosopher until he could "reach the foundation of ethics and find those universal principles from which all censure or approbation is ultimately derived." And he believed that he had found results of positive value for mankind.

The All-Important Distinction Between Judgments of Value and Judgments of Fact as Drawn by Hume

The consequence of what we have been saying is that Hume was *not* skeptical in this work of moral philosophy. Many have been confused by the striking difference between this *Inquiry* and the previous work on human understanding. There has, in fact, been a quite widespread failure to realize the importance for Hume, as a truth about the moral phenomena, of the real and necessary *distinction* between the judgment of value and conclusions of the understanding regarding truth and matters of fact and existence. This distinction Hume had pointed out early in his *Abstract* and it remained fundamental in his moral philosophy as perfected in this *Inquiry*.

We cannot do better than to look at the first statement in the *Abstract* of the important difference between "logic" and "ethics" which to us today seems a very paradoxical sort of opposition to set up. In that book review of the first part of his *Treatise* concerned with the understanding he informed the public: "The author has finished what regards logic" and then, toward the end of the *Abstract,* "I shall conclude the logics of this author." Now the aim of logic, he had said, is "to explain the principles and operations of our reasoning faculty," which means that the *whole* of the book on the understanding is a "logic." "By all that has been said the reader will easily perceive that the philosophy contained in this book is very skeptical and tends to give us a notion of the imperfections and narrow limits of human understanding." Yet, in spite of the skepticism, Hume announces the forthcoming work which is still a part of his *Treatise of Human Nature* but dealing with matters which "regard our tastes and sentiment," [8] the book *Of Morals.* Thus the skeptical "limits of human understanding" do not exclude such other moral possibilities of Human Nature.

Consider now the philosophy of the later *Inquiry Concerning Human Understanding,* the revision of Book I of the *Treatise.* The achievement of Hume as a "logician" (in his own terms) was to have defined clearly and precisely the factors involved in those operations of the mind which yield "knowledge and probability," respectively. "Respectively," we must say, because Hume distinguishes between "truth" that can be demonstrated and the "relations of ideas," and "belief" in "matters of fact and existence" which is the result of inference based on past experience. The interesting feature about belief is that though it has only the value of probability in logic it is indispensable for action in the world. On the strength of it men conduct their daily affairs and even embark on the adventures of science. Belief is one thing, then, and truth another. The two operations of the "reasoning faculty" are distinct and not reducible to each other.[9]

---

[8] See the *Abstract* in the Liberal Arts Press edition of *An Inquiry Concerning Human Understanding,* quotations from pp. 184, 193, 194; see also the Introduction, p. xxi.

[9] Cf. Liberal Arts Press edition, Introduction, pp. xxiv–xxxii.

Morals are "phenomena of human life" (*Inquiry Concerning Morals*, Section VI), or of man as a "sociable" and "active" being. They are *distinct* from any conclusions of reasoning, just as "beliefs" themselves are from demonstrative truths. Like beliefs, moreover, they are related to the active life. But they differ from active belief in that they do not assert simply matters of fact or existence but the *value* of the character of persons and their actions. This appraisal or evaluation is a quite distinctive phenomenon of human nature and it must be understood in its own right and never reduced to an affair of reason and knowledge. The prior exposure of "limits of human understanding" is thus a possible opportunity for some novel disclosures concerning the nature of human morals.

Hutcheson and Hume

The reference of morality and moral judgments to sentiment was in itself nothing new or original with Hume. Francis Hutcheson had previously argued for the foundation of morals on sentiment, and Hume followed Hutcheson and had great respect for his philosophy.[10] Yet one can observe a reluctance on Hume's part to take sides in any battle waged by the protagonists of REASON and SENTIMENT (so Hume prints the opposed watchwords), for "disputes with men pertinaciously obstinate in their principles" are apt to become futile and forced. Hume himself hints "that *reason* and *sentiment* concur in almost all moral determinations and conclusions," but that will be a *finding*, not a foreordained conclusion. For "men are now cured of their passion for hypotheses and systems . . . and will hearken to no arguments but those that are derived from experience" (Section I).

But we must start aright by observing this necessary distinction which we do actually experience between our moral determinations and the determinations of our reason or under-

[10] See the extensive and detailed discussion of Hume's relation to Hutcheson in Norman Kemp Smith, *The Philosophy of Hume*, Chap. II and elsewhere; consult the Index.

standing. The besetting vice of "modern inquirers" has been that they "have commonly endeavored to account for these (moral) distinctions by metaphysical reasonings and by deductions from the most abstract principles of the understanding." "As this is a question of fact, not of abstract science, we can only expect success by following the experimental method and deducing general maxims from a comparison of particular instances" (Section I).

There must, then, be fresh exploration of these moral phenomena of human life which are not on any account to be confused with the phenomena of human understanding. Moral judgments or valuations are distinct from conclusions of reasoning. Values are not the same sort of thing in the actual life of man as established facts. Their "source" or what they are derived from does not appear, in the first instance, to be reason but sentiment. But reason may have a role—and what it is must be ascertained by inquiry exactly as the foundation of ethics is to be learned. And there is hope, as Hume has said, of some "success."

Hume's Critics Misrepresent His Position on Moral Skepticism

This point of view from which Hume started was precisely what his contemporary critics were unable to appreciate—such men as James Beattie, Thomas Reid, and other self-styled "common sense" philosophers who managed only too successfully to misrepresent Hume in his lifetime.[11] The careful distinction Hume made between "decisions of morality" and "conclusions" of the understanding was interpreted as teaching a devastating moral skepticism. Such a judgment could easily estop any mind from following Hume in his *Inquiry*. And in fact it has taken a long time since then for readers to appreciate the significance of his particular way of making that essential distinction between the judgment of value and the judgment of fact when he insisted upon the difference between "sentiment" and "reason" in the operations of human nature. To the very end Hume had

11 See Norman Kemp Smith, *op. cit.*, pp. 520ff.

to be fighting for the recognition of that distinction, let alone developing any theory of their relationship, as can be seen in the predominant interest of his first Appendix, "Of Moral Sentiment." Today Hume's great discernment is at last being appreciated.[12]

III. THE ANALYSIS OF MORALS: PRINCIPAL POINTS

The first stage of inquiry is the identification of those qualities of mind or character which are *morally* judged by men "in common life." The mark by which we know them is the language we use in reference to them: they are "estimable" or "blamable," and more strongly still, "admirable" or "odious." Indeed there is a great variety of alternative "epithets" which range from approval or disapproval to "approbation" or "censure," and these latter forms carry with them a sense of some appropriate action to follow which will favor or condemn the "qualities of men" that are thus appraised. The connection of the judgment with *action* by the person who judges, and even by the society, is an essential point about the nature of a moral judgment.

1. THE EXPERIMENTAL METHOD

There is an observation to make at this juncture which will be pertinent on several subsequent occasions in study of the *Inquiry*. We ought always to remember that Hume's "experimental method" requires "deducing general maxims from a comparison of particular instances." Thus it is a mistake in the present case to ignore the *variety and degrees* of the expression of esteem or its opposite, or else to fix on some one of them, let us say, approval or disapproval, and *reduce* all the others to it. The single expression may then be taken as a "definition" and the others to be merely literary synonyms. But to follow Hume's

12 See Norman Kemp Smith, *op. cit.*, pp. 196-200; and R. M. Hare, *The Language of Morals* (Oxford, 1952), pp. 44f.

method one needs to keep all the "particular instances" in mind in order to understand the "general maxim." When Hume actually does give a "definition of virtue," very late in the book (where it should be according to empirical principles), he expects the reader to think of the various denotations which have been previously given in the discussion. Then he can safely say, perhaps: "It is the nature and, indeed, the definition of virtue, that it is *a quality of the mind agreeable to or approved of by everyone who considers or contemplates it*" (Section VIII, note to the heading). Read apart from the whole context of preceding inquiry and discussions, the "approval" seems very little different from an "agreeable" sentiment of pleasure. Later, in Appendix I, treating "Of Moral Sentiment," Hume ventures again to define virtue by reference to "the pleasing sentiment of approbation" which is more clearly active in tendency.[1] But in the light of the theories of approval and disapproval that have since sprung from these belated definitions, Hume might have been wiser, perhaps, to dispense with them altogether as he had *at one time planned to do.* Thus in Editions G to N (according to the classification in the Green and Grose edition) he declared "it will scarce be possible for us . . . to proceed . . . by beginning with exact definitions of virtue and vice which are the objects of our present inquiry." After edition N, however, Hume *substituted* for the passage containing that disclaimer of exact definition the extensive passage which we have considered, directing our attention to the "complication of mental qualities" which constitute "personal merit" and telling of his "method" of procedure. The change removed a possible safeguard against readers taking what he said in the eventual "definition" as an "exact definition" and then "deducing" things from it, which is quite contrary to the empirical method

---

[1] Rachel Kydd observes, "To say that a thing is an object of approval is to say something essentially different from 'I' or 'many people,' 'the majority,' or even 'everybody' have a feeling of liking for it, or are inclined to react to it with the expression 'Hurray.'

"Hume distinguishes approval from mere liking on two grounds . . . ," (*Reason and Conduct in Hume's Treatise*, Oxford, 1946), p. 170.

that Hume desired to follow. It is well, therefore, to keep the "complications" in view, and all the varied denotations of the language, for they may in their variety and complexity be alone adequate to that human experience which Hume is endeavoring faithfully to interpret.

The second stage of the inquiry, after having obtained the "collection" or "catalogue" of the qualities which are the objects of moral judgment, is that of scientific reasoning. The purpose then is to "discover the circumstances on both sides [the 'estimable' or the 'blamable'] which are common to these qualities." When these are known we shall have "those universal principles from which all censure or approbation is ultimately derived."

2. UTILITY AND THE SOCIAL VIRTUES

Morals are so intimately involved with life in society that it is natural to examine first the obviously "social virtues," such as benevolence, the virtue much celebrated by moralists in the eighteenth century, and justice, the most ancient of virtues.

The first discovery is that "there is one circumstance which never fails to be amply insisted on, namely, the happiness and satisfaction derived to society from his [the beneficent man's] intercourse and good offices" (Sect. II, Pt. II). This is generalized shortly, and with the addition of a new phrase: "In all determinations of morality, this circumstance of public utility is ever principally in view; . . ." At least "a *part* of their merit [that of the benevolent 'character and disposition'] we ought to ascribe to their utility."

Justice is Founded on Public Utility

Public utility is *always* a consideration when we express our moral approbation of any act or trait of benevolence, but it may not be the sole ground for our moral judgment. In the case of justice, however, it appears to be "the sole foundation of its merit." This is a more "curious and important" fact, worthy of some study.

An examination of the various kinds of justice discloses that they all "depend entirely on the particular state and condition in which men are placed, and owe their origin and existence to that *utility* which results to the public from their strict and regular observance . . . hence arises its [justice's] merit and moral obligation." Study of the laws concerning property, for instance, shows that an effort is constantly being made to find rules of its use and ownership "which are, on the whole, most *useful and beneficial*" and "by which the general *interest* of mankind is so much promoted" (Sect. III, Part I). The "interests of society" are ever the chief object in view when any decisions must be made as to justice.

Is it not a sufficient ground or "foundation" for the "duty" of justice "to observe that human society or even human nature could not subsist without the establishment of it." Justice quite "evidently tends to promote public utility and to support civil society," and it is precisely through "reflecting on that tendency" (Section III, Part II) that men have come to attribute merit to its general observance.

In this account of the "origin and nature" of justice Hume has been cautiously steering between several old theories and metaphysical controversies which could readily sidetrack the progress of empirical inquiry. One theory was rationalistic, that justice is founded on reason, and even the admired and "illustrious" Montesquieu is criticized, in passing, for still adhering to it in his definition of law or right as "founded on certain *rapports* or relations, which is a system that, in my opinion, never will be reconciled with true philosophy." Another theory was that of a natural or innate instinct of justice; a third, the rather prevalent theory akin to the sophistic view criticized in ancient days by Socrates, that justice is nothing but a matter of convention, that is, of what men are used to doing in their social relationships, and further the theory added that men are made accustomed to the conventional justice by the "artifice" of education (today we could render "education" with the term "indoctrination"). One consideration in the minds of those who had based justice on either reason or nature was to strengthen the duty or obligation to perform justly, since it really could not be evaded without flying in the face of the absolute necessity of things. In contrast, Hume was nearer the view of those who envisaged justice as some kind of convention or agreement and as being adaptable to the actual conditions of life in a given society, but he still held aloof from that conventional position. He admitted here that some "doubt" might be felt about his own proposal precisely because there is the obvious "influence of education and acquired habits." The doubt is whether there really is such "reflection," which his own theory required, upon the ultimate utility of actions or dispositions. It is very true, he admits, that "we are not, in every instance, conscious of any immediate reflection on the pernicious consequences of it [injustice]," for we "are apt much to continue mechanically, without recalling on every occasion the reflections which first determined us." Nevertheless, "even in common life"—not merely in the abstract world of the philosopher's solitary study —"we have every moment recourse to the principle of public utility, and ask, 'What must become of the world if such practices prevail?' 'How could society subsist under such disorders?' "

Hume wanted to keep the reader's attention upon this conception of utility and not permit him to be lured away to "speculative" issues. Nevertheless he recognized the necessity of dealing with these questions, for not to do so is to leave the honest inquirer doubtful of the adequacy of the discussion. Hence, it would seem, Hume devoted Appendix III to "Some Further Considerations with Regard to Justice."

A Resemblance to Kant

We may be permitted, however, to make our own independent observations upon the apparent similarity of this maxim which, Hume suggests, is ever in our mind—"What must become of the world, if such practices prevail?"—with Kant's first formula for the categorical imperative. The difference between the two ethics at this point appears only to be that as to the authority or commanding power of reason and the absoluteness of the consequent obligation. It is interesting to note, therefore, how John Dewey sought to effect a rapprochement of such an empirical ethic and the Kantian transcendental ethics, using the image of the moral man imaginatively going through a dramatic rehearsal in seeing what would happen in a world with or without the duty in question.[2]

The Virtues and Obligations of Men in Political Society

It is a truth of experience and history that human society cannot subsist without a "civil government," to use Locke's expression. Morals and the virtue of justice are indeed the prime essentials of existence, but the laws of society need further to be upheld and applied through the agencies of "political society." In treating of this subject Hume was drawing upon what was originally the third book of the *Treatise* that also supplied some materials for his *Political Discourses* which, it will be remembered, were produced the same year as the *Inquiry,* 1752, so that they may perhaps be considered as a companion work or supplement to it.[3] The point of chief interest in the *Inquiry* is that society in its political form only arises because of its utility, "the advantage it procures to society," and in particular that of "preserving peace and order among mankind," and, Hume adds in Appendix III, securing also the rights of property. It follows from this view of the utility of government that whatever conduct on the part of men is necessary or useful toward the proper performance of the function of government is also regarded with *moral* approbation. Hence the virtue of "allegiance" or "fidelity" to the State and its government. It is worth noting, incidentally, that Montesquieu in the *Spirit of the Laws* had made a great point about such "political virtue," so that it was very much in the public mind at that time, which may account, in part at least, for the *importance* Hume assigned

[2] See Dewey and Tufts, *Ethics,* XVI, 323f., "Deliberation as Dramatic Rehearsal" (New York, 1908).

[3] See *Hume's Political Essays,* Liberal Arts Press edition, Introduction.

it, placing it alongside of the virtues of benevolence and justice.

What happens in the relations among political societies themselves is instructive, too, for it provides valuable confirmation of this theory of utility. The "laws of nations" are rules useful in the "intercourse" of the nations; but they are not so obligatory as the laws of civil society. Now Hume is far indeed from being Machiavellian, for he holds that "alliances and treaties . . . would only be so much waste of parchment if they were not found by experience to have *some* influence and authority." Some authority, but not the *degree* of it found within the civil state. Thus we learn that "the *moral obligation* holds proportion with the *usefulness*." The usefulness is the key to interpretation in all these matters.

This instance, and several others cited, now reveal in general that the virtues and duties of men always have an essential relation to the existing human situation: "the public convenience [that is, utility] which regulates morals is inviolably established in the nature of man and of the world in which he lives." Thus the "reflection" which men make more or less consciously upon the tendency of actions or habits to be useful to society presupposes a relevant knowledge of the world in which men actually are living. Two acts of mind appear to be involved: knowing the facts of the situation, which is an operation of the understanding in Hume's sense, and the reflective estimate of the utility. More will have to be said about this later under "Questions and Criticisms."

Another pregnant remark here is the very last sentence of Section IV: "Common interest and utility beget infallibly a standard of right and wrong among the parties concerned." Hume does not pursue the questions which this statement naturally raises. The pertinence of the remark in this place, however, where the subject is the particular virtues and duties of men in *political* society, is worthy of some short comment. In general, actions in that context are judged right or wrong by reference to the observance or the infraction, as the case might be, of the laws of the State and its government. For Hobbes such conformity to law was the sole criterion alike of justice and of moral right or wrong, for he rejected any prior justice by which the laws of the State might be condemned. Morals, then, are defined by reference to laws, and the laws by reference to the "command" of the sovereign. Apparently Hume agrees that there is *no a priori rule* of justice and that right and wrong do come into being, as it were, from something antecedent to them in human experience. It is certainly *not* the case, however, that they are derived from political law, nor is it true that the law is the creature of a sovereign's reason and will. Instead, "common interest and utility beget" the standard—and "beget infallibly." Nothing is said about the sovereign Prince in this affair, and in this respect Hume agrees with Montesquieu that we are dealing with a social and moral phenomenon quite beyond the measures of political authority. In fact, we confront here, in "common interest and utility," both the source of all morals and the *raison d'être* of political society. How is this possible, this authority, so to speak, of *utility* in the life of mankind?

Thus the inquiry moves to the subject of Section V, "Why Utility Pleases." Let us put the question, however, in another way: what gives utility such a purchase on the human mind that it can affect our attitude toward persons and their behavior, produce peculiar reactions in us of sentiment, such as esteem or contempt, and even *move* us to act ourselves in accordance with our moral sentiments of approbation and disapprobation, or, in other words, with our moral judgments? That is what Hume is asking after his study of the social virtues and their corresponding duties or obligations. The crucial question is why utility has such significant effects in human life.

3. The Principle of Utility

But first we should realize what utility is through a study of its various denotations. The remark made earlier about Hume's "experimental method" of reaching principles by "comparison of particular instances" is again pertinent: it is well to recall to mind at least a number of the particular cases where the meaning of utility applies and thus get the "general" meaning. The varying language is, once again, essential, because it indicates those *different* particular examples which enable us to "deduce" or "induce" a general principle, the principle of utility. A brief review gives the following instances: utility is identified with "the tendency to promote the interests of our species," with "salutary consequences," with "the order of society, the harmony of families, the mutual support of friends" (Section II). It is found in that special kind of "convenience and advantage" which political government provides, namely "preserving peace and order" and securing property (Section IV). Usefulness is discerned in the "tendency to serve any person possessed of the particular qualities" (Section VI). In sum, utility is "everything that contributes to the happiness of society" (Conclusion, Section IX). Let us first attend to the expression "contributes" and to the other similar ones, such as promoting the interests of society, salutary consequences, order, harmony, mutual support, convenience, advantage. Utility is exhibited in all these instances and can only be appreciated in these particulars which constitute far more definite and concrete evidence than anything we have concerning "the happiness of society." For, as Aristotle had said, everyone has a vague idea of happiness standing for the whole good of life, whatever that is, but what one *means* by it depends on the kind of life he has had and what *particular things* in it he has come to cherish or prefer. On the other hand, utility is something we have experience of and can quite concretely determine "in common life." There is a special reason, moreover, why Hume should have thus regarded utility as a practical principle from which to derive morals. He was concurrently doing pioneering work in economics. Among his "Moral and Political Essays" were a number of studies of economics which had considerable originality. Adam Smith actually stood in the position of a pupil with respect to Hume, a pupil and a very dear friend.[4] Smith

---

4 See the letters to Adam Smith in Greig, *op. cit.* When the *Theory of the Moral Sentiments* appeared, Hume wrote Smith, "I am very well acquainted with Bourke [Edmund Burke], who was much taken with your book," and

was professor of moral philosophy and author of *The Theory of Moral Sentiments* as well as of *The Wealth of Nations*. Now in the economic life, according to both Hume and Adam Smith, one has daily experience of the fact that the utility and the relative values of goods are both determinable *without* any "hedonistic calculus," as it was to be later described, by which one might be supposed to assign the values of things according to the balance of pleasure and pain. The balance is determined rather by the exchange in the markets of commerce. There are prices, rents, interest, labor costs that are established publicly in some kind of evaluative relation with each other. Utility is thus a ponderable quality and capable of being decided without the aid of any philosopher's inner criteria for determining relative degrees of pleasure and pain. Utility is then a *real* foundation for those moral distinctions which arise whenever the interests of *society or the public* are in concern rather than the *private* interests of individuals.

Is Hume a Utilitarian?

A question cannot fail to have occurred to the reader long before this, namely, whether or not Hume should be called a "utilitarian." Surely a philosopher who envisages the "principle of utility" as the foundation of morals and the "social virtues" and duties would seem clearly to be a utilitarian in ethics. It may even seem strange indeed that Hume did not actually go on to the "greatest happiness principle," linking this inseparably with the principle of utility, as John Stuart Mill was to do a century later. It is true that Hume says at the very beginning of Section 11, Part II, "in displaying the praises of any humane, beneficent man, there is one circumstance which never fails to be amply insisted on, namely, the happiness and satisfaction derived to society . . ." And we quoted a passage from Section V, too, about the "happiness of society." Nonethe-

---

"I wish you had more particularly and fully proved that all kinds of sympathy are necessarily agreeable. This is the hinge of your system." To Adam Smith, July 28, 1759.

less the trend of Hume's thinking is in precisely the *reverse* direction, from the subjective to the objective conditions. Hume mentions happiness and then devotes all his attention to *utility* which is something that is quite objectively determined in practice. Moreover, we shall see, when Hume really does go beyond the principle of utility to some more ultimate or supreme principle, it is not to happiness as the supreme principle but "humanity." And this ultimate concern with "humanity," with the distinctively human quality of man and his life must be recognized as fully characteristic of Hume. He is not trafficking simply with that subjective pleasurable state of being which people generally think of as happiness. And here the ethics of Hume is again in perfect accord with "the principles of the ancients," and with Aristotle especially, as was noted earlier. Hume's affinities remain to the end with the old Greek and Latin writers and not with modern hedonists even if the later ones among them declare for a "universal hedonism." In Hume's own time, and shortly before he developed his ethics, Bishop Joseph Butler had already challenged in his "Sermons on Human Nature," and very successfully at that, the assumption that the object and motivation of all voluntary action is the enjoyment of pleasure. Butler substituted for such an oversimplified and narrow conception the endeavor of man's whole being to realize his own nature. And Hume had openly affiliated himself quite early in his career with Butler's moral philosophy [5] as well as Hutcheson's. But if we nowadays desire to assimilate Hume's philosophy to anything nearer our own time, it is a better choice to select either John Dewey or, strange as it may seem, Hegel rather than the author of *Utilitarianism*.[6]

[5] See *Abstract of the Treatise*, p. 184. For Butler, *Sermons Preached in the Rolls Chapel*, see Liberal Arts Press edition, *Five Sermons* (LLA 21).

[6] Compare with Hume's conception of "public utility," for example, Hegel's treatment of economics in the chapter on "Civil Society" in *The Philosophy of Right*.

4. The Principles of "Humanity" and "Social Sympathy in Human Nature"

Returning, after these preliminaries concerning utility, to the question posed, "Why Utility Pleases," we may seem to find in that title itself a contradiction of the interpretation of Hume which has just been proposed, namely, that he is not referring beyond the principle of utility to "the principle of happiness" in the sense of a pleasurable state of being. We must wrestle, therefore, with this topic of the place of pleasure, which is of course an ancient question in ethics.

The Question of Pleasure

Hume actually speaks very rarely of pleasure in the abstract. "Usefulness is agreeable . . ." he says, and "the very aspect of happiness, joy, prosperity, gives pleasure." There is a "pleasing sympathy"; "a sympathetic movement of pleasure or uneasiness" (Section V). Pleasure is experienced in all these contexts but it is only as an *attendant* circumstance. And what Hume is inquiring into is *why* utility *moves* men to feel and express themselves morally with respect to human character and actions. Thus if we look again at the phrase of the first quotation we see that it must be completed, whereupon it reads: "Usefulness is agreeable and *engages our approbation*." The "agreeable" quality is there and it suffuses the perception of usefulness and also the responsive approbation, yet *this* is not what "engages" us. The "why" refers not to the pleasure but to whatever it is that calls forth action which is *attended with* a pleasurable sentiment.

The "Active Energy" of Utility

At this point we should do well once again to collect the various particular expressions in which Hume draws attention to the motivating, dynamic character of utility. Our "catalogue" of these instances contains the following. In the case of justice "this circumstance of usefulness has, in general, the *strongest energy and most entire command* over our sentiments" (Section III, italics mine in this and the following quotations). "Public utility . . . must . . . *take hold* of some natural affection." "Everything which contributes to the happiness of society *recommends itself directly* to our approbation and good will." "In our serious occupations, in our careless amusements, this principle *still exerts its active energy*." "It appears . . . that . . . the useful tendency of the social virtues *moves us* not by any regard to self-interest but has *an influence much more universal and extensive*" (Section V). Why all that "influence," "active energy," "command," exerted by utility? That is the real question.

This view of the sense of the question is confirmed by a debate which Hume goes through with those who propose "self-love" as the sole motive of human life and the principle of ethics. The public utility of the social virtues "must please either from consideration of self-interest or from more generous motives." The alternatives here posed are in terms of *motive* or the moving power. What is it, or better, whence does this "energy" or "influence" come?

Why Utility Interests?

It will be helpful, perhaps, to recall again when reading that caption of Section V, "Why Utility Pleases," how very much Hume himself was steeped in the classical literature, for this may reflect itself in his manner of writing. In the Latin there are various expressions for "it pleases," "it is agreeable," "it interests me," which are all very close together in their meaning and usage, and are, indeed, variants of each other. "Utility pleases us" can be read as "utility *interests* us." Now we may further note how extensively Hume himself also uses this term "interest," for, though it is usually associated almost exclusively with "self-interest," he is careful to insert "self" or "private" when he uses interest with that reference. He is free, then, to speak of "the true interests of mankind" (Section II, Part II), "the common interest," and "the interests of mankind and society." Thus we may be authorized by Hume's own usage to put the question "Why Utility pleases" into this alternative form, "Why is it that utility interests us or engages our *interest?*" And then, seeing that utility itself means "contributing" to the interests of society, another question: Why do the interests of others or of society *interest us?* As warrant for this rendering we can cite the fact that Hume asks the very same question in this quite simple form: *"What is that to me?* There are few occasions when this question is not pertinent" (Section V, Part I).

The Answer

And what is the answer to this? We are so made that "we have humanity or a fellow feeling with others . . . this is experienced to be a principle in human nature." "It is needless to push our researches" beyond that principle. Here is something "original" in human nature (Section V, Part II, first footnote).

Now it is true that in his early *Treatise* Hume had attempted to explain this characteristic operation of sympathy in terms of the "principles of association," but this youthful venture is now renounced. There simply is "this social sympathy in human nature" and it is, for the purposes of this inquiry concerning morals, the ultimate principle.

It is this ultimate principle, call it "humanity" or "social sympathy," that makes men sensitive to the "social utility" of the acts and dispositions or virtues of men. It imparts the distinctively *moral* character to those sentiments of approbation and disapprobation, the character which distinguishes these sentiments from mere private likes and dislikes. This humanity, too, is what *moves* men to judge actions and character and to take personal action themselves according to their moral judgments.

It appears from Hume's own language that this ultimate principle is itself more complex than we realize at first. There are really two quite distinct functions indicated in the term "humanity" and "sympathy." Sympathy is an affective operation wherein the sentiments of men (including pleasure and pain) are "communicated" among them as they live in society. But "humanity" is given a different characterization in the next to last paragraph where it becomes "a concern for others." "Concern" betokens an active interest, an outgoing one that attends to others, and then sympathy comes into play.

Hume appears to have been very loath to reduce "these principles of humanity and sympathy" to any one single principle or common denominator. They are distinct but they are also intimately related or co-operating factors in human life, and together they are "the true origin of morals." [7]

Digression on the Resemblance to Kant in this Matter of an Ultimate Interest

Students of Kant will have been struck by the fact that Kant, too, has to refer to something ultimate which cannot be explained further by reference to anything else. Toward the end of the *Fundamental Principles of the Metaphysic of Morals* Kant speaks of the "interest" of reason in moral law as being the limit of our ethical knowledge; there *is* this interest, and it is *a motive* manifested in the fact of moral duty. Hume's "humanity" or "concern for others" is likewise an ultimate interest of

---

[7] Hume does not ignore the complexity of human motivation at any time, and especially the way "self-love" is mingled with almost everything men feel and do. His discussion is in fact a running encounter with "the selfish theory of morals" and with the "deduction of morals from self-love or a regard to private interest, which is an obvious thought." The reader should attend carefully to Hume's examination of this theory at many different places throughout the *Inquiry*, notably in Sections V, VI, IX, and of course the whole of Appendix II, "Of Self-Love." For an adequate appreciation of the argument on this subject one should read Bishop Butler's *Sermons Preached in the Rolls Chapel*, especially the three Sermons on Human Nature (reprinted in Liberal Arts Press edition).

man (not reason) and it is also a *motive* of action and manifested in behavior where "the particular sentiments of self-love" are "frequently controlled and limited" (Section IX, Part I).

How General Standards are "Infallibly Begotten"

"The present theory," as Hume now calls it, has been the outcome of an inquiry into "the chief part of morals, which has a reference to mankind and our fellow creatures," and the inquiry has shown how utility can be the chief, and in some cases, the "sole source" of what men value as "the social virtues." It has argued that those moral values and practices cannot be deduced from the principle of self-love but require a reference to sympathy and a concern for others which are fundamental principles of our human nature. These principles operate "in the world we live in" (Section IV). Furthermore, they have a part even in constituting that world, for the active concern for others brings men into relations with each other and in these relationships and in each other's presence sympathy "communicates" their sentiments and tendencies of behavior among them and thus brings them further into community. So the same principles that are responsible for the moral sentiments and moral values develop the society of men with each other. And "the intercourse of the sentiments . . . in society and conversation makes us form some general unalterable standard by which we may approve or disapprove of characters and manners" (Section V, Part II). Here then is the answer to the question raised at the close of Section IV concerning the formation of general standards. The theory makes it clear how, without invoking reason, men can reach those principles by which they actually judge moral matters. The public standards of ethics which are referred to by men no more originate in "the faculty of reasoning" than do morals or the virtues and duties themselves.

Further Confirmation of the Theory

It is a mark of the "experimental method" that if the theory be true and useful, it uncovers new data that will in turn confirm it. The "present theory" has been reached by study of the "social virtues." It discloses that humanity and sympathy conjoined operate in producing these moral phenomena. Now it appears that the double principles of sympathy with and the concern for one's fellow man work other effects in human life, phenomena *analogous* to moral valuations and not exactly the same. These cases are similar to those of concomitant variations employed in the search for causes and effects, and they both furnish a corroboration of the theory and reveal some new aspects of the phenomena brought into the picture. Hume devotes Sections VI-VII to these confirmatory studies.

It is a rather unexpected fact about man that we can even value morally and approve of qualities belonging to another person that *are only useful to that person*. In other words, it is not always necessary that there be a discernible *public* utility. Usefulness to anybody, even someone other than ourselves and in a situation where we derive no benefit, is still ground for our judgment of esteem or approbation. This fact must utterly balk the protagonists of "the selfish theory of morals," for they are obliged by hypothesis to argue that we must always see some benefit or advantage for ourselves if we are to be interested and approve. But it is, nevertheless, the fact that even where we cannot possibly be affected by the doings of the person envisaged we have, through sympathy with him, an appreciation of the good of his useful qualities for him and even, indeed, of their immediate agreeableness or value.

The Assimilation of Quasi-Moral Values

Many kinds of characteristic traits which we thus value by virtue of sympathy are cited by Hume, often with reference to historical examples. And here, with his penchant for classical

culture, Hume includes among the moral or quasi-moral characters such things as "bodily-endowments," "beauty," "talents,"
which moderns would not so classify.[8] Hume's contention is
nonetheless that the same operations of judgment take place in
respect of these qualities as in the case of the obviously "social
and moral" qualities and he insists on being guided by "taste
and sentiment" in these matters and on giving, as he rather
superbly declares, "a natural, unforced interpretation of the
phenomena of human life" (Section VI, end of Part I).

We shall not go into further detail about these sections VI-
VIII. They demonstrate in one form or another the "contagion
and sympathy" that operate among men and "communicate"
their sentiments to each other, and it is always a case of that
"same social sympathy . . . or fellow feeling with human happiness or misery."

IV. CONCLUSION. HUME'S THEORY OF MORALS

Personal Merit

"Personal merit" is the phenomenon of human life with
which this inquiry began and to which its conclusion must re-
vert. It is a fact that "in common life" merit is attributed to
persons because of their "possession of mental qualities" which
are "valuable." The inquiry has shown that these valuable
qualities are always either *"useful* or *agreeable,* the *utile* or the
dulce" either to the person himself who has them or to other
persons. This is the first general truth that comes out of this
investigation, the first of the principles concerning morals.

It is a principle gleaned from experience and established by
the examination of the actual instances in which we find men

---

[8] See the Second Reflection in Appendix IV, "Of Some Verbal Disputes."
Note that Kant in the opening section of his *Fundamental Principles* marks
an absolute distinction between the goodness of talent and the good will or
moral character—here taking sharp issue, implicitly at any rate, with Hume.
Cf. Liberal Arts Press edition (Tr. Abbott).

ascribing merit or its opposite to persons. It is a truth obvious
to anyone who studies the phenomenon of merit if he has not
been previously perverted by philosophical "systems and hypotheses."

"The Natural, Unforced Interpretation"

At the outset Hume wanted to avoid becoming embroiled in
the typical controversies of philosophers in which the protagonists battle obstinately for their previously espoused "principles," and he believed that he had succeeded and given "a
natural, unforced interpretation of the phenomena of human
life." He hoped that the "natural understanding" of the reader
would freely draw the obvious conclusion from the facts—facts,
moreover, which are matters of common experience, where men
have the means of checking the evidence.

The Ingredient of Humanity in Man

However, there are disputes that occur on the "vulgar" level,
too, as well as in philosophical circles. One such dispute con-
cerns "the *degrees* of benevolence or self-love which prevail in
human nature." It has not been necessary, fortunately, to take
a position on the issue because the question has not naturally
arisen in the investigation. "The present theory" does not raise
it because according to it there is no absolute opposition between the *selfish* and *social* sentiments or dispositions. Human
life is an interplay of both sorts of sentiments. And one cannot
determine beforehand any necessary proportion or prevalence
of one over the other. "It is sufficient for our present purpose,
if it be allowed that there is some benevolence, however small,
infused in our bosom, some spark of friendship for humankind,
some particle of the dove kneaded into our frame along with
the elements of the wolf and serpent."

The Development of Morality

Let it only be granted that there are such sentiments in man concerning others, if ever so weak in the individuals, and we are now able to see how morals originate and eventually come to have considerable influence in human affairs, so that we must reckon them in when we draw up a true portraiture of human nature and life in society.

The story of morals, according to "the present theory," is as follows: The sentiments in man that are concerned with his fellow man, however feeble, will nonetheless initially "produce a cool preference of what is useful and serviceable to mankind above what is pernicious and dangerous." This "preference" constitutes in reality "a moral distinction." The preference or judgment is first felt as a sentiment, "a general sentiment of blame and approbation." But it has an *active* character as well, "a tendency, however faint, to the objects of the one and a proportional aversion to those of the other."

The "sentiment of humanity" in and by itself lacks strength as compared with "avarice, ambition, vanity," or any other passion classed under self-love, but it proves to have a potentiality or rather a mobilizing power so that the moral distinctions which show themselves at first as only preferences of sentiment become powerful factors, as morals, in the life of man.

The Concurrence of Humanity in the Lives of Men, and its Power

The passions of self-love, it must first be noted, are all particular ones and do not concern themselves with any general or common object. Men motivated by them are apt to be at odds with each other in action and not agreeing upon any common object. Herein lies the advantage of the sentiment of humanity, that it is "common to all men." "The humanity of one man is the humanity of everyone, and the same object touches this

passion in all human creatures." And the same moral sentiments of "general censure or applause" result and are expressed
in the common language. Through the expression of these
"universal sentiments of censure or approbation . . . virtue and
vice . . . become known; morals are recognized; certain general
ideas are framed of human conduct and behavior. Such
measures are expected from men in such situations. This action
is determined to be conformable to our abstract rule [the
standard]; that other, contrary. And by such universal principles are the particular sentiments of self-love frequently controlled and limited." Thus morality arises and develops and the
standards of morality come to have some measure of authority
in the active life of man in society.

Social Intercourse Engenders Common Standards

Something must be added in further support of this conclusion "that moral sentiments are found of such influence in
life." The principles of morality, viz., humanity and sympathy,
"we must remark, are social and universal: they form the *party*
of mankind against vice and disorder, its common enemy. And
as the benevolent concern for others [i.e., humanity] is diffused . . . over all men and is the same in all, it occurs more
frequently in discourse, is cherished in society and conversation, and the blame and approbation consequent on it are
thereby roused . . ."

Other Aids and Reinforcement of the Standards of Morality

Further reinforcement comes naturally from a "passion" that
would usually be considered a purely selfish one, "the love of
fame." Yet it actually contributes "force to moral sentiment,"
and in this wise: "By our continual and earnest pursuit of a
character, a name, a reputation in the world, we bring our own
deportment and conduct frequently in review and consider
how they appear in the eyes of those who approach and regard

us. This constant habit of surveying ourselves, as it were, in reflection, keeps alive all the sentiments of right and wrong and begets, in noble natures, a certain reverence for themselves as well as others. . . ." Here is a picture of "the most perfect morality."

The Ethical Image of Man

And Hume paints at the very end of the Conclusion his ethical image of man. It is the person who with his other traits of self-love has benevolence, friendship, humanity, kindness, whose "happiness" consists of "inward peace of mind, consciousness of integrity, a satisfactory review of our conduct," "the invaluable enjoyment of a character . . . above all the peaceful reflection on one's own conduct." These Hume calls "the natural pleasures" which "are really without price, both because they are below all price in their attainment and above it in their enjoyment."

The Eloquent Moral Philosopher

This eloquent sentence concludes the *Inquiry*. Here Hume is, for the nonce, the moral philosopher writing in the style which he had earlier professed that he would avoid: "As virtue, of all objects, is allowed to be the most valuable, this species of philosopher paint her in her most amiable colors, borrowing all helps from poetry and eloquence . . . to please the imagination and gain the affections." [1] And in the present *Inquiry* it is said at the outset that those philosophers who stressed the importance of sentiment have had this as the essential end of their work; "the end of all moral speculation is to teach us our duty." Hume then proceeded in his own book to portray how "what is honorable, what is fair, what is becoming, what is noble, what is generous, takes possession of the heart and animates us to em-

[1] See *Philosophical Essays Concerning Human Understanding*, Liberal Arts Press edition, p. 15.

brace and maintain it" (Sect. I). Well, it seems that Hume knew that fine art of portrayal to touch men's souls, as well as the logical art and the method of scientific inquiry.

V. FURTHER QUESTIONS, AND CRITICISM

Avoiding "intricate speculations which are unfit for moral discourses" Hume had postponed several questions to a set of Appendices. One question is concerned with the relative part played by reason and sentiment in all moral decisions and judgments; another with the relationship between self-love and the benevolent element or the sentiment of humanity; a third with the nature of justice, how far it is natural and how far "artificial"; and the fourth, with the validity of the distinction made in theory between the "intellectual" and "moral endowments" and between the "voluntary" and involuntary.

The Underlying Basic Question that of the Function of Reason

All these questions, in one way or another, hark back for Hume to the basic question as to the place and function of reason in the moral life.

The Argument about Self-Love—Hobbes, Butler, and Hume

The theory of ethics, for instance, which had centered on the principle of self-love was obliged to introduce subtle calculations of self-interest in order to evade the obvious reality of altruistic interest or concern. Even Bishop Butler, who had valiantly argued against Hobbes' "selfish theory," still assumed that self-love within its own limits, and not usurping the place of benevolence, was largely a rational or at least a "reflective affair" in that man conceived of his own personal happiness as an end and then intelligently organized his life toward that end. Butler then envisaged the role of a superior authority, "conscience," but this was also called the "principle of reflection" as the ultimate control over the narrow reflection in self-love. And Butler had sighed: "Had it [the principle of reflection or conscience] power as it hath authority," the life of man would approach the divine commandment to love one's neighbor as oneself. While Hume followed Butler in his *criticism* of the psychology of the selfish theory, he took leave of him when he attributed to "the principle of reflection" any such prevailing power. No! "Reason, being cool and disengaged, is no motive to action" (Appendix I).

This negative judgment on Hume's part has involved him in subsequent criticism even at the hands of those who have admired him. He seems too sure of this *exclusion* of reason from a role which had been traditionally ascribed to it ever since those ancients whom he usually admired so much.

Hume's Treatment of Reason

There was a hint, which actually read like a promise, in the beginning of the *Inquiry:* "I am apt to suspect . . . that *reason* and *sentiment* concur in almost all moral determinations and conclusions" (Section I). The reader, for his part, is apt to suppose that Hume will later engage in a "reconciling project," as in his other writings.[1] The following statements in Appendix I show how reason and sentiment "concur." "One principal foundation of moral praise being supposed to lie in the usefulness of any quality or action, it is evident that *reason* must enter for a considerable share in all decisions of this kind, since nothing but that faculty can instruct us in the tendencies of qualities and actions, and point out their beneficial consequences to society and to their possessor. . . . But though reason, when fully

[1] This phrase is used in the *Philosophical Essays Concerning Human Understanding*, Liberal Arts Press edition, p. 104, with reference to "Liberty and Necessity." It is also used in *Hume's Political Essays*, Liberal Arts Press edition, Introduction, xxixff., and the essay "Of the Origin of Government," pp. 41f., where it is a problem of reconciling "authority and liberty."

asserted and improved, be sufficient to instruct us in the pernicious or useful tendency . . . it is not alone sufficient to produce any moral blame or approbation. . . . It is requisite a *sentiment* should here display itself, in order to give a preference to the useful above the pernicious tendencies . . . *reason* instructs us in the several tendencies of action, and *humanity* makes a distinction in favor of those which are useful and beneficial." "Twist and turn this matter as you will you must have recourse to decisions of sentiment." "It appears evident that the ultimate ends of human actions can never, in any case, be accounted for by reason."

Now there are several cases, in the course of the investigation, when Hume has actually allowed to reason an efficacy other than that solely of instruction concerning facts and tendencies. It is true that at no time does he appear to attribute any originative role to reason. It cannot determine ends or make decisions of preference and value. But reason seems to "concur" not in the sense of an outsider doing a serviceable job of instruction but as an insider giving weight to and influencing the morality of action. A case of that merely instrumental function of reason, for instance, may be seen in the study of benevolence where almsgiving is "naturally praised," but when we know more about the consequences of so doing, "we retract our first sentiment and adjust anew the boundaries of moral good and evil" (Section II). In the case of justice, too, "our regards to justice" are enlarged "in proportion as we become acquainted with the extensive utility of that virtue" (Section III). In "Why Utility Pleases," however, it is pointed out how "the judgment corrects or *endeavors to correct* the appearance" in the case where we distinguish the "character" of a person from "fortune" or "accidental consequences." Now in this last case, the "endeavor" of the judgment is an attribute that wants explaining. For "endeavor" belongs wholly, according to the theory, to sentiment and not to reason.

The question is not merely a verbal one as to whether we shall call this judgment an act of reason or not. It is the *function* that is performed that is important, not the "faculty." And here it seems, a motive-character is attributed to the judgment which actively discriminates between the accidents of experience and reality.

More puzzling still is the tacit confession, if we may put it thus, of the eloquent words of the Conclusion. That the eloquence should touch and move us is not the point but rather the fact about which Hume the moralist is so eloquent, viz., that "surveying ourselves, as it were, in reflection, keeps alive all the sentiments of right and wrong, and begets in noble natures," etc. This *vitalizing* role of "surveying ourselves," how is it possible without our accrediting to the mind in its role of surveying a *power* so to *affect* the feelings and to "beget self-reverence." And to take a less seductive case, the moral standards which are also "begotten," and "infallibly" so, are *positive influences* upon action, for they have an active part, not merely an instructive role, in that amazing phenomenon where "self-love [is] frequently controlled and limited" (Section IX, Part I).

In other words, "reflection" and "judgment" seem to enter, by Hume's admissions, into the *motivation* of human life as well as do the sentiments. But the present Introduction is not the place to develop an amendment to Hume's theory, if that be possible; we can aim here only to acquaint the student of the *Inquiry* with the important criticisms of Hume. It will be sufficient for this purpose if we now quote the views of two scholars who have examined Hume's moral philosophy from within and offered constructive criticism. Writing about *Reason and Conduct in Hume's Treatise,* Rachel Kydd has said (and these conclusions seem to apply equally well to the *Inquiry*): "Our general conclusion is that he (Hume) does in fact allow, both explicitly and implicitly, a far greater power to reason than is often supposed. He makes it perfectly plain that theoretical judgments both empirical and *a priori* have a very great influence on action, and that this influence is a common one which partakes in the determining, if not of all, yet at least of a great many acts. . . ." [2]

[2] Rachel Kydd: *Reason and Conduct in Hume's Treatise.* See Chapter IV, "Empirical Reason and Conduct," and p. 138.

And in conclusion: "It is precisely his views on practical reason which should have enabled, and indeed did logically commit him, to say that moral conduct does depend on reason. . . . The view that our duties depend on reason alone Hume has utterly destroyed. They are indeed dependent upon practical judgments, but such judgments can only be empirical. What they assert depends materially on the natural dispositions of the agents about whom they are made, and, hence, what it is rational or a duty to do remains essentially conditioned by the empirical nature of man." [3]

In the Concluding Comments of his book *The Philosophy of David Hume,* Norman Kemp Smith writes as follows: "Should judgments genuinely cognitive in character have to be recognized as entering into belief—as ultimately, by implication, Hume himself admits is the case—the capital positions in his ethics, no less than in his general philosophy, will at once be endangered. For if, as then follows—a further step than Hume has given any sign of taking—judgments cognitive in character have similarly to be allowed as entering into all judgments of moral approval and disapproval, i.e., if moral judgments involve judgments of *apprehension* as well as of *appreciation,* the whole question of the interrelations of feeling and reason—so fundamental in his ethics, and from his ethics carried over into his general philosophy—may have to be very differently viewed. The problem, too, of moral obligation may then be found to demand a quite different answer from any that Hume has been able to give. On these, as on other questions of *theory,* Hume's ethics is integral to his general philosophical outlook, and stands or falls together with it." [4]

The Problem of Moral Obligation

In the above quotation Kemp Smith has indicated that the problem of moral obligation is not satisfactorily solved. Ever since Kant focused attention upon moral obligation as the

---

[3] *Ibid,* Chapter V, "Reason and Morality," p. 189.
[4] Norman Kemp Smith, *The Philosophy of David Hume,* pp. 565f.

crucial question for ethics and analyzed the conditions of its possibility as a phenomenon of human existence, this criticism has been leveled at Hume's moral philosophy. Indeed, it is customary to present the deficiency of any empirical ethics by citing Hume on this score and pointing out that there is really no room for the "ought" in such a philosophy.

Let us first consider what Hume has said concerning the problem of moral obligation. The first thing that strikes one is that he does not actually regard it as much of a problem, for this is what he says in his "Conclusion": "There remains nothing but briefly to consider our interested *obligation* to it" [virtue]. The very juxtaposition of these terms "interested *obligation*" seems paradoxical to us if we are versed in that immense tradition of ethics that derives from Kant: "interest" and "obligation" seem rather to be utterly opposed, quite as much as "inclination" and "duty" are. What can Hume mean, then, by such a conjunction of words, "interested obligation"?

Prior to the answer to that question must come another as to what "obligation," without any adjective, meant in the day and age of Hume? Obligation was, however, a special form of "duty" and not coextensive with it in application. And so we must first take up "duty."

Speaking the language of "common life," Hume referred to duties in connection with the virtues as something entailed by them. Virtue is a valued quality of the person in his conduct of life in society; it is a quality that has a *moral* value and evokes a *moral* approbation because called for by the common principle of humanity in us; and the moral quality being a disposition to act in a certain way, action is expected so that a duty follows naturally from the fact of our appreciation and recognition of any virtue. The approbation carries with it the duty to perform accordingly. There is no separation in the process, so to speak, between moral *approbation* and moral duty—the one slides into the other.

Given the working of the principle of humanity, be it only in small dosage in each person, given the social existence of mankind which makes the common ingredient of humanity a potent influence in the moral sentiments of all persons, and given an intelligence of the facts of the situation and the consequences of any action, men have all they need for the moral conduct of life. No new inducement is necessary to make them perform the particular duties that correspond to the particular virtues to which they give their approbation and which they "ought" to put into practice. Thus the problem of man is not that of duty but of intelligence and humanity.

It is worthy of notice, too, that Hume *first* begins to speak of "obligation," as distinct from duty, in his study of justice. From the usefulness "alone" of justice "arises its merit *and moral obligation*" (Section III). Nothing is said about obligation in connection with the virtues of benevolence—the nearest expression to it being in the phrase "the ties of friendship approach, in a fond observance of each obliging office, to those of love and inclination" (Section II). Incidentally, this easy approximation of duty ("office") to "inclination" is symptomatic of the spirit of Hume's ethics, and it is seen again in the Conclusion where virtue is divested of her "dismal dress" and "talks not of useless austerities and rigors, suffering and self-denial." But to return to the special character of duty when it is "moral obligation." The association of obligation with justice and with political society in Hume's philosophy was thoroughly in the general tradition of political philosophy up to that time. Obligation was originally a Roman law concept. In a substantive sense it is whatever man is required to do by law and with the sanctions of law, that is, with the ultimate enforcement of the obligation through an exercise of the power of the state if the person does not voluntarily perform his duty as a member of civil society. Obligation does stand there in a sort of *contrast* with inclination and even with voluntary action. There is always a political power envisaged beyond the person who lies under any obligation. Now at the time Hume was writing, this concept of obligation was undergoing an alteration, notably in the work of a contemporary with whom he had an unfortunate quarrel later, J. J. Rousseau. At the time of the publication of Hume's *Inquiry,* however, Rousseau had not produced his *Dis-*

course on the Origin of Inequality (1754) where he gave his own eloquent account of man and his morals, an account quite at odds with the optimism of the day, which even Hume mirrored, and tending toward a view of morality which in Kant's writings was destined to be "full of austerity and rigor." For our purpose here all we need to consider about Rousseau's philosophical ideas is that he was the first to internalize obligation, so to speak, that is, to call a moral obligation one where the sanction lay within man himself and was no longer located in the power of the state or government. As Rousseau expressed the change of meaning: "there is a difference between a power we are forced to obey and one that we are *obliged* to recognize." And connected with this inner obligation of the person was the idea that it is a consequence of man's essential freedom, and hence "moral liberty" consists in "obeying a law that we prescribe to ourselves."[5] Of course, it is also true for Rousseau that this self-prescribed law had to be a law of men in their society with each other, so that behind the free obligation of the individual person is the "general will" of the whole community of free persons. This obligation still carried with it the lurking imagery of a source of law and right larger than and comprehensive of the individual person, and a source having weight and obliging power. Now it appears that the same kind of imagery was operating in the thinking of Hume. For he objected as much as both Rousseau and Montesquieu were doing to Hobbes' extremely legalistic view that the only real obligation in any proper sense is that of enforcement of law by the sovereign government of the state. Instead of Hobbes' sovereign, Rousseau put the whole body politic, the society of free men united by their own act, in one body authorized to lay down the laws that express their will, their "general will." Now a parallel may be instituted with Hume on this last point: the common principle

[5] For further discussion of Rousseau's position concerning obligation and its significance in the modern world see the editor's "The Meaning of Obligation" in *Contemporary Idealism in America*, edited by Clifford Barrett, (New York, 1930); also *Jean Jacques Rousseau, Moralist* (New York, 1934), 2 vols.

of "humanity" is the source of all morals among men exactly as the general will is the source of the moral laws—"moral" because expressive of the free and common will of men. Instead of the general and common will, we have a common principle of humanity which looks to the "general interests of society" as Rousseau's general will looks to the general good of society. Thus Hume no less than Rousseau took obligation out of the precincts of external government and established it as the internal governance of men where their humanity dictates what is to be done, that is, what their *obligation* is.

Hume was satisfied, apparently, with the prescription by humanity envisaged in the *moral approbation*. That approbation is the thing. In it is funded the force and power of the sentiment of humanity, many times reinforced by the presence of that same sentiment in all men, and it is made at once precise and general by the social intercourse of men and their use of general language to communicate their sentiments and values. What more is needed for moral obligation than such a fund of power so humanely employed in defining the virtues and duties of men?

So we must conclude that Hume's ethics place the emphasis upon the *factor of moral approbation* and treat moral obligation as derivative from it—and this is precisely what his own Conclusion says.

But why the problem of "interested obligation"? This can be answered very simply or "briefly," when we realize how obligation follows naturally from moral approbation. We know that obligation, in the individual person, is the very dictate of his own humanity as well as the humanity of other persons and we can also see that it is "the true interest of each individual" to *be* moral and to "practice every moral duty" and to rejoice in the virtues of every person. To ask about "interested obligation" then is to ask how men are to see and grasp with their intelligence that they will find their "self-interest" and their "greater happiness" realized and satisfied in living a moral life. The interest in their own personal happiness, called by Butler self-love, is always present in mankind. Like Butler,

Hume is arguing that "self-love" and "humanity" (in Butler's case "conscience"), though often different, are never ultimately opposed, but that men who intelligently seek their true happiness and have the most extensive views of their own interest and happiness will find it all satisfied in the practice of moral virtue.

There is no point in going on further to a discussion of obligation in the light of Kant's fundamental relocation of the essential problem of ethics along the very lines from which Hume shied away, and which he characterized as too "austere and rigorous." Instead of confronting men with "suffering and self-denial" to move them to act as moral beings, Hume found it more natural and "unforced" to speak in a final burst of eloquence about virtue with her "most engaging charms" and about "the invaluable enjoyment of a character" and the priceless and supreme "satisfaction" that attends "the peaceful reflection on one's own conduct."

VI. CONCLUSION

The contemporary reader of Hume will have some difficulty in reconciling this Hume of the *Inquiry Concerning Morals* with the traditional view of him as a skeptic. This was the error of his own contemporaries, the "common sense" philosophers, his critics. The source of their mistake was, among other things, their seeing him as merely a successor to Locke and Berkeley. Following only his study of knowledge they saw him confessing to a "philosophical skepticism," paying no attention to the very subtlety of such a phrase, and the possibility that apart from the philosophical problems concerning understanding there could well be natural belief and adherence to moral values. The pattern of interpretation of Hume has altered little since those first criticisms, even with the advent of histories of philosophy that profess to offer large perspectives and also, as history should, pay attention to individuality and novelty. Hume is still classed with "subjective idealism"; he does, it is true, draw the "logical" conclusion that it ends in skepticism. How then can he talk, for instance, about "persons" when he inquires into morals and morality? Strange it is to find this Hume of the traditional image starting off a work on morals with the notion of "personal merit" and proceeding to analyze it. Moreover, he does not analyze it away but on the contrary reaches a "foundation of ethics" and "universal principles." Hume thus constructive seems a paradoxical figure. But there he is, so presenting himself in this *Inquiry.* It is certainly not the case that he was throwing a sop to respectability in the language and argument of this book. He told personal friends what he said eventually in *My Own Life,* that this book was the best in all respects of any that he had ever written. If we are willing to allow, as Kemp Smith says, that "Hume was his own best critic," we should accept the Hume revealed in this work as an authentic Hume and redress our whole view of his philosophy by taking account of this important aspect of it.

All his life as a writer of philosophy Hume had one central theme which he had developed after the arduous researches of his youth—the theme of Human Nature and the distinctive nature of man. His various writings interpret man with reference to a variety of characteristic phenomena of human life in the world. In the intellectual aspect men have beliefs for which there cannot be found any rational ground or warrant. Yet men live in a world "peopled" by such beliefs which go beyond ascertainable evidence. Man is of such a nature that he can form such beliefs and live by them. And the realm of morals is another set of phenomena of human nature no less significant and even more striking. Here human beings themselves are treated not as mere facts but as persons that have personal characteristics which are a matter of "concern" and which men regard in a peculiar light, with a favoring sort of regard, so that they want to see those qualities of human merit, those virtues, realized more fully in their "social and active life," and of course the unfavorable qualities discouraged. Morals are a great tribute to human nature. They do not, however, involve men in the quandaries of "understanding" as some of our important beliefs about existence do. The moral life sustains the tests of reflection and experience and it leads to a happier social existence where men are conscious of worth in each other and even "reverence" others as well as themselves. The lessons of the *Inquiry* are salutary even if they are not the best lessons of Hume's philosophy—and yet he did say of the *book* that it was "incomparably the best," on all counts, of all his writings!

CHARLES W. HENDEL

SELECTED BIBLIOGRAPHY

HUME'S WORKS AND LETTERS

A Treatise of Human Nature, Books I and II (1739), and Book III (1740).

Essays, Moral and Political (Vol. I: 1741; Vol. II: 1742).

An Enquiry Concerning Human Understanding (1748).

An Enquiry Concerning the Principles of Morals (1751).

Political Discourses (1752).

History of England (1754-62).

Four Dissertations (1757):
  (1) Natural History of Religion
  (2) Of the Passions
  (3) Of Tragedy
  (4) Of the Standard of Taste

Dialogues Concerning Natural Religion (1779).

The Letters of David Hume, edited by J. Y. T. Greig (Oxford, 1932).

The Letters of David Hume, edited by R. Klibansky and E. C. Mossner (Oxford, 1952).

COLLECTED WORKS

The Philosophical Works of David Hume. 4 vols. Edinburgh: Adam Black and William Tait, 1826.

The Philosophical Works of David Hume. 4 vols. Boston: Little, Brown and Company, 1854.

The Philosophical Works of David Hume, edited by T. H. Green and T. H. Grose. 4 vols. London: Longmans, Green and Company, 1898.

CURRENT EDITIONS OF HUME'S WORKS

An Abstract of a Treatise of Human Nature (1740), edited with an Introduction by J. M. Keynes and P. Sraffa, Cambridge, 1938.

An Inquiry Concerning Human Understanding, edited with an Introduction by C. W. Hendel. "The Library of Liberal Arts" No. 49. New York, 1955.

David Hume's Political Essays, edited with an Introduction by C. W. Hendel. "The Library of Liberal Arts" No. 34. New York, 1953.

Hume's Dialogues Concerning Natural Religion, edited with an Introduction by Norman Kemp Smith. Oxford, 1935.

Hume's Enquiries, edited by L. A. Selby-Bigge. Oxford, 1902.

Hume's Moral and Political Philosophy, edited by Henry D. Aiken. New York, 1948.

Hume's Treatise, edited with an analytical index by L. A. Selby-Bigge. Oxford, 1941.

Selections from Hume, edited by C. W. Hendel. "The Modern Student's Library." New York, 1927.

WORKS ON HUME

Broad, C. D., *Five Types of Ethical Theory.* New York, 1930.

Burton, J. H., *Life and Correspondence of David Hume.* 2 vols. Edinburgh, 1846.

Church, R. W., *Hume's Theory of the Understanding.* Ithaca, 1935.

Greig, J. Y. T., *David Hume.* New York, 1931.

Hare, R. M., *The Language of Morals.* Oxford, 1952, pp. 44f.

Hedenius, Ingemar, *Studies in Hume's Ethics,* Upsala and Stockholm, 1935.

Hendel, C. W., *Studies in the Philosophy of David Hume.* Princeton, 1925.

Huxley, T. H., *Hume.* London, 1879.

Kemp Smith, Norman, *Dialogues Concerning Natural Religion.* Oxford, 1935.

———— *The Philosophy of Hume.* London, 1941.

Kuypers, M. S., *Studies in the Eighteenth Century Background of Hume's Empiricism.* Minneapolis, 1930.

Kydd, Rachel M., *Reason and Conduct in Hume's Treatise.* Oxford, 1946.

Laing, B. M., *David Hume.* London, 1932.

Laird, John, *Hume's Philosophy of Human Nature.* London, 1932.

Lechartier, Georges, *David Hume; moraliste et sociologue.* Paris, 1900.

MacNabb, D. I. C., *David Hume: His Theory of Knowledge and Morality.* "Hutchinson's University Library," 1951.

Maund, Constance, *Hume's Theory of Knowledge.* Macmillan, 1937.

Moore, George, *Principia Ethica.*

Morris, C. R., *Locke, Berkeley, Hume.* Oxford, 1931.

Mossner, E. C., *The Life of David Hume.* Austin, 1941.

——— *Forgotten Hume: Le bon David.* New York, 1943.

——— "Was Hume a Tory Historian?" *Journal of the History of Ideas,* II (1941), 225-36.

Passmore, J. A., *Hume's Intentions.* Cambridge, 1952.

Plamenatz, John P., *The English Utilitarians.* Oxford, 1949.

Price, H. H., *Hume's Theory of the External World.* Oxford, 1940.

Ross, W. D., *Human Nature and Utility in Hume's Social Philosophy.* Berea, Ky., 1942.

Sabine, George H., *A History of Political Theory.* New York, 1937; revised edition, 1950.

Shearer, Edna A., *Hume's Place in Ethics.* Bryn Mawr, 1915.

Smith, A. H., *A Treatise on Knowledge.* Oxford, 1943.

Stephen, Leslie, *History of English Thought in the Eighteenth Century.* London, 1876.

——— *The English Utilitarians.* 3 vols. London, 1900.

Stevenson, Charles L., *Ethics and Language.* Yale University Press, New Haven, 1944. Chap. XII, "Some Related Theories," 5 Hume, pp. 273-6.

Taylor, A. E., *David Hume and the Miraculous.* Cambridge, 1927.

ARTICLES

Falk, W. D., "Obligation and Rightness," *Philosophy* (July, 1945).

McGilvary, E. V., "Altruism in Hume's *Treatise,*" *Philosophical Review,* Vol. XII, No. 3 (May, 1903).

Oake, Roger B., "Montesquieu and Hume," *Modern Language Quarterly,* II (1941), 25-41.

NOTE ON THE TEXT

The present edition of the *Inquiry Concerning the Principles of Morals* is reprinted from the first edition of Hume's collected philosophical writings, *The Philosophical Works of David Hume,* published in 1826 by Adam Black and William Tait. The text is based on the version published in 1777 (Edition R), and has been carefully compared with the text as edited by T. H. Green and T. H. Grose (published by Longmans, Green and Co.), and by L. A. Selby-Bigge (published by Oxford University Press).

The reading of the two texts has been adopted where they were at variance with the third, and the most plausible chosen where all three were at variance, as happened in a few cases. All corrections, however, were minor and did not materially alter the text.

The editor of the edition of 1826 stated that he had taken care to compare the edition of 1777 with former editions and "where any alterations were discovered, not merely verbal but illustrative of the philosophical opinions of the author, to add these as notes to the passages where they occur." These notes have been retained, supplemented in the present edition, and compared with the notes in Hume's *Essays* (1912, edited by T. H. Green and T. H. Grose).

It is customary to designate by letter the various editions published during Hume's lifetime. The references in the footnotes are to the listings given in the Green-Grose edition, which are reprinted on the following page.

The present edition also includes a reprint of the author's essay, "A Dialogue," which Hume always considered part of his moral writings.

The publishers' editorial staff has supplied translations of foreign-language passages and helpful supplementary notes, which have been bracketed. Spelling and punctuation have been revised throughout to conform to present-day American usage.

O. P.

A *Essays Moral and Political.* The First Edition. Edinburgh, 1742.

B Ditto. The Second Edition, Corrected. Edinburgh, 1742.

C *Essays Moral and Political,* Volume II. Edinburgh, 1742.

D *Essays Moral and Political.* The Third Edition, Corrected with Additions. London, 1748.

E *Philosophical Essays concerning Human Understanding.* London, 1748.

F Ditto. The Second Edition, with Additions and Corrections. London, 1751.

G *An Enquiry concerning the Principles of Morals.* London, 1751.

H *Political Discourses.* Edinburgh, 1752.

I Ditto. The Second Edition. Edinburgh, 1752.

K *Essays and Treatises on Several Subjects.* Four volumes. London and Edinburgh, 1753-1754.

L *Four Dissertations: I. The Natural History of Religion. II. Of the Passions. III. Of Tragedy. IV. Of the Standard of Taste.* London, 1757.

M *Essays and Treatises on Several Subjects.* A New Edition. London and Edinburgh, 1758.

N Ditto. Four volumes. London and Edinburgh, 1760.

O Ditto. Two volumes. London and Edinburgh, 1764.

P Ditto. Two volumes. London and Edinburgh, 1768.

Q Ditto. Four volumes. London and Edinburgh, 1770.

R Ditto. Two volumes. London and Edinburgh, 1777.

AN INQUIRY CONCERNING
THE PRINCIPLES OF MORALS

SECTION I

OF THE GENERAL PRINCIPLES OF MORALS

Disputes with men pertinaciously obstinate in their principles are, of all others, the most irksome, except, perhaps, those with persons entirely disingenuous,[1] who really do not believe the opinions they defend, but engage in the controversy from affectation, from a spirit of opposition, or from a desire of showing wit and ingenuity superior to the rest of mankind. The same blind adherence to their own arguments is to be expected in both: the same contempt of their antagonists, and the same passionate vehemence in enforcing sophistry and falsehood. And as reasoning is not the source whence either disputant derives his tenets, it is in vain to expect that any logic which speaks not to the affections will ever engage him to embrace sounder principles.

Those who have denied the reality of moral distinctions may be ranked among the disingenuous disputants; nor is it conceivable that any human creature could ever seriously believe that all characters and actions were alike entitled to the affection and regard of everyone. The difference which nature has placed between one man and another is so wide, and this difference is still so much further widened by education, example, and habit that, where the opposite extremes come at once under our apprehension, there is no skepticism so scrupulous, and scarce any assurance so determined, as absolutely to deny all distinction between them. Let a man's insensibility be ever so great, he must often be touched with the images of *right* and *wrong;* and let his prejudices be ever so obstinate, he must observe that others are susceptible of like impressions. The only way, therefore, of converting an antagonist of this kind is to leave him to himself. For, finding that nobody keeps up the

---

[1] [Entirely disingenuous: added in Edition M.]

controversy with him, it is probable he will at last of himself, from mere weariness come over to the side of common sense and reason.

There has been a controversy started of late, much better worth examination, concerning the general foundation of morals; whether they be derived from *reason* or from *sentiment;* whether we attain the knowledge of them by a chain of argument and induction or by an immediate feeling and finer internal sense; whether, like all sound judgment of truth and falsehood, they should be the same to every rational, intelligent being, or whether, like the perception of beauty and deformity, they be founded entirely on the particular fabric and constitution of the human species.

The ancient philosophers, though they often affirm that virtue is nothing but conformity to reason, yet, in general, seem to consider morals as deriving their existence from taste and sentiment. On the other hand, our modern inquirers, though they also talk much of the beauty of virtue and deformity of vice, yet have commonly endeavored to account for these distinctions by metaphysical reasonings and by deductions from the most abstract principles of the understanding. Such confusion reigned in these subjects that an opposition of the greatest consequence could prevail between one system and another, and even in the parts of almost each individual system, and yet nobody, till very lately, was ever sensible of it. The elegant [2] Lord Shaftesbury, who first gave occasion to remark this distinction, and who, in general, adhered to the principles of the ancients, is not himself entirely free from the same confusion.

It must be acknowledged that both sides of the question are susceptible of specious arguments. Moral distinctions, it may be said, are discernible by pure *reason:* else, whence the many disputes that reign in common life, as well as in philosophy, with regard to this subject; the long chain of proofs often produced on both sides, the examples cited, the authorities appealed to, the analogies employed, the fallacies detected, the

2 [Elegant and sublime: Editions G and K.]

inferences drawn, and the several conclusions adjusted to their proper principles? Truth is disputable, not taste: what exists in the nature of things is the standard of our judgment; what each man feels within himself is the standard of sentiment. Propositions in geometry may be proved, systems in physics may be controverted, but the harmony of verse, the tenderness of passion, the brilliancy of wit must give immediate pleasure. No man reasons concerning another's beauty, but frequently concerning the justice or injustice of his actions. In every criminal trial, the first object of the prisoner is to disprove the facts alleged and deny the actions imputed to him; the second, to prove that, even if these actions were real, they might be justified as innocent and lawful. It is confessedly by deductions of the understanding that the first point is ascertained: how can we suppose that a different faculty of the mind is employed in fixing the other ?

On the other hand, those who would resolve all moral deter-minations into *sentiments* may endeavor to show that it is im-possible for reason ever to draw conclusions of this nature. To virtue, say they, it belongs to be *amiable,* and vice *odious.* This forms their very nature or essence. But can reason or argu-mentation distribute these different epithets to any subjects and pronounce beforehand that this must produce love, and that hatred? Or what other reason can we ever assign for these affections but the original fabric and formation of the human mind, which is naturally adapted to receive them?

The end of all moral speculations is to teach us our duty, and, by proper representations of the deformity of vice and beauty of virtue, beget correspondent habits, and engage us to avoid the one, and embrace the other. But is this ever to be expected from inferences and conclusions of the understanding, which of themselves have no hold of the affections or set in motion the active powers of men? They discover truths. But where the truths which they discover are indifferent and beget no desire or aversion, they can have no influence on conduct and behavior. What is honorable, what is fair, what is becom-ing, what is noble, what is generous takes possession of the heart and animates us to embrace and maintain it. What is intelligible, what is evident, what is probable, what is true procures only the cool assent of the understanding, and, gratifying a speculative curiosity, puts an end to our researches.

Extinguish all the warm feelings and prepossessions in favor of virtue, and all disgust or aversion to vice; render men totally indifferent toward these distinctions; and morality is no longer a practical study, nor has any tendency to regulate our lives and actions.

These arguments on each side (and many more might be produced) are so plausible that I am apt to suspect they may, the one as well as the other, be solid and satisfactory, and that *reason* and *sentiment* concur in almost all moral determinations and conclusions. The final sentence, it is probable, which pronounces characters and actions amiable or odious, praiseworthy or blamable; that which stamps on them the mark of honor or infamy, approbation or censure; that which renders morality an active principle and constitutes virtue our happiness, and vice our misery—it is probable, I say, that this final sentence depends on some internal sense or feeling which nature has made universal in the whole species. For what else can have an influence of this nature? But in order to pave the way for such a sentiment and give a proper discernment of its object, it is often necessary, we find, that much reasoning should precede, that nice distinctions be made, just conclusions drawn, distant comparisons formed, complicated relations examined, and general facts fixed and ascertained. Some species of beauty, especially the natural kinds, on their first appearance command our affection and approbation; and where they fail of this effect, it is impossible for any reasoning to redress their influence or adapt them better to our taste and sentiment. But in many orders of beauty, particularly those of the finer arts, it is requisite to employ much reasoning in order to feel the proper sentiment; and a false relish may frequently be corrected by argument and reflection. There are just grounds to conclude that moral beauty partakes much of this latter species and demands the assistance of our intellectual faculties in order to give it a suitable influence on the human mind.

But though this question concerning the general principles of morals be curious and important, it is needless for us at present to employ further care in our researches concerning it. For if we can be so happy, in the course of this inquiry, as to discover the true origin of morals, it will then easily appear how far either sentiment or reason enters into all determinations of this nature.[3] [4 In order to attain this purpose, we shall endeavor to follow a very simple method: we shall analyze that complication of mental qualities which form what, in common life, we call "personal merit"; we shall consider every attribute of the mind which renders a man an object either of esteem and affection or of hatred and contempt; every habit or sentiment or faculty which, if ascribed to any person, implies either praise or blame and may enter into any panegyric or satire of his character and manners. The quick sensibility, which, on this head, is so universal among mankind, gives a philosopher sufficient assurance that he can never be considerably mistaken in framing the catalogue or incur any danger of misplacing the objects of his contemplation: he needs only enter into his own breast for a moment and consider whether or not he should desire to have this or that quality ascribed to him, and whether

[3] See Appendix I, "Concerning Moral Sentiment."

[4] [The passage within brackets was inserted in edition O. Instead, editions G to N carried the following statement: "Meanwhile, it will scarce be possible for us, ere this controversy is fully decided, to proceed in that accurate manner, required in the sciences; by beginning with exact definitions of virtue and vice, which are the objects of our present inquiry. But we shall do what may justly be esteemed as satisfactory. We shall consider the matter as an object of experience. We shall call *every quality or action of the mind,* virtuous, *which is attended with the general approbation of mankind;* and we shall denominate vicious, *every quality which is the object of general blame or censure.* These qualities we shall endeavor to collect; and after examining, on both sides, the several circumstances in which they agree 'tis hoped we may, at last, reach the foundation of ethics, and find those universal principles, from which all moral blame or approbation is ultimately derived."]

such or such an imputation would proceed from a friend or an enemy. The very nature of language guides us almost infallibly in forming a judgment of this nature; and as every tongue possesses one set of words which are taken in a good sense, and another in the opposite, the least acquaintance with the idiom suffices, without any reasoning, to direct us in collecting and arranging the estimable or blamable qualities of men. The only object of reasoning is to discover the circumstances on both sides which are common to these qualities—to observe that particular in which the estimable qualities agree, on the one hand, and the blamable, on the other; and thence to reach the foundation of ethics and find those universal principles from which all censure or approbation is ultimately derived.] As this is a question of fact, not of abstract science, we can only expect success by following the experimental method and deducing general maxims from a comparison of particular instances. The other scientifical method, where a general abstract principle is first established, and is afterwards branched out into a variety of inferences and conclusions, may be more perfect in itself, but suits less the imperfection of human nature and is a common source of illusion and mistake, in this as well as in other subjects. Men are now cured of their passion for hypotheses and systems in natural philosophy, and will hearken to no arguments but those which are derived from experience. It is full time they should attempt a like reformation in all moral disquisitions and reject every system of ethics, however subtle or ingenious, which is not founded on fact and observation.

[5] We shall begin our inquiry on this head by the consideration of the social virtues; Benevolence and Justice. The explication of them will probably give us an opening by which the others may be accounted for.

[5] [This paragraph was added in Edition O.]

SECTION II [1]

OF BENEVOLENCE

PART I

IT may be esteemed, perhaps, a superfluous task to prove that the benevolent or softer affections [2] are *estimable* and, wherever they appear, engage the approbation and good will of mankind. The epithets, *sociable, good-natured, humane, merciful, grateful, friendly, generous, beneficent,* or their equivalents, are known in all languages, and universally express the highest merit which human nature is capable of attaining. Where these amiable qualities are attended with birth and power and eminent abilities, and display themselves in the good government or useful instruction of mankind, they seem even to raise the possessors of them above the rank of *human nature* and make them approach, in some measure, to the divine. Exalted capacity, undaunted courage, prosperous success —these may only expose a hero or politician to the envy and ill will of the public. But as soon as the praises are added of humane and beneficent, when instances are displayed of lenity, tenderness, or friendship, envy itself is silent or joins the general voice of approbation and applause.

When Pericles, the great Athenian statesman and general, was on his deathbed, his surrounding friends, deeming him now insensible, began to indulge their sorrow for their expiring patron by enumerating his great qualities and successes, his conquests and victories, the unusual length of his administration, and his nine trophies erected over the enemies of the republic. *You forget,* cries the dying hero who had heard all, *you forget the most eminent of my praises, while you dwell so much*

---

[1] [In Editions G to Q this Section was introduced by paragraphs, forming Part I, which subsequently appeared as Appendix II, "Of Self-Love."]

[2] [Are virtuous—engage the esteem, approbation, and etc.: Editions G to N.]

*on those vulgar advantages in which fortune had a principal
share. You have not observed that no citizen has ever yet worn
mourning on my account.*[3]

In men of more ordinary talents and capacity, the social virtues become, if possible, still more essentially requisite, there
being nothing eminent, in that case, to compensate for the want
of them, or preserve the person from our severest hatred as well
as contempt. A high ambition, an elevated courage is apt, says
Cicero, in less perfect characters, to degenerate into a turbulent
ferocity. The more social and softer virtues are there chiefly to
be regarded. These are always good and amiable.[4]

The principal advantage which Juvenal discovers in the extensive capacity of the human species is that it renders our benevolence also more extensive and gives us larger opportunities
of spreading our kindly influence than what are indulged to the
inferior creation.[5] It must, indeed, be confessed that by doing
good only can a man truly enjoy the advantages of being eminent. His exalted station, of itself, but the more exposes him to
danger and tempest. His sole prerogative is to afford shelter to
inferiors who repose themselves under his cover and protection.

But I forget that it is not my present business to recommend
generosity and benevolence, or to paint in their true colors all
the genuine charms of the social virtues. These, indeed, sufficiently engage every heart, on the first apprehension of them;
and it is difficult to abstain from some sally or panegyric, as
often as they occur in discourse or reasoning. But our object
here being more the speculative than the practical part of
morals, it will suffice to remark (what will readily, I believe, be
allowed) that no qualities are more entitled to the general good
will and approbation of mankind than beneficence and humanity, friendship and gratitude, natural affection and public
spirit, or whatever proceeds from a tender sympathy with
others and a generous concern for our kind and species. These,
wherever they appear, seem to transfuse themselves, in a man-

---

[3] Plutarch in *Pericle* 38.
[4] Cicero *de Officiis,* lib. i.
[5] Sat. xv. 139f.

ner, into each beholder, and to call forth, in their own behalf, the same favorable and affectionate sentiments which they exert on all around.

PART II [1]

We may observe that in displaying the praises of any humane, beneficent man there is one circumstance which never fails to be amply insisted on—namely, the happiness and satisfaction derived to society from his intercourse and good offices. To his parents, we are apt to say, he endears himself by his pious attachment and duteous care still more than by the connections of nature. His children never feel his authority but when employed for their advantage. With him, the ties of love are consolidated by beneficence and friendship. The ties of friendship approach, in a fond observance of each obliging office, to those of love and inclination. His domestics and dependents have in him a sure resource, and no longer dread the power of fortune but so far as she exercises it over him. From him the hungry receive food, the naked clothing, the ignorant and slothful skill and industry. Like the sun, an inferior minister of Providence, he cheers, invigorates, and sustains the surrounding world.

If confined to private life, the sphere of his activity is narrower, but his influence is all benign and gentle. If exalted into a higher station, mankind and posterity reap the fruit of his labors.

As these topics of praise never fail to be employed, and with success, where we would inspire esteem for anyone, may it not thence be concluded that the *utility* resulting from the social virtues forms, at least, a *part* of their merit, and is one source of that approbation and regard so universally paid to them?

When we recommend even an animal or a plant as *useful* and *beneficial,* we give it an applause and recommendation suited to its nature. As, on the other hand, reflection on the baneful influence of any of these inferior beings always inspires us with

[1] [Part III in Editions G to Q.]

the sentiment of aversion. The eye is pleased with the prospect of cornfields and loaded vineyards, horses grazing, and flocks pasturing; but flies the view of briars and brambles affording shelter to wolves and serpents.

A machine, a piece of furniture, a vestment, a house well contrived for use and convenience is so far beautiful and is contemplated with pleasure and approbation. An experienced eye is here sensible to many excellences which escape persons ignorant and uninstructed.

Can anything stronger be said in praise of a profession, such as merchandise or manufacture, than to observe the advantages which it procures to society? And is not a monk and inquisitor enraged when we treat his order as useless or pernicious to mankind?

The historian exults in displaying the benefit arising from his labors. The writer of romance alleviates or denies the bad consequences ascribed to his manner of composition.

In general, what praise is implied in the simple epithet "useful"! What reproach in the contrary!

Your gods, says Cicero,[2] in opposition to the Epicureans, cannot justly claim any worship or adoration with whatever imaginary perfections you may suppose them endowed. They are totally useless and inactive. Even the Egyptians, whom you so much ridicule, never consecrated any animal but on account of its utility.

The skeptics assert,[3] though absurdly, that the origin of all religious worship was derived from the utility of inanimate objects, as the sun and moon to the support and well-being of mankind. This is also the common reason assigned by historians for the deification of eminent heroes and legislators.[4]

To plant a tree, to cultivate a field, to beget children—meritorious acts, according to the religion of Zoroaster.

In all determinations of morality, this circumstance of public utility is ever principally in view; and wherever disputes arise,

---

[2] *De Nat. Deor.* lib. i. 36.
[3] Sext. *Emp. adversus Math.* lib. viii. [ix. 394, 18.]
[4] Diod. Sic. *passim.*

either in philosophy or common life, concerning the bounds of duty, the question cannot, by any means, be decided with greater certainty than by ascertaining, on any side, the true interests of mankind. If any false opinion, embraced from appearances, has been found to prevail, as soon as further experience and sounder reasoning have given us juster notions of human affairs, we retract our first sentiment and adjust anew the boundaries of moral good and evil.

Giving alms to common beggars is naturally praised, because it seems to carry relief to the distressed and indigent. But when we observe the encouragement thence arising to idleness and debauchery, we regard that species of charity rather as a weakness than a virtue.

Tyrannicide, or the assassination of usurpers and oppressive princes, was highly extolled in ancient times, because it both freed mankind from many of these monsters and seemed to keep the others in awe whom the sword or poniard could not reach. But history and experience having since convinced us that this practice increases the jealousy and cruelty of princes, a Timoleon and a Brutus, though treated with indulgence on account of the prejudices of their times, are now considered as very improper models for imitation.

Liberality in princes is regarded as a mark of beneficence. But when it occurs that the homely bread of the honest and industrious is often thereby converted into delicious cates for the idle and the prodigal, we soon retract our heedless praises. The regrets of a prince for having lost a day were noble and generous; but had he intended to have spent it in acts of generosity to his greedy courtiers, it was better lost than misemployed after that manner.

Luxury, or a refinement on the pleasures and conveniences of life, had long been supposed the source of every corruption in government, and the immediate cause of faction, sedition, civil wars, and the total loss of liberty. It was therefore universally regarded as a vice, and was an object of declamation to all satirists and severe moralists. Those who prove, or attempt to prove, that such refinements rather tend to the increase of industry, civility, and arts regulate anew our *moral* as well as *political* sentiments and represent as laudable or innocent what had formerly been regarded as pernicious and blamable.

Upon the whole, then, it seems undeniable that nothing can bestow more merit on any human creature than the sentiment of benevolence in an eminent degree, and that a *part,* at least, of its merit arises from its tendency to promote the interests of our species and bestow happiness on human society. We carry our view into the salutary consequences of such a character and disposition; and whatever has so benign an influence and forwards so desirable an end is beheld with complacency and pleasure. The social virtues are never regarded without their beneficial tendencies, nor viewed as barren and unfruitful. The happiness of mankind, the order of society, the harmony of families, the mutual support of friends are always considered as the result of the gentle dominion over the breasts of men.

How considerable a *part* of their merit we ought to ascribe to their utility will better appear from future disquisitions,[5] as well as the reason why this circumstance has such a command over our esteem and approbation.[6]

SECTION III

OF JUSTICE

PART I

THAT Justice is useful to society, and consequently that *part* of its merit, at least, must arise from that consideration, it would be a superfluous undertaking to prove. That public utility is the *sole* origin of Justice, and that reflections on the beneficial consequences of this virtue are the *sole* foundation

---

[5] Sect. III: "Of Justice," and Sect. IV: "Of Political Society."
[6] Sect. V: "Why Utility Pleases."

of its merit, this proposition, being more curious and important, will better deserve our examination and inquiry.

Let us suppose that nature has bestowed on the human race such profuse *abundance* of all *external* conveniences that, without any uncertainty in the event, without any care or industry on our part, every individual finds himself fully provided with whatever his most voracious appetites can want or luxurious imagination wish or desire. His natural beauty, we shall suppose, surpasses all acquired ornaments: the perpetual clemency of the seasons renders useless all clothes or covering; the raw herbage affords him the most delicious fare; the clear fountain the richest beverage. No laborious occupation required: no tillage, no navigation. Music, poetry, and contemplation form his sole business; conversation, mirth, and friendship, his sole amusement.

It seems evident that in such a happy state every other social virtue would flourish and receive tenfold increase; but the cautious, jealous virtue of justice would never once have been dreamed of. For what purpose make a partition of goods where everyone has already more than enough? Why give rise to property where there cannot possibly be any injury? Why call this object *mine* when, upon the seizing of it by another, I need but stretch out my hand to possess myself of what is equally valuable? Justice, in that case, being totally *useless*, would be an idle ceremonial and could never possibly have place in the catalogue of virtues.

We see, even in the present necessitous condition of mankind, that, wherever any benefit is bestowed by nature in an unlimited abundance, we leave it always in common among the whole human race and make no subdivisions of right and property. Water and air, though the most necessary of all objects, are not challenged as the property of individuals; nor can any man commit injustice by the most lavish use and enjoyment of these blessings. In fertile, extensive countries, with few inhabitants, land is regarded on the same footing. And no topic is so much insisted on, by those who defend the liberty of the seas, as the unexhausted use of them in navigation. Were the advantages procured by navigation as inexhaustible, these reasoners had never had any adversaries to refute, nor had any claims ever been advanced of a separate, exclusive dominion over the ocean.

It may happen in some countries, at some periods, that there be established a property in water, none in land,[1] if the latter be in greater abundance than can be used by the inhabitants, and the former be found with difficulty and in very small quantities.

Again: suppose that, though the necessities of the human race continue the same as at present, yet the mind is so enlarged and so replete with friendship and generosity that every man has the utmost tenderness for every man, and feels no more concern for his own interest than for that of his fellows: It seems evident that the *use* of Justice would, in this case, be suspended by such an extensive benevolence, nor would the divisions and barriers of property and obligation have ever been thought of. Why should I bind another, by a deed or promise, to do me any good office when I know that he is already prompted by the strongest inclination to seek my happiness and would of himself perform the desired service, except the hurt he thereby receives be greater than the benefit accruing to me; in which case he knows that, from my innate humanity and friendship, I should be the first to oppose myself to his imprudent generosity? Why raise landmarks between my neighbor's field and mine when my heart has made no division between our interests, but shares all his joys and sorrows with the same force and vivacity as if originally my own? Every man, upon this supposition, being a second self to another, would trust all his interests to the discretion of every man without jealousy, without partition, without distinction. And the whole human race would form only one family where all would lie in common and be used freely, without regard to property; but cautiously too, with an entire regard to the necessities of each individual, as if our own interests were most intimately concerned.

In the present disposition of the human heart, it would per-

[1] Genesis, Chaps. 13 and 21.

haps be difficult to find complete instances of such enlarged affections; but still we may observe that the case of families approaches toward it; and the stronger the mutual benevolence is among the individuals, the nearer it approaches, till all distinction of property be, in a great measure, lost and confounded among them. Between married persons, the cement of friendship is by the laws supposed so strong as to abolish all division of possessions, and has often, in reality, the force ascribed to it. And it is observable that, during the ardor of new enthusiasms, when every principle is inflamed into extravagance, the community of goods has frequently been attempted; and nothing but experience of its inconveniences, from the returning or disguised selfishness of men, could make the imprudent fanatics adopt anew the ideas of justice and of separate property. So true is it that this virtue derives its existence entirely from its necessary *use* to the intercourse and social state of mankind.

To make this truth more evident, let us reverse the foregoing suppositions and, carrying everything to the opposite extreme, consider what would be the effect of these new situations. Suppose a society to fall into such want of all common necessaries that the utmost frugality and industry cannot preserve the greater number from perishing and the whole from extreme misery: it will readily, I believe, be admitted that the strict laws of justice are suspended in such a pressing emergency and give place to the stronger motives of necessity and self-preservation. Is it any crime, after a shipwreck, to seize whatever means or instrument of safety one can lay hold of, without regard to former limitations of property? Or if a city besieged were perishing with hunger, can we imagine that men will see any means of preservation before them and lose their lives from a scrupulous regard to what, in other situations, would be the rules of equity and justice? The *use* and *tendency* of that virtue is to procure happiness and security, by preserving order in society. But where the society is ready to perish from extreme necessity, no greater evil can be dreaded from violence and injustice, and every man may now provide for himself by all the means which prudence can dictate or humanity permit. The public, even in less urgent necessities, opens granaries without the consent of proprietors, as justly supposing that the authority of magistracy may, consistent with equity, extend so far. But were any number of men to assemble without the tie of laws or civil jurisdiction, would an equal partition of bread in a famine, though effected by power and even violence, be regarded as criminal or injurious?

Suppose, likewise, that it should be a virtuous man's fate to fall into the society of ruffians, remote from the protection of laws and government, what conduct must he embrace in that melancholy situation? He sees such a desperate rapaciousness prevail, such a disregard to equity, such contempt of order, such stupid blindness to future consequences, as must immediately have the most tragical conclusion and must terminate in destruction to the greater number and in a total dissolution of society to the rest. He, meanwhile, can have no other expedient than to arm himself, to whomever the sword he seizes, or the buckler, may belong; to make provision of all means of defense and security. And his particular regard to justice being no longer of *use* to his own safety or that of others, he must consult the dictates of self-preservation alone, without concern for those who no longer merit his care and attention.

When any man, even in political society, renders himself by his crimes obnoxious to the public, he is punished by the laws in his goods and person; that is, the ordinary rules of justice are, with regard to him, suspended for a moment, and it becomes equitable to inflict on him, for the *benefit* of society, what otherwise he could not suffer without wrong or injury.

The rage and violence of public war, what is it but a suspension of justice among the warring parties who perceive that this virtue is now no longer of any *use* or advantage to them? The laws of war, which then succeed to those of equity and justice, are rules calculated for the *advantage* and *utility* of that particular state in which men are now placed. And were a civilized nation engaged with barbarians who observed no rules even of war, the former must also suspend their observance of them where they no longer serve to any purpose, and must render every action or rencounter as bloody and pernicious as possible to the first aggressors.

Thus the rules of equity or justice depend entirely on the particular state and condition in which men are placed, and owe their origin and existence to that *utility* which results to the public from their strict and regular observance. Reverse, in any considerable circumstance, the condition of men: produce extreme abundance or extreme necessity, implant in the human breast perfect moderation and humanity or perfect rapaciousness and malice; by rendering justice totally *useless,* you thereby totally destroy its essence and suspend its obligation upon mankind.

The common situation of society is a medium amidst all these extremes. We are naturally partial to ourselves and to our friends, but are capable of learning the advantage resulting from a more equitable conduct. Few enjoyments are given us from the open and liberal hand of nature; but by art, labor, and industry we can extract them in great abundance. Hence the ideas of property become necessary in all civil society; hence justice derives its usefulness to the public; and hence alone arises its merit and moral obligation.

These conclusions are so natural and obvious that they have not escaped even the poets in their descriptions of the felicity attending the golden age or the reign of Saturn. The seasons in that first period of nature were so temperate, if we credit these agreeable fictions, that there was no necessity for men to provide themselves with clothes and houses, as a security against the violence of heat and cold: the rivers flowed with wine and milk; the oaks yielded honey; and Nature spontaneously produced her greatest delicacies. Nor were these the chief advantages of that happy age. Tempests were not alone removed from nature, but those most furious tempests were unknown to human breasts which now cause such uproar and engender such confusion. Avarice, ambition, cruelty, selfishness were never heard of; cordial affection, compassion, sympathy were the only movements with which the mind was yet acquainted. Even the punctilious distinction of *mine* and *thine* was banished from among that happy race of mortals and carried with it the very notion of property and obligation, justice and injustice.

This *poetical* fiction of the *golden age* is, in some respects, of a piece with the *philosophical* fiction of the *state of nature;* only that the former is represented as the most charming and most peaceable condition which can possibly be imagined, whereas the latter is painted out as a state of mutual war and violence attended with the most extreme necessity. On the first origin of mankind, we are told, their ignorance and savage nature were so prevalent that they could give no mutual trust, but must each depend upon himself and his own force or cunning for protection and security. No law was heard of; no rule of justice known; no distinction of property regarded; power was the only measure of right; and a perpetual war of all against all was the result of men's untamed selfishness and barbarity.[2]

2 This fiction of a state of nature as a state of war was not first started by Mr. Hobbes, as is commonly imagined. Plato endeavors to refute a hypothesis very like it in the 2d, 3d, and 4th books *de Republica.* Cicero, on the contrary, supposes it certain and universally acknowledged in the following passage.* "Quis enim vestrum, judices, ignorat, ita naturam rerum tulisse, ut quodam tempore homines, nondum neque naturali, neque civili jure descripto, fusi per agros ac dispersi vagarentur, tantumque haberent, quantum manu ac viribus, per caedem ac vulnera, aut eripere, aut retinere potuissent? Qui igitur primi virtute et consilio praestanti exstiterunt, ii perspecto genere humanae docilitatis atque ingenii, dissipatos unum in locum congregarunt, eosque ex feritate illa ad justitiam atque mansuetudinem transduxerunt. Tum res ad communem utilitatem, quas publicas appellamus, tum conventicula hominum, quae postea civitates nominatae sunt, tum domicilia conjuncta, quas urbes dicimus, invento et divino et humano jure, moenibus sepserunt. Atque inter hanc vitam perpolitam humanitate, et illam immanem, nihil tam interest, quam JUS atque VIS. Horum utro uti nolimus, altero est utendum. Vim volumus extingui? Jus valeat necesse est, id est, judicia, quibus omne jus continetur. Judicia displicent, aut nulla sunt? Vis dominetur necesse est. Haec vident omnes."— PRO SEXT, 1. 42.†

* [Editions G to N add: "Which is the only authority I shall cite for these reasonings: not imitating in this the example of Pufendorf, nor even that of Grotius, who think a verse from Ovid or Plautus or Petronius a necessary warrant for every moral truth; or the example of Mr. Woollaston, who has constant recourse to Hebrew and Arabic authors for the same purpose."]

Whether such a condition of human nature could ever exist or, if it did, could continue so long as to merit the appellation of a state may justly be doubted. Men are necessarily born in a family society at least and are trained up by their parents to some rule of conduct and behavior. But this must be admitted, that, if such a state of mutual war and violence was ever real, the suspension of all laws of justice, from their absolute inutility, is a necessary and infallible consequence.

The more we vary our views of human life, and the newer and more unusual the lights are in which we survey it, the more shall we be convinced that the origin here assigned for the virtue of justice is real and satisfactory.

Were there a species of creatures intermingled with men which, though rational, were possessed of such inferior strength, both of body and mind, that they were incapable of all resistance and could never, upon the highest provocation, make us feel the effects of their resentment, the necessary consequence, I think, is that we should be bound, by the laws of humanity, to give gentle usage to these creatures, but should not, properly speaking, lie under any restraint of justice with regard to them, nor could they possess any right or property exclusive of such arbitrary lords. Our intercourse with them could not be called society, which supposes a degree of equality,

---

† ["For is there anyone among you, gentlemen of the jury, who does not know that nature brought it about that there was a time when neither natural nor civil law was yet defined and men roamed scattered and dispersed over the fields and only had what they were able to seize and keep with violent hands through slaughter and wounds? Accordingly, those who first were eminent by reason of their outstanding virtue and judgment recognized the kind of teachability and intelligence inherent in man, gathered the dispersed in one place, and transformed them from savagery into justice and gentleness. Then affairs were organized to the common advantage, which we call public affairs; then associations came into being, which were later called states; then dwelling places were joined together, to which we give the name of 'cities,' and enclosed with walls, after divine and human law had been invented. Nothing so marks the difference between this highly civilized life of ours and that early monstrous way of life as 'law' and 'violence.' If we refuse to employ one of them, we have to use the other. If we want violence to be extirpated, we must of necessity let law prevail, that is, the verdicts in which all law is contained. If we dislike the verdicts or they are not enforced, violence must necessarily rule. That is clear to all." *Pro P. Sextio (For Publius Sextius)*, 1. 42.]

but absolute command on the one side, and servile obedience on the other. Whatever we covet, they must instantly resign. Our permission is the only tenure by which they hold their possessions, our compassion and kindness the only check by which they curb our lawless will; and as no inconvenience ever results from the exercise of a power so firmly established in nature, the restraints of justice and property, being totally *useless,* would never have place in so unequal a confederacy.

This is plainly the situation of men with regard to animals; and how far these may be said to possess reason I leave it to others to determine. The great superiority of civilized Europeans above barbarous Indians tempted us to imagine ourselves on the same footing with regard to them and made us throw off all restraints of justice, and even of humanity, in our treatment of them. In many nations, the female sex are reduced to like slavery and are rendered incapable of all property, in opposition to their lordly masters. But though the males, when united, have in all countries bodily force sufficient to maintain this severe tyranny, yet such are the insinuations, address, and charms of their fair companions that women are commonly able to break the confederacy and share with the other sex in all the rights and privileges of society.

Were the human species so framed by nature as that each individual possessed within himself every faculty requisite both for his own preservation and for the propagation of his kind, were all society and intercourse cut off between man and man by the primary intention of the Supreme Creator, it seems evident that so solitary a being would be as much incapable of justice as of social discourse and conversation. Where mutual regards and forbearance serve to no manner of purpose, they would never direct the conduct of any reasonable man. The headlong course of the passions would be checked by no reflection on future consequences. And as each man is here supposed to love himself alone and to depend only on himself and his own activity for safety and happiness, he would on every occasion, to the utmost of his power, challenge the preference above every other being, to none of which he is bound by any ties, either of nature or of interest.

But suppose the conjunction of the sexes to be established in nature, a family immediately arises, and particular rules being found requisite for its subsistence, these are immediately embraced, though without comprehending the rest of mankind within their prescriptions. Suppose that several families unite together into one society which is totally disjoined from all others, the rules which preserve peace and order enlarge themselves to the utmost extent of that society, but, becoming then entirely useless, lose their force when carried one step farther. But again, suppose that several distinct societies maintain a kind of intercourse for mutual convenience and advantage, the boundaries of justice still grow larger, in proportion to the largeness of men's views and the force of their mutual connections. History, experience, reason sufficiently instruct us in this natural progress of human sentiments and in the gradual enlargement of our regards to justice, in proportion as we become acquainted with the extensive utility of that virtue.

PART II

IF we examine the *particular* laws by which justice is directed and property determined, we shall still be presented with the same conclusions. The good of mankind is the only object of all these laws and regulations. Not only is it requisite for the peace and interest of society that men's possessions should be separated, but the rules which we follow in making the separation are such as can best be contrived to serve further the interests of society.

We shall suppose that a creature possessed of reason, but unacquainted with human nature, deliberates with himself what *rules* of justice or property would best promote public interest and establish peace and security among mankind: his most obvious thought would be to assign the largest possessions to the most extensive virtue and give everyone the power of doing good, proportioned to his inclination. In a perfect theocracy, where a being infinitely intelligent governs by particular volitions, this rule would certainly have place and might serve to the wisest purposes. But were mankind to execute such a law, so great is the uncertainty of merit, both from its natural obscurity and from the self-conceit of each individual, that no determinate rule of conduct would ever result from it; and the total dissolution of society must be the immediate consequence. Fanatics may suppose *that dominion is founded on grace,* and *that saints alone inherit the earth;* but the civil magistrate very justly puts these sublime theorists on the same footing with common robbers and teaches them, by the severest discipline, that a rule which in speculation may seem the most advantageous to society may yet be found in practice totally pernicious and destructive.

That there were *religious* fanatics of this kind in England during the civil wars, we learn from history; though it is probable that the obvious *tendency* of these principles excited such horror in mankind, as soon obliged the dangerous enthusiasts to renounce, or at least conceal, their tenets. Perhaps the *levellers,*[1] who claimed an equal distribution of property, were a kind of *political* fanatics which arose from the religious species, and more openly avowed their pretensions; as carrying a more plausible appearance, of being practicable in themselves as well as useful to human society.

It must, indeed, be confessed that nature is so liberal to mankind that, were all her presents equally divided among the species and improved by art and industry, every individual would enjoy all the necessaries and even most of the comforts of life, nor would ever be liable to any ills but such as might accidentally arise from the sickly frame and constitution of his body. It must also be confessed that wherever we depart from this equality we rob the poor of more satisfaction than we add

1 [The Levellers were an influential political party of Puritans which arose in the Army of the Long Parliament about 1647. More radical and more secular in their political thinking than the Independents, the Levellers advocated a levelling of all ranks and social distinctions.]

to the rich, and that the slight gratification of a frivolous vanity in one individual frequently costs more than bread to many families, and even provinces. It may appear withal that the rule of equality, as it would be highly *useful,* is not altogether *impracticable,* but has taken place, at least in an imperfect degree, in some republics, particularly that of Sparta, where it was attended, it is said, with the most beneficial consequences. Not to mention that the *agrarian* laws, so frequently claimed in Rome, and carried into execution in many Greek cities, proceeded, all of them, from the general idea of the utility of this principle.

But historians, and even common sense, may inform us that, however specious these ideas of *perfect* equality may seem, they are really at bottom *impracticable;* and were they not so, would be extremely *pernicious* to human society. Render possessions ever so equal, men's different degrees of art, care, and industry will immediately break that equality. Or if you check these virtues, you reduce society to the most extreme indigence and, instead of preventing want and beggary in a few, render it unavoidable to the whole community. The most rigorous inquisition, too, is requisite to watch every inequality on its first appearance; and the most severe jurisdiction to punish and redress it. But besides that so much authority must soon degenerate into tyranny and be exerted with great partialities: who can possibly be possessed of it in such a situation as is here supposed? Perfect equality of possessions, destroying all subordination, weakens extremely the authority of magistracy and must reduce all power nearly to a level, as well as property.

We may conclude, therefore, that, in order to establish laws for the regulation of property, we must be acquainted with the nature and situation of man, must reject appearances which may be false, though specious; and must search for those rules which are, on the whole, most *useful* and *beneficial:* vulgar sense and slight experience are sufficient for this purpose, where men give not way to too selfish avidity or too extensive enthusiasm.

Who sees not, for instance, that whatever is produced or improved by a man's art or industry ought forever to be secured to him in order to give encouragement to such *useful* habits and accomplishments? That the property ought also to descend to children and relations, for the same *useful* purpose? That it may be alienated by consent in order to beget that commerce and intercourse which is so *beneficial* to human society? And that all contracts and promises ought carefully to be fulfilled in order to secure mutual trust and confidence, by which the general *interest* of mankind is so much promoted?

Examine the writers on the laws of nature and you will always find that, whatever principles they set out with, they are sure to terminate here at last and to assign, as the ultimate reason for every rule which they establish, the convenience and necessities of mankind. A concession thus extorted, in opposition to systems, has more authority than if it had been made in prosecution of them.

What other reason, indeed, could writers ever give why this must be *mine* and that *yours,* since uninstructed nature, surely, never made any such distinction? The objects which receive those appellations are of themselves foreign to us; they are totally disjoined and separated from us; and nothing but the general interests of society can form the connection.

Sometimes the interests of society may require a rule of justice in a particular case, but may not determine any particular rule, among several which are all equally beneficial. In that case the *slightest* analogies are laid hold of in order to prevent that indifference and ambiguity which would be the source of perpetual dissension. Thus possession alone, and first possession, is supposed to convey property where nobody else has any preceding claim and pretension. Many of the reasonings of lawyers are of this analogical nature and depend on very slight connections of the imagination.

Does anyone scruple, in extraordinary cases, to violate all regard to the private property of individuals and sacrifice to public interest a distinction which had been established for the sake of that interest? The safety of the people is the supreme law: all other particular laws are subordinate to it and depend-

ent on it; and if, in the *common* course of things, they be followed and regarded, it is only because the public safety and
interest *commonly* demand so equal and impartial an administration.

Sometimes both *utility* and *analogy* fail and leave the laws of
justice in total uncertainty. Thus it is highly requisite that
prescription or long possession should convey property; but
what number of days or months or years should be sufficient for
that purpose it is impossible for reason alone to determine.
Civil laws here supply the place of the natural *code* and assign
different terms for prescription, according to the different
utilities proposed by the legislature. Bills of exchange and
promissory notes, by the laws of most countries, prescribe
sooner than bonds and mortgages and contracts of a more for-
mal nature.

In general, we may observe that all questions of property are
subordinate to the authority of civil laws, which extend, re-
strain, modify, and alter the rules of natural justice, according
to the particular *convenience* of each community. The laws
have, or ought to have, a constant reference to the constitution
of government, the manners, the climate, the religion, the commerce, the situation of each society. A late author [2] of genius,
as well as learning, has prosecuted this subject at large, and has
established from these principles a system of political knowledge which abounds in ingenious and brilliant thoughts, and
is not wanting in solidity.[3]

[2] [Editions G and K read: "Of great genius as well as extensive learning
. . . the best system of political knowledge, that, perhaps, has ever yet been
communicated to the world."]

[3] The author of *L'Esprit des Loix* [Montesquieu]. This illustrious writer,
however, sets out with a different theory and supposes all right to be
founded on certain *rapports* or relations, which is a system that, in my
opinion, never will be reconciled with true philosophy. Father Malebranche,
as far as I can learn, was the first that started this abstract theory of morals,
which was afterwards adopted by Cudworth,* Clarke, and others; and as
it excludes all sentiment and pretends to found everything on reason, it has
not wanted followers in this philosophic age. See Section I, Appendix I.
With regard to justice, the virtue here treated of, the inference against this

What is a man's property? Anything which it is lawful for him, and for him alone, to use. *But what rule have we by which we can distinguish these objects?* Here we must have recourse to statutes, customs, precedents, analogies, and a hundred other circumstances—some of which are constant and inflexible, some variable and arbitrary. But the ultimate point, in which they all professedly terminate, is the interest and happiness of human society. Where this enters not into consideration, nothing can appear more whimsical, unnatural, and even superstitious than all or most of the laws of justice and of property.

Those who ridicule vulgar superstitions and expose the folly of particular regards to meats, days, places, postures, apparel have an easy task, while they consider all the qualities and relations of the objects and discover no adequate cause for that affection or antipathy, veneration or horror, which have so mighty an influence over a considerable part of mankind. A Syrian would have starved rather than taste pigeons; an

---

theory seems short and conclusive. Property is allowed to be dependent on civil laws; civil laws are allowed to have no other object but the interest of society. This, therefore, must be allowed to be the sole foundation of property and justice. Not to mention that our obligation itself to obey the magistrate and his laws is founded on nothing but the interests of society.

If the ideas of justice sometimes do not follow the dispositions of civil law, we shall find that these cases, instead of objections, are confirmations of the theory delivered above. Where a civil law is so perverse as to cross all the interests of society, it loses all its authority, and men judge by the ideas of natural justice, which are conformable to those interests. Sometimes also civil laws, for useful purposes, require a ceremony or form to any deed; and where that is wanting, their decrees run contrary to the usual tenor of justice; but one who takes advantage of such chicanes is not commonly regarded as an honest man. Thus the interests of society require that contracts be fulfilled; and there is not a more material article either of natural or civil justice. But the omission of a trifling circumstance will often, by law, invalidate a contract *in foro humano,* but not *in foro conscientiae,* as divines express themselves. In these cases, the magistrate is supposed only to withdraw his power of enforcing the right, not to have altered the right. Where his intention extends to the right and is conformable to the interests of society, it never fails to alter the right—a clear proof of the origin of justice and of property, as assigned above.

* [The reference to Cudworth was added in Edition O.]

Egyptian would not have approached bacon; but if these species of food be examined by the senses of sight, smell, or taste, or scrutinized by the sciences of chemistry, medicine, or physics, no difference is ever found between them and any other species, nor can that precise circumstance be pitched on which may afford a just foundation for the religious passion. A fowl on Thursday is lawful food; on Friday abominable: eggs, in this house and in this diocese, are permitted during Lent; a hundred paces farther, to eat them is a damnable sin. This earth or building yesterday was profane; today, by the muttering of certain words, it has become holy and sacred. Such reflections as these, in the mouth of a philosopher, one may safely say, are too obvious to have any influence, because they must always, to every man, occur at first sight; and where they prevail not of themselves, they are surely obstructed by education, prejudice, and passion, not by ignorance or mistake.

It may appear to a careless view, or rather a too abstracted reflection, that there enters a like superstition into all the sentiments of justice; and that, if a man expose its object, or what we call property, to the same scrutiny of sense and science, he will not, by the most accurate inquiry, find any foundation for the difference made by moral sentiment. I may lawfully nourish myself from this tree; but the fruit of another of the same species, ten paces off, it is criminal for me to touch. Had I worn this apparel an hour ago, I had merited the severest punishment; but a man, by pronouncing a few magical syllables, has now rendered it fit for my use and service. Were this house placed in the neighboring territory, it had been immoral for me to dwell in it; but being built on this side the river, it is subject to a different municipal law, and [4] by its becoming mine I incur no blame or censure. The same species of reasoning, it may be thought, which so successfully exposes superstition is also applicable to justice; nor is it possible, in the one case more than in the other, to point out in the object that precise quality or circumstance which is the foundation of the sentiment.

But there is this material difference between *superstition* and

[4] [By its becoming mine: added in Edition Q.]

justice, that the former is frivolous, useless, and burdensome; the latter is absolutely requisite to the well-being of mankind and existence of society. When we abstract from this circumstance (for it is too apparent ever to be overlooked), it must be confessed that all regards to right and property seem entirely without foundation, as much as the grossest and most vulgar superstition. Were the interests of society nowise concerned, it is as unintelligible why another's articulating certain sounds, implying consent, should change the nature of my actions with regard to a particular object, as why the reciting of a liturgy by a priest, in a certain habit and posture, should dedicate a heap of brick and timber and render it thenceforth and forever sacred.[5]

[5] It is evident that the will or consent alone never transfers property, nor causes the obligation of a promise (for the same reasoning extends to both); but the will must be expressed by words or signs in order to impose a tie upon any man. The expression, being once brought in as subservient to the will, soon becomes the principal part of the promise; nor will a man be less bound by his word, though he secretly give a different direction to his intention and withhold the assent of his mind. But though the expression makes, on most occasions, the whole of the promise, yet it does not always so; and one who should make use of any expression of which he knows not the meaning, and which he uses without any sense of the consequences, would not certainly be bound by it. Nay, though he know its meaning, yet if he uses it in jest only, and with such signs as evidently show that he has no serious intentions of binding himself, he would not lie under any obligation of performance; but it is necessary that the words be a perfect expression of the will, without any contrary signs. Nay, even this we must not carry so far as to imagine that one whom, by our quickness of understanding, we conjecture, from certain signs, to have an intention of deceiving us is not bound by his expression or verbal promise, if we accept of it; but must limit this conclusion to those cases where the signs are of a different nature from those of deceit. All these contradictions are easily accounted for if justice arise entirely from its usefulness to society; but will never be explained on any other hypothesis.

It is remarkable that the moral decisions of the *Jesuits,* and other relaxed casuists, were commonly formed in prosecution of some such subtleties of reasoning as are here pointed out, and proceeded as much from the habit of scholastic refinement as from any corruption of the heart, if we may follow the authority of Mons. Bayle. See his *Dictionary,* article "Loyola." And why has the indignation of mankind risen so high against these casuists, but

These reflections are far from weakening the obligations of justice, or diminishing anything from the most sacred attention to property. On the contrary, such sentiments must acquire new force from the present reasoning. For what stronger foundation can be desired or conceived for any duty than to observe that human society, or even human nature, could not subsist without the establishment of it, and will still arrive at greater degrees of happiness and perfection, the more inviolable the regard is which is paid to that duty?

⁶ The dilemma seems obvious: as justice evidently tends to promote public utility and to support civil society, the sentiment of justice is either derived from our reflecting on that tendency or, like hunger, thirst, and other appetites, resentment, love of life, attachment to offspring, and other passions, arises

---

because everyone perceived that human society could not subsist were such practices authorized, and that morals must always be handled with a view to public interest more than philosophical regularity? If the secret direction of the intention, said every man of sense, could invalidate a contract, where is our security? And yet a metaphysical schoolman might think that where an intention was supposed to be requisite, if that intention really had no place, no consequence ought to follow and no obligation be imposed. The casuistical subtleties may not be greater than the subtleties of lawyers, hinted at above; but as the former are *pernicious,* and the latter *innocent* and even *necessary,* this is the reason of the very different reception they meet with from the world.

* [It is a doctrine of the church of Rome, that the priest, by a secret direction of his intention, can invalidate any sacrament. This position is derived from a strict and regular prosecution of the obvious truth, that empty words alone, without any meaning or intention in the speaker, can never be attended with any effect. If the same conclusion be not admitted in reasonings concerning civil contracts, where the affair is allowed to be of so much less consequence than the eternal salvation of thousands, it proceeds entirely from men's sense of the danger and inconvenience of the doctrine in the former case. And we may thence observe that, however positive, arrogant, and dogmatical any superstition may appear, it never can convey any thorough persuasion of the reality of its objects, or put them, in any degree, on a balance with the common incidents of life which we learn from daily observation and experimental reasoning.]

* [This paragraph was added in Edition O.]

⁶ [Edition Q omits all between this point and the concluding paragraph of the section "rule of philosophizing."]

from a simple original instinct in the human breast, which nature has implanted for like salutary purposes.[7] If the latter be the case, it follows that property, which is the object of justice, is also distinguished by a simple, original instinct, and is not ascertained by any argument or reflection. But who is there that ever heard of such an instinct? Or is this a subject in which new discoveries can be made? We may as well expect to discover in the body new senses which had before escaped the observation of all mankind.

But further, though it seems a very simple proposition to say that nature, by an instinctive sentiment, distinguishes property, yet in reality we shall find that there are required for that purpose ten thousand different instincts, and these employed about objects of the greatest intricacy and nicest discernment. For when a definition of *property* is required, that relation is found to resolve itself into any possession acquired by occupation, by industry, by prescription, by inheritance, by contract, etc. Can we think that nature, by an original instinct, instructs us in all these methods of acquisition?

These words, too, inheritance and contract, stand for ideas infinitely complicated; and to define them exactly a hundred volumes of laws, and a thousand volumes of commentators have not been found sufficient. Does nature, whose instincts in men are all simple, embrace such complicated and artificial objects and create a rational creature without trusting anything to the operation of his reason?

But even though all this were admitted, it would not be satisfactory. Positive laws can certainly transfer property. It is by another original instinct that we recognize the authority of kings and senates and mark all the boundaries of their jurisdiction? Judges, too, even though their sentence be erroneous and illegal, must be allowed, for the sake of peace and order, to have decisive authority and ultimately to determine property.

7 [Edition N omits the preceding sentence, and reads instead: "If justice arose from a simple, original instinct in the human breast, without any reflection, even on those obvious interests of society, which absolutely require that virtue, it follows," etc.]

Have we original, innate ideas of praetors, and chancellors, and juries? Who sees not that all these institutions arise merely from the necessities of human society?

All birds of the same species, in every age and country, build their nests alike: in this we see the force of instinct. Men, in different times and places, frame their houses differently: here we perceive the influence of reason and custom. A like inference may be drawn from comparing the instinct of generation and the institution of property.

How great soever the variety of municipal laws, it must be confessed that their chief outlines pretty regularly concur, because the purposes to which they tend are everywhere exactly similar. In like manner, all houses have a roof and walls, windows and chimneys, though diversified in their shape, figure, and materials. The purposes of the latter, directed to the conveniences of human life, discover not more plainly their origin from reason and reflection than do those of the former, which point all to a like end.

I need not mention the variations which all the rules of property receive from the finer turns and connections of the imagination, and from the subtleties and abstractions of law topics and reasonings. There is no possibility of reconciling this observation to the notion of original instincts.

What alone will beget a doubt concerning the theory on which I insist is the influence of education and acquired habits, by which we are so accustomed to blame injustice that we are not, in every instance, conscious of any immediate reflection on the pernicious consequences of it. The views the most familiar to us are apt, for that very reason, to escape us; and what we have very frequently performed from certain motives we are apt likewise to continue mechanically, without recalling, on every occasion, the reflections which first determined us. The convenience, or rather necessity, which leads to justice is so universal and everywhere points so much to the same rules that the habit takes place in all societies; and it is not without some scrutiny that we are able to ascertain its true origin. The matter, however, is not so obscure but that, even in common life, we have every moment recourse to the principle of public utility and ask, *What must become of the world, if such practices prevail? How could society subsist under such disorders?* Were the distinction or separation of possessions entirely useless, can anyone conceive that it ever should have obtained in society?

Thus we seem, upon the whole, to have attained a knowledge of the force of that principle here insisted on, and can determine what degree of esteem or moral approbation may result from reflections on public interest and utility. The necessity of justice to the support of society is the *sole* foundation of that virtue; and since no moral excellence is more highly esteemed, we may conclude that this circumstance of usefulness has, in general, the strongest energy and most entire command over our sentiments. It must therefore be the source of a considerable part of the merit ascribed to humanity, benevolence, friendship, public spirit, and other social virtues of that stamp; as it is the *sole* source of the moral approbation paid to fidelity, justice, veracity, integrity, and those other estimable and useful qualities and principles. It is entirely agreeable to the rules of philosophy, and even of common reason, where any principle has been found to have a great force and energy in one instance, to ascribe to it a like energy in all similar instances.[8] This indeed is Newton's chief rule of philosophizing.[9]

SECTION IV

OF POLITICAL SOCIETY

HAD every man sufficient *sagacity* to perceive, at all times, the strong interest which binds him to the observance of justice and equity, and *strength of mind* sufficient to persevere in a

[8] [This sentence is printed as a note in Editions G to P; and they also call it the *second* rule.]

[9] *Principia,* lib. iii.

steady adherence to a general and a distant interest, in opposition to the allurements of present pleasure and advantage, there had never, in that case, been any such thing as government or political society; but each man, following his natural liberty, had lived in entire peace and harmony with all others. What need of positive law where natural justice is of itself a sufficient restraint? Why create magistrates where there never arises any disorder or iniquity? Why abridge our native freedom when, in every instance, the utmost exertion of it is found innocent and beneficial? It is evident that, if government were totally useless, it never could have place, and that the *sole* foundation of the duty of *allegiance* is the *advantage* which it procures to society by preserving peace and order among mankind.

When a number of political societies are erected and maintain a great intercourse together, a new set of rules are immediately discovered to be *useful* in that particular situation, and accordingly take place under the title of "Laws of Nations." Of this kind are the sacredness of the person of ambassadors, abstaining from poisoned arms, quarter in war, with others of that kind which are plainly calculated for the *advantage* of states and kingdoms in their intercourse with each other.

The rules of justice, such as prevail among individuals, are not entirely suspended among political societies. All princes pretend a regard to the rights of other princes, and some, no doubt, without hypocrisy. Alliances and treaties are every day made between independent states, which would only be so much waste of parchment if they were not found, by experience, to have some influence and authority. But here is the difference between kingdoms and individuals. Human nature cannot, by any means, subsist without the association of individuals; and that association never could have place were no regard paid to the laws of equity and justice. Disorder, confusion, the war of all against all are the necessary consequences of such a licentious conduct. But nations can subsist without intercourse. They may even subsist, in some degree, under a general war. The observance of justice, though useful among them, is not guarded by so strong a necessity as among individuals; and the *moral obliga-*

tion holds proportion with the *usefulness*. All politicians will allow, and most philosophers, that *reasons of state* may, in particular emergencies, dispense with the rules of justice and invalidate any treaty or alliance, where the strict observance of it would be prejudicial, in a considerable degree, to either of the contracting parties. But nothing less than the most extreme necessity, it is confessed, can justify individuals in a breach of promise or an invasion of the properties of others.

In a confederated commonwealth, such as the Achaean [1] republic of old or the Swiss Cantons and United Provinces in modern times—as the league has here a peculiar *utility*, the conditions of union have a peculiar sacredness and authority, and a violation of them would be regarded as no less, or even as more, criminal than any private injury or injustice.

The long and helpless infancy of man requires the combination of parents for the subsistence of their young; and that combination requires the virtue of chastity or fidelity to the marriage bed. Without such a *utility*, it will readily be owned that such a virtue would never have been thought of.[2]

wrong

---

1 [Hume refers to the second Achaean League, a federation of Greek city-states, which flourished in the third and second centuries B.C.; to the federation now known (*i.e.*, since 1803) as Switzerland; and to the United Provinces of Holland. The "peculiar utility" of the federation in all three cases was that the states joined the respective leagues for the purpose of common defense, while retaining in other matters complete sovereignty.]

2 The only solution which Plato gives to all the objections that might be raised against the community of women established in his imaginary commonwealth is Κάλλιστα γὰρ δὴ τοῦτο καὶ λέγεται καὶ λελέξεται, ὅτι τὸ μὲν ὠφέλιμον καλόν, τὸ δὲ βλαβερὸν αἰσχρόν.* *Scite enim istud et dicitur et dicetur, Id quod utile sit honestum esse, quod autem inutile sit turpe esse.* *De Rep.* lib. v. p. 457. ex. edit. Serrani. And this maxim will admit of no doubt where public utility is concerned, which is Plato's meaning. And indeed, to what other purpose do all the ideas of chastity and modesty serve? *Nisi utile est quod facimus, frustra est gloria,*† says Phaedrus. Καλὸν τῶν βλαβερῶν οὐδέν ‡ says Plutarch, *De vitioso pudore. Nihil eorum quae damnosa sunt, pulchrum est.*‡ The same was the opinion of the Stoics. Φασὶν οὖν οἱ Στωικοὶ ἀγαθὸν εἶναι ὠφέλειαν ἢ οὐχ ἕτερον ὠφελείας, ὠφέλειαν μὲν λέγοντες τὴν ἀρετὴν καὶ τὴν σπουδαίαν πρᾶξιν.**

* ["For it is an excellent statement and will always be an excellent statement, that whatever is useful is noble, and what is harmful is base."]

An infidelity of this nature is much more *pernicious* in women than in *men*. Hence the laws of chastity are much stricter over the one sex than over the other.

These rules have all a reference to generation; and yet women past childbearing are no more supposed to be exempted from them than those in the flower of their youth and beauty. *General rules* are often extended beyond the principle whence they first arise, and this in all matters of taste and sentiment. It is a vulgar story at Paris that during the rage of the Mississippi [3] a humpbacked fellow went every day into the Rue de Quincempoix, where the stockjobbers met in great crowds, and was well paid for allowing them to make use of his hump as a desk, in order to sign their contracts upon it. Would the fortune which he raised by this expedient make him a handsome fellow, though it be confessed that personal beauty arises very much from ideas of utility? The imagination is influenced by associations of ideas which, though they arise at first from the judgment, are not easily altered by every particular exception that occurs to us. To which we may add, in the present case of chastity, that the example of the old would be pernicious to the young; and that women, continually foreseeing that a certain time would bring them the liberty of indulgence, would naturally advance that period and think more lightly of this whole duty so requisite to society.

Those who live in the same family have such frequent opportunities of license of this kind that nothing could preserve purity of manners were marriage allowed among the nearest relations or any intercourse of love between them ratified by

---

† ["If our actions are not useful, there is no point to glory."]

‡ ["Nothing that is harmful is good," says Plutarch, (*On False Shame*).]

** ["The Stoics, then, assert that good is 'utility and nothing other than utility,' meaning by 'utility' virtue and right action." Sextus Empiricus iii. 20.]

3 [The Mississippi Scheme was a plan to meet the financial needs of Louis XV through the issuance of bank notes guaranteed by the king, but actually based on the anticipated exploitation of the French Mississippi territory. The originator of the plan was John Law, a Scottish economist and speculator. The Scheme lasted three years and was marked by wild speculations.]

law and custom. Incest, therefore, being *pernicious* in a superior degree, has also a superior turpitude and moral deformity annexed to it.

What is the reason why, by the Athenian laws, one might marry a half sister by the father, but not by the mother? Plainly this: the manners of the Athenians were so reserved that a man was never permitted to approach the women's apartment, even in the same family, unless where he visited his own mother. His stepmother and her children were as much shut up from him as the women of any other family, and there was as little danger of any criminal correspondence between them. Uncles and nieces, for a like reason, might marry at Athens, but neither these, nor half brothers and sisters, could contract that alliance at Rome, where the intercourse was more open between the sexes. Public utility is the cause of all these variations.

To repeat to a man's prejudice anything that escaped him in private conversation, or to make any such use of his private letters, is highly blamed. The free and social intercourse of minds must be extremely checked where no such rules of fidelity are established.

Even in repeating stories, whence we can foresee no ill consequences to result, the giving of one's author is regarded as a piece of indiscretion, if not of immorality. These stories, in passing from hand to hand, and receiving all the usual variations, frequently come about to the persons concerned and produce animosities and quarrels among people whose intentions are the most innocent and inoffensive.

To pry into secrets, to open or even read the letters of others, to play the spy upon their words and looks and actions—what habits more inconvenient in society? What habits, of consequence, more blamable?

This principle is also the foundation of most of the laws of good manners—a kind of lesser morality calculated for the ease of company and conversation. Too much or too little ceremony are both blamed; and everything which promotes ease, without an indecent familiarity, is useful and laudable.

Constancy in friendships, attachments, and familiarities is

commendable and is requisite to support trust and good correspondence in society. But in places of general, though casual, concourse, where the pursuit of health and pleasure brings people promiscuously together, public convenience has dispensed with this maxim, and custom there promotes an unreserved conversation for the time, by indulging the privilege of dropping afterward every indifferent acquaintance without breach of civility or good manners.

Even in societies which are established on principles the most immoral, and the most destructive to the interests of the general society, there are required certain rules which a species of false honor, as well as private interest, engages the members to observe. Robbers and pirates, it has often been remarked, could not maintain their pernicious confederacy did they not establish a new distributive justice among themselves and recall those laws of equity which they have violated with the rest of mankind.

I hate a drinking companion, says the Greek proverb, who never forgets. The follies of the last debauch should be buried in eternal oblivion in order to give full scope to the follies of the next.

Among nations where an immoral gallantry, if covered with a thin veil of mystery, is in some degree authorized by custom, there immediately arises a set of rules calculated for the convenience of that attachment. The famous court or parliament of love in Provence formerly decided all difficult cases of this nature.

In societies for play there are laws required for the conduct of the game; and these laws are different in each game. The foundation, I own, of such societies is frivolous, and the laws are in a great measure, though not altogether, capricious and arbitrary. So far is there a material difference between them and the rules of justice, fidelity, and loyalty. The general societies of men are absolutely requisite for the subsistence of the species; and the public convenience, which regulates morals, is inviolably established in the nature of man, and of the world in which he lives. The comparison, therefore, in these respects is very imperfect. We may only learn from it the necessity of rules wherever men have any intercourse with each other.

They cannot even pass each other on the road without rules. Wagoners, coachmen, and postilions have principles by which they give the way; and these are chiefly founded on mutual ease and convenience. Sometimes also they are arbitrary, at least dependent on a kind of capricious analogy, like many of the reasonings of lawyers.[4]

To carry the matter further, we may observe that it is impossible for men so much as to murder each other without statutes and maxims, and an idea of justice and honor. War has its laws as well as peace; and even that sportive kind of war, carried on among wrestlers, boxers, cudgel players, gladiators, is regulated by fixed principles. Common interest and utility beget infallibly a standard of right and wrong among the parties concerned.

SECTION V

WHY UTILITY PLEASES

PART I

IT seems so natural a thought to ascribe to their utility the praise which we bestow on the social virtues that one would expect to meet with this principle everywhere in moral writers as the chief foundation of their reasoning and inquiry. In common life we may observe that the circumstance of utility is always appealed to, nor is it supposed that a greater eulogy can

---

[4] That the lighter machine yield to the heavier, and in machines of the same kind, that the empty yield to the loaded; this rule is founded on convenience. That those who are going to the capital take place of those who are coming from it; this seems to be founded on some idea of the dignity of the great city, and of the preference of the future to the past. From like reasons, among footwalkers, the right hand entitles a man to the wall, and prevents jostling, which peaceable people find very disagreeable and inconvenient.

be given to any man than to display his usefulness to the public and enumerate the services which he has performed to mankind and society. What praise, even of an inanimate form, if the regularity and elegance of its parts destroy not its fitness for any useful purpose! And how satisfactory an apology for any disproportion or seeming deformity if we can show the necessity of that particular construction for the use intended! A ship appears more beautiful to an artist, or one moderately skilled in navigation, where its prow is wide and swelling beyond its poop, than if it were framed with a precise geometrical regularity, in contradiction to all the laws of mechanics. A building whose doors and windows were exact squares would hurt the eye by that very proportion as ill-adapted to the figure of a human creature, for whose service the fabric was intended. What wonder then that a man whose habits and conduct are hurtful to society and dangerous or pernicious to everyone who has an intercourse with him should, on that account, be an object of disapprobation and communicate to every spectator the strongest sentiment of disgust and hatred? [1]

[1] We ought not to imagine, because an inanimate object may be useful as well as a man, that therefore it ought also, according to this system, to merit the appellation of *virtuous*. The sentiments excited by utility are, in the two cases, very different; and the one is mixed with affection, esteem, approbation, etc., and not the other. In like manner, an inanimate object may have good color and proportions as well as a human figure. But can we ever be in love with the former? There are a numerous set of passions and sentiments of which thinking, rational beings are, by the original constitution of nature, the only proper objects: and though the very same qualities be transferred to an insensible, inanimate being, they will not excite the same sentiments. The beneficial qualities of herbs and minerals are, indeed, sometimes called their *virtues;* but this is an effect of the caprice of language, which ought not to be regarded in reasoning. For though there be a species of approbation attending even inanimate objects when beneficial, yet this sentiment is so weak, and so different from that which is directed to beneficent magistrates or statesmen, that they ought not to be ranked under the same class or appellation.

A very small variation of the object, even where the same qualities are preserved, will destroy a sentiment. Thus, the same beauty, transferred to a different sex, excites no amorous passion where nature is not extremely perverted.

But perhaps the difficulty of accounting for these effects of usefulness, or its contrary, has kept philosophers from admitting them into their systems of ethics, and has induced them rather to employ any other principle in explaining the origin of moral good and evil. But it is no just reason for rejecting any principle confirmed by experience that we cannot give a satisfactory account of its origin, nor are able to resolve it into other, more general principles. And if we would employ a little thought on the present subject we need be at no loss to account for the influence of utility and to deduce it from principles the most known and avowed in human nature.

From the apparent usefulness of the social virtues it has readily been inferred by skeptics, both ancient and modern, that all moral distinctions arise from education, and were at first invented, and afterwards encouraged, by the art of politicians in order to render men tractable and subdue their natural ferocity and selfishness, which incapacitated them for society. This principle, indeed, of precept and education must so far be owned to have a powerful influence that it may frequently increase or diminish, beyond their natural standard, the sentiments of approbation or dislike; and may even, in particular instances, create, without any natural principle, a new sentiment of this kind, as is evident in all superstitious practices and observances. But that *all* moral affection or dislike arises from this origin will never surely be allowed by any judicious inquirer. Had nature made no such distinction, founded on the original constitution of the mind, the words *honorable* and *shameful, lovely* and *odious, noble* and *despicable* had never had place in any language, nor could politicians, had they invented these terms, ever have been able to render them intelligible or make them convey any idea to the audience. So that nothing can be more superficial than this paradox of the skeptics; and it were well if, in the abstruser studies of logic and metaphysics, we could as easily obviate the cavils of that sect as in the practical and more intelligible sciences of politics and morals.

The social virtues must, therefore, be allowed to have a natu-

ral beauty and amiableness, which at first, antecedent to all
precept or education, recommends them to the esteem of uninstructed mankind and engages their affections. And as the public utility of these virtues is the chief circumstance whence they
derive their merit, it follows that the end which they have a
tendency to promote must be some way agreeable to us and
take hold of some natural affection. It must please either from
considerations of self-interest or from more generous motives
and regards.

It has often been asserted that as every man has a strong connection with society and perceives the impossibility of his solitary subsistence, he becomes, on that account, favorable to all
those habits or principles which promote order in society and
insure to him the quiet possession of so inestimable a blessing.
As much as we value our own happiness and welfare, as much
must we applaud the practice of justice and humanity by
which alone the social confederacy can be maintained and
every man reap the fruits of mutual protection and assistance.

This deduction of morals from self-love, or a regard to private interest, is an obvious thought and has not arisen wholly
from the wanton sallies and sportive assaults of the skeptics.
To mention no others, Polybius, one of the gravest and most
judicious as well as most moral writers of antiquity, has assigned this selfish origin of all our sentiments of virtue.[2] But
though the solid, practical sense of that author and his aversion

---

[2] Undutifulness to parents is disapproved of by mankind, προορωμένους
τὸ μέλλον, καὶ συλλογιζομένους ὅτι τὸ παραπλήσιον ἑκάστοις αὐτῶν
συγκυρήσει.* Ingratitude for a like reason (though he seems there to mix
a more generous regard) συναγανακτοῦντας μὲν τῷ πέλας, ἀναφέροντας δ'
ἐπ' αὐτοὺς τὸ παραπλήσιον, ἐξ ὧν ὑπογίγνεταί τις ἔννοια παρ' ἑκάστῳ τῆς
τοῦ καθήκοντος δυνάμεως καὶ θεωρίας.† (Ed. Gronovius.) Perhaps the historian only meant that our sympathy and humanity was more enlivened by
our considering the similarity of our case with that of the person suffering,
which is a just sentiment.

   * ["anticipating (scil. they) the future, and reckoning that something
similar will happen to each of them."]

   † ["getting irritated along with the other man (their 'neighbor') and
imagining themselves in a similar situation. Hence, in each of them there
arises a notion of the meaning and of the theory of the 'befitting.'" vi. 4.]

to all vain subtleties render his authority on the present subject very considerable, yet is not this an affair to be decided by authority; and the voice of nature and experience seems plainly to oppose the selfish theory.

We frequently bestow praise on virtuous actions performed in very distant ages and remote countries, where the utmost subtlety of imagination would not discover any appearance of self-interest or find any connection of our present happiness and security with events so widely separated from us.

A generous, a brave, a noble deed performed by an adversary commands our approbation, while, in its consequences, it may be acknowledged prejudicial to our particular interest.

When private advantage concurs with general affection for virtue, we readily perceive and avow the mixture of these distinct sentiments, which have a very different feeling and influence on the mind. We praise, perhaps, with more alacrity where the generous, humane action contributes to our particular interest; but the topics of praise, which we insist on, are very wide of this circumstance. And we may attempt to bring over others to our sentiments, without endeavoring to convince them that they reap any advantage from the actions which we recommend to their approbation and applause.

Frame the model of a praiseworthy character consisting of all the most amiable moral virtues: give instances in which these display themselves after an eminent and extraordinary manner; you readily engage the esteem and approbation of all your audience, who never so much as inquire in what age and country the person lived who possessed these noble qualities—a circumstance, however, of all others the most material to self-love, or a concern for our own individual happiness.

Once on a time a statesman, in the shock and contest of parties, prevailed so far as to procure by his eloquence the banishment of an able adversary; whom he secretly followed, offering him money for his support during his exile and soothing him with topics of consolation in his misfortunes. *Alas!* cries the banished statesman, *with what regret must I leave my friends in this city where even enemies are so generous!* Virtue, though in an enemy, here pleased him; and we also give it the just tribute of praise and approbation; nor do we retract these sentiments when we hear that the action passed at Athens about two thousand years ago, and that the persons' names were Aeschines and Demosthenes.

What is that to me? There are few occasions when this question is not pertinent; and had it that universal, infallible influence supposed, it would turn into ridicule every composition, and almost every conversation, which contain any praise or censure of men and manners.

It is but a weak subterfuge, when pressed by these facts and arguments, to say that we transport ourselves, by the force of imagination, into distant ages and countries and consider the advantage which we should have reaped from these characters had we been contemporaries and had any commerce with the persons. It is not conceivable how a *real* sentiment or passion can ever arise from a known *imaginary* interest, especially when our *real* interest is still kept in view and is often acknowledged to be entirely distinct from the imaginary, and even sometimes opposite to it.

A man brought to the brink of a precipice cannot look down without trembling; and the sentiment of *imaginary* danger actuates him, in opposition to the opinion and belief of *real* safety. But the imagination is here assisted by the presence of a striking object, and yet prevails not, except it be also aided by novelty and the unusual appearance of the object. Custom soon reconciles us to heights and precipices, and wears off these false and delusive terrors. The reverse is observable in the estimates which we form of characters and manners; and the more we habituate ourselves to an accurate scrutiny of morals, the more delicate feeling do we acquire of the most minute distinctions between vice and virtue. Such frequent occasion, indeed, have we in common life to pronounce all kinds of moral determinations that no object of this kind can be new or unusual to us, nor could any *false* views or prepossessions maintain their ground against an experience so common and familiar. Experience being chiefly what forms the associations of ideas, it is impossible that any association could establish and support itself in direct opposition to that principle.

Usefulness is agreeable and engages our approbation. This is a matter of fact confirmed by daily observation. But *useful?* For what? For somebody's interest surely. Whose interest then? Not our own only, for our approbation frequently extends further. It must therefore be the interest of those who are served by the character or action approved of; and these, we may conclude, however remote, are not totally indifferent to us. By opening up this principle we shall discover one great source of moral distinctions.

PART II

Self-love is a principle in human nature of such extensive energy, and the interest of each individual is in general so closely connected with that of the community, that those philosophers were excusable who fancied that all our concern for the public might be resolved into a concern for our own happiness and preservation. They saw, every moment, instances of approbation or blame, satisfaction or displeasure toward characters and actions; they denominated the objects of these sentiments *virtues* or *vices;* they observed that the former had a tendency to increase the happiness, and the latter the misery of mankind; they asked whether it were possible that we could have any general concern for society or any disinterested resentment of the welfare or injury of others; they found it simpler to consider all these sentiments as modifications of self-love, and they discovered a pretense at least for this unity of principle in that close union of interest which is so observable between the public and each individual.

But notwithstanding this frequent confusion of interests, it is easy to attain what natural philosophers, after Lord Bacon, have affected to call the *experimentum crucis,* or that experiment which points out the right way in any doubt or ambiguity. We have found instances in which private interest was separate from public; in which it was even contrary, and yet we observed the moral sentiment to continue, notwithstanding this disjunction of interests. And wherever these distinct interests sensibly concurred, we always found a sensible increase of the sentiment and a more warm affection to virtue and detestation of vice, or what we properly call "gratitude" and "revenge." Compelled by these instances we must renounce the theory which accounts for every moral sentiment by the principle of self-love. We must adopt a more public affection and allow that the interests of society are not, even on their own account, entirely indifferent to us. Usefulness is only a tendency to a certain end; and it is a contradiction in terms that anything pleases as means to an end where the end itself nowise affects us. If usefulness, therefore, be a source of moral sentiment, and if this usefulness be not always considered with a reference to self, it follows that everything which contributes to the happiness of society recommends itself directly to our approbation and good will. Here is a principle which accounts, in great part for the origin of morality: and what need we seek for abstruse and remote systems when there occurs one so obvious and natural? [1]

Have we any difficulty to comprehend the force of humanity and benevolence? Or to conceive that the very aspect of happiness, joy, prosperity gives pleasure; that of pain, suffering, sorrow communicates uneasiness? The human countenance, says Horace,[2] borrows smiles or tears from the human countenance

[1] It is needless to push our researches so far as to ask, why we have humanity or a fellow-feeling with others? It is sufficient that this is experienced to be a principle in human nature. We must stop somewhere in our examination of causes; and there are, in every science, some general principles beyond which we cannot hope to find any principle more general. No man is absolutely indifferent to the happiness and misery of others. The first has a natural tendency to give pleasure, the second pain. This everyone may find in himself. It is not probable that these principles can be resolved into principles more simple and universal, whatever attempts may have been made to that purpose. But if it were possible, it belongs not to the present subject; and we may here safely consider these principles as original—happy if we can render all the consequences sufficiently plain and perspicuous!

[2] Ut ridentibus arrident, ita flentibus adflent
    Humani vultus.*   HOR.

* ["As the human face smiles at those who smile, so does it weep at those who weep." Horace, The Art of Poetry, 101-102.]

Reduce a person to solitude and he loses all enjoyment, except either of the sensual or speculative kind; and that because the movements of his heart are not forwarded by correspondent movements in his fellow creatures. The signs of sorrow and mourning, though arbitrary, affect us with melancholy, but the natural symptoms, tears and cries and groans, never fail to infuse compassion and uneasiness. And if the effects of misery touch us in so lively a manner, can we be supposed altogether insensible or indifferent toward its causes when a malicious or treacherous character and behavior are presented to us?

We enter, I shall suppose, into a convenient, warm, well-contrived apartment: we necessarily receive a pleasure from its very survey because it presents us with the pleasing ideas of ease, satisfaction, and enjoyment. The hospitable, good-humored, humane landlord appears. This circumstance surely must embellish the whole, nor can we easily forbear reflecting, with pleasure, on the satisfaction which results to everyone from his intercourse and good offices.

His whole family, by the freedom, ease, confidence, and calm enjoyment diffused over their countenances, sufficiently express their happiness. I have a pleasing sympathy in the prospect of so much joy, and can never consider the source of it without the most agreeable emotions.

He tells me that an oppressive and powerful neighbor had attempted to dispossess him of his inheritance and had long disturbed all his innocent and social pleasures. I feel an immediate indignation arise in me against such violence and injury.

But it is no wonder, he adds, that a private wrong should proceed from a man who had enslaved provinces, depopulated cities, and made the field and scaffold stream with human blood. I am struck with horror at the prospect of so much misery and am actuated by the strongest antipathy against its author.

In general, it is certain that wherever we go, whatever we reflect on or converse about, everything still presents us with the view of human happiness or misery and excites in our breast a sympathetic movement of pleasure or uneasiness. In our serious occupations, in our careless amusements, this principle still exerts its active energy.

A man who enters the theater is immediately struck with the view of so great a multitude participating of one common amusement, and experiences, from their very aspect, a superior sensibility or disposition of being affected with every sentiment which he shares with his fellow creatures.

He observes the actors to be animated by the appearance of a full audience and raised to a degree of enthusiasm which they cannot command in any solitary or calm moment.

Every movement of the theater, by a skillful poet, is communicated, as it were, by magic to the spectators, who weep, tremble, resent, rejoice, and are inflamed with all the variety of passions which actuate the several personages of the drama.

Where any event crosses our wishes and interrupts the happiness of the favorite characters, we feel a sensible anxiety and concern. But where their sufferings proceed from the treachery, cruelty, or tyranny of an enemy, our breasts are affected with the liveliest resentment against the author of these calamities.

It is here esteemed contrary to the rules of art to represent anything cool and indifferent. A distant friend, or a confidant, who has no immediate interest in the catastrophe ought, if possible, to be avoided by the poet, as communicating a like indifference to the audience and checking the progress of the passions.

Few species of poetry are more entertaining than *pastoral;* and everyone is sensible that the chief source of its pleasure arises from those images of a gentle and tender tranquillity which it represents in its personages, and of which it communicates a like sentiment to the reader. Sannazarius, who transferred the scene to the seashore, though he presented the most magnificent object in nature, is confessed to have erred in his choice. The idea of toil, labor, and danger suffered by the fisherman is painful, by an unavoidable sympathy which attends every conception of human happiness or misery.

When I was twenty, says a French poet, Ovid was my favorite. Now I am forty, I declare for Horace. We enter, to be sure, more readily into sentiments which resemble those we feel every day; but no passion, when well represented, can be entirely indifferent to us, because there is none of which every man has not within him at least the seeds and first principles. It is the business of poetry to bring every affection near to us by lively imagery and representation, and make it look like truth and reality; a certain proof that, wherever the reality is found, our minds are disposed to be strongly affected by it.

Any recent event or piece of news by which the fate of states, provinces, or many individuals is affected is extremely interesting even to those whose welfare is not immediately engaged. Such intelligence is propagated with celerity, heard with avidity, and inquired into with attention and concern. The interest of society appears, on this occasion, to be in some degree the interest of each individual. The imagination is sure to be affected, though the passions excited may not always be so strong and steady as to have great influence on the conduct and behavior.

The perusal of a history seems a calm entertainment, but would be no entertainment at all did not our hearts beat with correspondent movements to those which are described by the historian.

Thucydides and Guicciardin support with difficulty our attention while the former describes the trivial rencounters of the small cities of Greece and the latter the harmless wars of Pisa. The few persons interested, and the small interest, fill not the imagination and engage not the affections. The deep distress of the numerous Athenian army before Syracuse, the danger which so nearly threatens Venice—these excite compassion; these move terror and anxiety.

The indifferent, uninteresting style of Suetonius, equally with the masterly pencil of Tacitus, may convince us of the cruel depravity of Nero or Tiberius; but what a difference of sentiment! While the former coldly relates the facts, the latter sets before our eyes the venerable figures of a Soranus and a Thrasea, intrepid in their fate and only moved by the melting sorrows of their friends and kindred. What sympathy then touches every human heart! What indignation against the tyrant whose causeless fear or unprovoked malice gave rise to such detestable barbarity!

If we bring these subjects nearer, if we remove all suspicion of fiction and deceit, what powerful concern is excited, and how much superior, in many instances, to the narrow attachments of self-love and private interest! Popular sedition, party zeal, a devoted obedience to factious leaders—these are some of the most visible, though less laudable, effects of this social sympathy in human nature.

The frivolousness of the subject, too, we may observe, is not able to detach us entirely from what carries an image of human sentiment and affection.

When a person stutters and pronounces with difficulty, we even sympathize with this trivial uneasiness and suffer for him. And it is a rule in criticism that every combination of syllables or letters which gives pain to the organs of speech in the recital appears also, from a species of sympathy, harsh and disagreeable to the ear. Nay, when we run over a book with our eye, we are sensible of such unharmonious composition, because we still imagine that a person recites it to us and suffers from the pronunciation of these jarring sounds. So delicate is our sympathy!

Easy and unconstrained postures and motions are always beautiful: an air of health and vigor is agreeable; clothes which warm, without burdening the body, which cover, without imprisoning the limbs, are well fashioned. In every judgment of beauty the feelings of the person affected enter into consideration and communicate to the spectator similar touches of pain or pleasure.[3] What wonder, then, if we can pronounce no judgment concerning the character and conduct of men without

---

[3] "Decentior equus cujus astricta sunt ilia; sed idem velocior. Pulcher aspectu sit athleta, cujus lacertos exercitatio expressit; idem certamini paratior. Nunquam enim *species* ab *utilitate* dividitur. Sed hoc quidem discernere modici judicii est." * Quintilian *Inst*. lib. viii. cap. 3.

* ["A horse whose flanks are drawn tightly together is more seemly; but it is also swifter. An athlete whose upper arms are well-developed through exercise may be more beautiful to look at; but he is also better prepared for the contest. For looks can never be separated from usefulness. But to draw a distinction between them is a mark of mediocre judgment."]

considering the tendencies of their actions and the happiness or misery which thence arises to society? What association of ideas would ever operate were that principle here totally inactive? [4]

If any man, from a cold insensibility or narrow selfishness of temper, is unaffected with the images of human happiness or misery, he must be equally indifferent to the images of vice and virtue; as, on the other hand, it is always found that a warm concern for the interests of our species is attended with a delicate feeling of all moral distinctions—a strong resentment of injury done to men, a lively approbation of their welfare. In this particular, though great superiority is observable of one man above another, yet none are so entirely indifferent to the interests of their fellow creatures as to perceive no distinctions of moral good and evil, in consequence of the different tendencies of actions and principles. How, indeed, can we suppose it possible in anyone who wears a human heart that, if there be subjected to his censure one character or system of conduct which is beneficial, and another which is pernicious to his species or community, he will not so much as give a cool preference to the former or ascribe to it the smallest merit or regard? Let us suppose a person ever so selfish, let private interest have engrossed ever so much his attention, yet in instances where that is not concerned he must unavoidably feel *some* propensity to the

4 In proportion to the station which a man possesses, according to the relations in which he is placed, we always expect from him a greater or less degree of good, and, when disappointed, blame his inutility; and much more do we blame him, if any ill or prejudice arises from his conduct and behavior. When the interests of one country interfere with those of another, we estimate the merits of a statesman by the good or ill which results to his own country from his measures and counsels, without regard to the prejudice which he brings on its enemies and rivals. His fellow citizens are the objects which lie nearest the eye while we determine his character. And as nature has implanted in everyone a superior affection to his own country, we never expect any regard to distant nations where a competition arises. Not to mention that while every man consults the good of his own community, we are sensible that the general interest of mankind is better promoted than by any loose indeterminate views to the good of a species, whence no beneficial action could ever result for want of a duly limited object on which they could exert themselves.

good of mankind and make it an object of choice, if everything else be equal. Would any man who is walking alone tread as willingly on another's gouty toes, whom he has no quarrel with, as on the hard flint and pavement? There is here surely a difference in the case. We surely take into consideration the happiness and misery of others in weighing the several motives of action, and incline to the former where no private regards draw us to seek our own promotion or advantage by the injury of our fellow creatures. And if the principles of humanity are capable, in many instances, of influencing our actions, they must, at all times, have *some* authority over our sentiments and give us a general approbation of what is useful to society, and blame of what is dangerous or pernicious. The degrees of these sentiments may be the subject of controversy, but the reality of their existence, one should think, must be admitted in every theory or system.

A creature absolutely malicious and spiteful, were there any such in nature, must be worse than indifferent to the images of vice and virtue. All his sentiments must be inverted, and directly opposite to those which prevail in the human species. Whatever contributes to the good of mankind, as it crosses the constant bent of his wishes and desires, must produce uneasiness and disapprobation; and, on the contrary, whatever is the source of disorder and misery in society must, for the same reason, be regarded with pleasure and complacency. Timon, who, probably from his affected spleen more than any inveterate malice, was denominated the man-hater, embraced Alcibiades with great fondness. *Go on, my boy!* cried he, *acquire the confidence of the people; you will one day, I foresee, be the cause of great calamities to them.*[5] Could we admit the two principles of the Manichaeans,[6] it is an infallible consequence that their sentiments of human actions, as well as of everything else, must be totally opposite, and that every instance of justice and humanity, from its necessary tendency, must please the one deity

[5] Plutarch in *Vita Alcib.* 16.
[6] [The two principles are the identification in Manichaeism of good with light, and evil with darkness.]

and displease the other. All mankind so far resemble the good principle that where interest or revenge or envy perverts not our disposition, we are always inclined, from our natural philanthropy, to give the preference to the happiness of society and, consequently, to virtue above its opposite. Absolute, unprovoked, disinterested malice has never, perhaps, place in any human breast; or if it had, must there pervert all the sentiments of morals as well as the feelings of humanity. If the cruelty of Nero be allowed entirely voluntary, and not rather the effect of constant fear and resentment, it is evident that Tigellinus, preferably to Seneca or Burrhus, must have possessed his steady and uniform approbation.

A statesman or patriot who serves our own country in our own time has always a more passionate regard paid to him than one whose beneficial influence operated on distant ages or remote nations, where the good resulting from his generous humanity, being less connected with us, seems more obscure and affects us with a less lively sympathy. We may own the merit to be equally great, though our sentiments are not raised to an equal height in both cases. The judgment here corrects the inequalities of our internal emotions and perceptions, in like manner as it preserves us from error in the several variations of images presented to our external senses. The same object, at a double distance, really throws on the eye a picture of but half the bulk, yet we imagine that it appears of the same size in both situations; because we know that, on our approach to it, its image would expand on the eye, and that the difference consists not in the object itself, but in our position with regard to it. And indeed, without such a correction of appearances, both in internal and external sentiment, men could never think or talk steadily on any subject while their fluctuating situations produce a continual variation on objects and throw them into such different and contrary lights and positions.[7]

7 For a like reason, the tendencies of actions and characters, not their real accidental consequences, are alone regarded in our moral determinations or general judgments, though in our real feeling or sentiment we cannot help paying greater regard to one whose station, joined to virtue, renders him really useful to society, than to one who exerts the social virtues only in

The more we converse with mankind, and the greater social intercourse we maintain, the more shall we be familiarized to these general preferences and distinctions without which our conversation and discourse could scarcely be rendered intelligible to each other. Every man's interest is peculiar to himself, and the aversions and desires which result from it cannot be supposed to affect others in a like degree. General language, therefore, being formed for general use, must be molded on some more general views and must affix the epithets of praise or blame in conformity to sentiments which arise from the general interests of the community. And if these sentiments, in most men, be not so strong as those which have a reference to private good, yet still they must make some distinction, even in persons the most depraved and selfish, and must attach the notion of good to a beneficent conduct, and of evil to the contrary. Sympathy, we shall allow, is much fainter than our concern for ourselves, and sympathy with persons remote from us much fainter than that with persons near and contiguous; but for this very reason it is necessary for us, in our calm judgments and discourse concerning the characters of men, to neglect all these differences and render our sentiments more public and social. Besides that we ourselves often change our situation in this particular; we every day meet with persons who are in a situation different from us, and who could never converse with us were we to remain constantly in that position and point of view which is peculiar to ourselves. The intercourse of sentiments, therefore, in society and conversation makes us form some gen-

---

good intentions and benevolent affections. Separating the character from the fortune by an easy and necessary effort of thought, we pronounce these persons alike, and give them the same general praise. The judgment corrects, or endeavors to correct, the appearance, but is not able entirely to prevail over sentiment.

Why is this peach tree said to be better than that other, but because it produces more or better fruit? And would not the same praise be given it, though snails or vermin had destroyed the peaches before they came to full maturity? In morals, too, is not *the tree known by the fruit?* And cannot we easily distinguish between nature and accident, in the one case as well as in the other?

eral unalterable standard by which we may approve or disapprove of characters and manners. And though the heart takes not part entirely with those general notions, nor regulates all its love and hatred by the universal, abstract differences of vice and virtue without regard to self or the persons with whom we are more intimately connected, yet have these moral differences a considerable influence; and being sufficient, at least, for discourse, serve all our purposes in company, in the pulpit, in the theater, and in the schools.[8]

Thus, in whatever light we take this subject, the merit ascribed to the social virtues appears still uniform and arises chiefly from that regard which the natural sentiment of benevolence engages us to pay to the interests of mankind and society. If we consider the principles of the human make, such as they appear to daily experience and observation, we must, *a priori,* conclude it impossible for such a creature as man to be totally indifferent to the well or ill-being of his fellow creatures, and not readily, of himself, to pronounce, where nothing gives him any particular bias, that what promotes their happiness is good, what tends to their misery is evil, without any further regard or consideration. Here then are the faint rudiments at least, or outlines, of a *general* distinction between actions; and in proportion as the humanity of the person is supposed to increase, his connection with those who are injured or benefited, and his lively conception of their misery or happiness, his consequent censure or approbation acquires proportionable vigor. There is no necessity that a generous action, barely mentioned in an old history or remote gazette, should communicate any strong feelings of applause and admiration. Virtue, placed at such a distance, is like a fixed star which, though to the eye of

---

[8] It is wisely ordained by nature that private connections should commonly prevail over universal views and considerations, otherwise our affections and actions would be dissipated and lost for want of a proper limited object. Thus a small benefit done to ourselves, or our near friends, excites more lively sentiments of love and approbation than a great benefit done to a distant commonwealth; but still we know here, as in all the senses, to correct these inequalities by reflection, and retain a general standard of vice and virtue, founded chiefly on general usefulness.

reason it may appear as luminous as the sun in his meridian, is so infinitely removed as to affect the senses neither with light nor heat. Bring this virtue nearer, by our acquaintance or connection with the persons, or even by an eloquent recital of the case, our hearts are immediately caught, our sympathy enlivened, and our cool approbation converted into the warmest sentiments of friendship and regard. These seem necessary and infallible consequences of the general principles of human nature, as discovered in common life and practice.

Again, reverse these views and reasonings: consider the matter *a posteriori;* and, weighing the consequences, inquire if the merit of social virtue be not, in a great measure, derived from the feelings of humanity with which it affects the spectators. It appears to be matter of fact that the circumstance of *utility,* in all subjects, is a source of praise and approbation; that it is constantly appealed to in all moral decisions concerning the merit and demerit of actions; that it is the *sole* source of that high regard paid to justice, fidelity, honor, allegiance, and chastity; that it is inseparable from all the other social virtues, humanity, generosity, charity, affability, lenity, mercy, and moderation; and, in a word, it is a foundation of the chief part of morals which has a reference to mankind and our fellow creatures.

It appears also that in our general approbation of characters and manners the useful tendency of the social virtues moves us not by any regards to self-interest, but has an influence much more universal and extensive. It appears that a tendency to public good and to the promoting of peace, harmony, and order in society does always, by affecting the benevolent principles of our frame, engage us on the side of the social virtues. And it appears, as an additional confirmation, that these principles of humanity and sympathy enter so deeply into all our sentiments and have so powerful an influence as may enable them to excite the strongest censure and applause. The present theory is the simple result of all these inferences, each of which seems founded on uniform experience and observation.

Were it doubtful whether there were any such principle in

our nature as humanity or a concern for others, yet when we see, in numberless instances, that whatever has a tendency to promote the interest of society is so highly approved of, we ought thence to learn the force of the benevolent principle, since it is impossible for anything to please as means to an end where the end is totally indifferent. On the other hand, were it doubtful whether there were implanted in our nature any general principle of moral blame and approbation, yet when we see, in numberless instances, the influence of humanity, we ought thence to conclude that it is impossible, but that everything which promotes the interests of society must communicate pleasure, and what is pernicious give uneasiness. But when these different reflections and observations concur in establishing the same conclusion, must they not bestow an undisputed evidence upon it?

It is, however, hoped that the progress of this argument will bring a further confirmation of the present theory, by showing the rise of other sentiments of esteem and regard from the same or like principles.

SECTION VI

OF QUALITIES USEFUL TO OURSELVES

PART I [1]

It seems evident that where a quality or habit is subjected to our examination, if it appear in any respect prejudicial to the person possessed of it, or such as incapacitates him for business and action, it is instantly blamed and ranked among his faults and imperfections. Indolence, negligence, want of order and

[1] [In Editions G to N this Section was introduced by paragraphs, forming Part I, which subsequently appeared as Appendix IV, "Of Some Verbal Disputes."]

method, obstinacy, fickleness, rashness, credulity—these qualities were never esteemed by anyone indifferent to a character, much less extolled as accomplishments or virtues. The prejudice resulting from them immediately strikes our eye and gives us the sentiment of pain and disapprobation.

No-quality, it is allowed, is absolutely either blamable or praiseworthy. It is all according to its degree. A due medium, say the Peripatetics, is the characteristic of virtue. But this medium is chiefly determined by utility. A proper celerity, for instance, and dispatch in business, is commendable. When defective, no progress is ever made in the execution of any purpose. When excessive, it engages us in precipitate and ill-concerted measures and enterprises. By such reasonings we fix the proper and commendable mediocrity in all moral and prudential disquisitions, and never lose view of the advantages which result from any character or habit.

Now, as these advantages are enjoyed by the person possessed of the character, it can never be *self-love* which renders the prospect of them agreeable to us, the spectators, and prompts our esteem and approbation. No force of imagination can convert us into another person and make us fancy that we, being that person, reap benefit from those valuable qualities which belong to him. Or if it did, no celerity of imagination could immediately transport us back into ourselves and make us love and esteem the person as different from us. Views and sentiments so opposite to known truth, and to each other, could never have place, at the same time, in the same person. All suspicion, therefore, of selfish regards is here totally excluded.

It is a quite different principle which actuates our bosom, and interests us in the felicity of the person whom we contemplate. Where his natural talents and acquired abilities give us the prospect of elevation, advancement, a figure in life, prosperous success, a steady command over fortune, and the execution of great or advantageous undertakings, we are struck with such agreeable images and feel a complacency and regard immediately arise toward him. The ideas of happiness, joy, triumph, prosperity are connected with every circumstance of his character and diffuse over our minds a pleasing sentiment of sympathy and humanity.[2]

Let us suppose a person originally framed so as to have no manner of concern for his fellow creatures, but to regard the happiness and misery of all sensible beings with greater indifference than even two contiguous shades of the same color. Let us suppose, if the prosperity of nations were laid on the one hand, and their ruin on the other, and he were desired to choose, that he would stand like the schoolman's ass, irresolute and undetermined between equal motives, or rather like the same ass between two pieces of wood or marble, without any inclination or propensity to either side. The consequence, I believe, must be allowed just that such a person, being absolutely unconcerned either for the public good of a community or the private utility of others, would look on every quality, however pernicious or however beneficial to society or to its possessor, with the same indifference as on the most common and uninteresting object.

But if, instead of this fancied monster, we suppose a *man* to form a judgment or determination in the case, there is to him a plain foundation of preference where everything else is equal; and however cool his choice may be, if his heart be selfish or if the persons interested be remote from him, there must still be a choice or distinction between what is useful and what is perni-

[2] One may venture to affirm that there is no human creature to whom the appearance of happiness (where envy or revenge has no place) does not give pleasure; that of misery, uneasiness. This seems inseparable from our make and constitution. But they are only the more generous minds that are thence prompted to seek zealously the good of others, and to have a real passion for their welfare. With men of narrow and ungenerous spirits, this sympathy goes not beyond a slight feeling of the imagination, which serves only to excite sentiments of complacency or censure, and makes them apply to the object either honorable or dishonorable appellations. A griping miser, for instance, praises extremely *industry* and *frugality* even in others, and sets them, in his estimation, above all the other virtues. He knows the good that results from them, and feels that species of happiness with a more lively sympathy than any other you could represent to him; though perhaps he would not part with a shilling to make the fortune of the industrious man whom he praises so highly.

cious. Now this distinction is the same, in all its parts, with the *moral distinction* whose foundation has been so often, and so much in vain, inquired after. The same endowments of the mind, in every circumstance, are agreeable to the sentiment of morals and to that of humanity; the same temper is susceptible of high degrees of the one sentiment and of the other; and the same alteration in the objects, by their nearer approach or by connections, enlivens the one and the other. By all the rules of philosophy, therefore, we must conclude that these sentiments are originally the same, since in each particular, even the most minute, they are governed by the same laws and are moved by the same objects.

Why do philosophers infer, with the greatest certainty, that the moon is kept in its orbit by the same force of gravity that makes bodies fall near the surface of the earth, but because these effects are, upon computation, found similar and equal? And must not this argument bring as strong conviction in moral as in natural disquisitions?

To prove, by any long detail, that all the qualities useful to the possessor are approved of, and the contrary censured, would be superfluous. The least reflection on what is every day experienced in life will be sufficient. We shall only mention a few instances in order to remove, if possible, all doubt and hesitation.

The quality the most necessary for the execution of any useful enterprise is *discretion*, by which we carry on a safe intercourse with others, give due attention to our own and to their character, weigh each circumstance of the business which we undertake, and employ the surest and safest means for the attainment of any end or purpose. To a Cromwell, perhaps, or a De Retz, discretion may appear an aldermanlike virtue, as Dr. Swift calls it; and being incompatible with those vast designs to which their courage and ambition prompted them, it might really, in them, be a fault or imperfection. But in the conduct of ordinary life no virtue is more requisite, not only to obtain success, but to avoid the most fatal miscarriages and disappointments. The greatest parts without it, as observed by an elegant writer, may be fatal to their owner; as Polyphemus, deprived of his eye, was only the more exposed on account of his enormous strength and stature.

The best character, indeed, were it not rather too perfect for human nature, is that which is not swayed by temper of any kind, but alternately employs enterprise and caution, as each is *useful* to the particular purpose intended. Such is the excellence which St. Evremond ascribes to Maréchal Turenne, who displayed every campaign, as he grew older, more temerity in his military enterprises; and being now, from long experience, perfectly acquainted with every incident in war, he advanced with greater firmness and security in a road so well-known to him. Fabius, says Machiavelli, was cautious; Scipio enterprising; and both succeeded because the situation of the Roman affairs, during the command of each, was peculiarly adapted to his genius, but both would have failed had these situations been reversed. He is happy whose circumstances suit his temper; but he is more excellent who can suit his temper to any circumstances.

What need is there to display the praises of *industry* and to extol its advantages, in the acquisition of power and riches, or in raising what we call a *fortune* in the world? The tortoise, according to the fable, by his perseverance gained the race of the hare, though possessed of much superior swiftness. A man's time, when well husbanded, is like a cultivated field of which a few acres produce more of what is useful to life than extensive provinces, even of the richest soil, when overrun with weeds and brambles.

But all prospect of success in life, or even of tolerable subsistence, must fail where a reasonable *frugality* is wanting. The heap, instead of increasing, diminishes daily and leaves its possessor so much more unhappy, as, not having been able to confine his expenses to a large revenue, he will still less be able to live contentedly on a small one. The souls of men, according to Plato,[3] inflamed with impure appetites, and losing the body, which alone afforded means of satisfaction, hover about the earth and haunt the places where their bodies are deposited, possessed with a longing desire to recover the lost organs of sensation. So may we see worthless prodigals, having consumed

3 *Phaedo* 81.

their fortune in wild debauches, thrusting themselves into
every plentiful table and every party of pleasure, hated even by
the vicious and despised even by fools.

The one extreme of frugality is *avarice,* which, as it both deprives a man of all use of his riches and checks hospitality and
every social enjoyment, is justly censured on a double account.
Prodigality, the other extreme, is commonly more hurtful to a
man himself; and each of these extremes is blamed above the
other, according to the temper of the person who censures, and
according to his greater or less sensibility to pleasure, either social or sensual.

[4] Qualities often derive their merit from complicated sources.
Honesty, fidelity, truth are praised for their immediate tendency to promote the interests of society; but after those virtues
are once established upon this foundation, they are also considered as advantageous to the person himself, and as the source
of that trust and confidence which can alone give a man any
consideration in life. One becomes contemptible, no less than
odious, when he forgets the duty which, in this particular, he
owes to himself as well as to society.

Perhaps this consideration is one *chief* source of the high
blame which is thrown on any instance of failure among women
in point of *chastity.* The greatest regard which can be acquired
by that sex is derived from their fidelity; and a woman becomes
cheap and vulgar, loses her rank, and is exposed to every insult,
who is deficient in this particular. The smallest failure is here
sufficient to blast her character. A female has so many opportunities of secretly indulging these appetites that nothing can give
us security but her absolute modesty and reserve; and where a
breach is once made it can scarcely ever be fully repaired. If a
man behave with cowardice on one occasion, a contrary conduct reinstates him in his character. But by what action can a
woman whose behavior has once been dissolute be able to assure us that she has formed better resolutions and has self-command enough to carry them into execution?

All men, it is allowed, are equally desirous of happiness; but
few are successful in the pursuit: one considerable cause is the

[4] [This paragraph and the next were added in Edition N.]

want of *strength* of *mind,* which might enable them to resist the temptation of present ease or pleasure and carry them forward in the search of more distant profit and enjoyment. Our affections, on a general prospect of their objects, form certain rules of conduct and certain measures of preference of one above another: and these decisions, though really the result of our calm passions and propensities (for what else can pronounce any object eligible, or the contrary), are yet said, by a natural abuse of terms, to be the determinations of pure *reason* and reflection. But when some of these objects approach nearer to us, or acquire the advantages of favorable lights and positions which catch the heart or imagination, our general resolutions are frequently confounded, a small enjoyment preferred, and lasting shame and sorrow entailed upon us. And however poets may employ their wit and eloquence in celebrating present pleasure and rejecting all distant views to fame, health, or fortune, it is obvious that this practice is the source of all dissoluteness and disorder, repentance and misery. A man of a strong and determined temper adheres tenaciously to his general resolutions and is neither seduced by the allurements of pleasure nor terrified by the menaces of pain, but keeps still in view those distant pursuits by which he at once insures his happiness and his honor.

Self-satisfaction, at least in some degree, is an advantage which equally attends the *fool* and the *wise man;* but it is the only one; nor is there any other circumstance in the conduct of life where they are upon an equal footing. Business, books, conversation—for all of these a fool is totally incapacitated, and, except condemned by his station to the coarsest drudgery, remains a *useless* burden upon the earth. Accordingly it is found that men are extremely jealous of their character in this particular; and many instances are seen of profligacy and treachery the most avowed and unreserved; none of bearing patiently the imputation of ignorance and stupidity. Dicaearchus, the Macedonian general who, as Polybius tells us,[5] openly erected one altar to impiety, another to injustice, in or-

---

[5] Lib. xvii, cap. 35.

der to bid defiance to mankind, even he, I am well assured, would have started at the epithet of *fool* and have meditated revenge for so injurious an appellation. Except the affection of parents, the strongest and most indissoluble bond in nature, no connection has strength sufficient to support the disgust arising from this character. Love itself, which can subsist under treachery, ingratitude, malice, and infidelity, is immediately extinguished by it when perceived and acknowledged; nor are deformity and old age more fatal to the dominion of that passion. So dreadful are the ideas of an utter incapacity for any purpose or undertaking, and of continued error and misconduct in life!

When it is asked whether a quick or slow apprehension be most valuable; whether one that at first view penetrates far into a subject, but can perform nothing upon study, or a contrary character which must work out everything by dint of application; whether a clear head or a copious invention; whether a profound genius or a sure judgment—in short, what character or peculiar turn of understanding is more excellent than another, it is evident that we can answer none of these questions without considering which of those qualities capacitates a man best for the world and carries him farthest in any undertaking.

If refined sense and exalted sense be not so *useful* as common sense, their rarity, their novelty, and the nobleness of their objects make some compensation and render them the admiration of mankind, as gold, though less serviceable than iron, acquires from its scarcity a value which is much superior.

The defects of judgment can be supplied by no art or invention; but those of *memory* frequently may, both in business and in study, by method and industry, and by diligence in committing everything to writing; and we scarcely ever hear a short memory given as a reason for a man's failure in any undertaking. But in ancient times, when no man could make a figure without the talent of speaking, and when the audience were too delicate to bear such crude undigested harangues as our extemporary orators offer to public assemblies, the faculty of memory was then of the utmost consequence, and was accordingly much more valued than at present. Scarce any great genius is mentioned in antiquity who is not celebrated for this talent; and Cicero enumerates it among the other sublime qualities of Caesar himself.[6]

Particular customs and manners alter the usefulness of qualities; they also alter their merit. Particular situations and accidents have, in some degree, the same influence. He will always be more esteemed who possesses those talents and accomplishments which suit his station and profession than he whom fortune has misplaced in the part which she has assigned him. The private or selfish virtues are in this respect more arbitrary than the public and social. In other respects they are, perhaps, less liable to doubt and controversy.

In this kingdom, such continued ostentation of late years has prevailed among men in *active* life with regard to *public spirit,* and among those in *speculative* with regard to *benevolence,* and so many false pretensions to each have been no doubt detected that men of the world are apt, without any bad intention, to discover a sullen incredulity on the head of those moral endowments, and even sometimes absolutely to deny their existence and reality. In like manner I find that of old the perpetual cant of the Stoics and Cynics concerning *virtue,* their magnificent professions and slender performances,[7] bred a disgust in mankind; and Lucian, who, though licentious with regard to pleasure, is yet, in other respects, a very moral writer, cannot sometimes talk of virtue, so much boasted, without be-

---

6 Fuit in illo ingenium, ratio, memoria, literae, cura, cogitatio, diligentia, etc.* *Philip.* 2. 45.

   * ["He was a man of genius, judgment, memory, culture, conscientiousness, thought, industry," etc. Cicero, *Second Philippic,* xlv. 116.]

7 [Hume refers here to the ascetic aspects of the teachings of both schools, which is, of course, only one part of their ethical doctrines. His general observation that the representatives of these schools did not live up to their own teaching reflects a prejudice; the sincerity of their teaching need not be doubted, and many representatives of both schools lived exemplary lives. A good summary of the ethical theory of the Stoics is given in Epictetus' *Enchiridion. Cf.* Higginson's translation of this work in the "Library of Liberal Arts" (New York: Liberal Arts Press).]

traying symptoms of spleen and irony.[8] But surely this peevish
delicacy, whencever it arises, can never be carried so far as to
make us deny the existence of every species of merit and all
distinction of manners and behavior. Besides *discretion,
caution, enterprise, industry, assiduity, frugality, economy,
good sense, prudence, discernment*—besides these endowments,
I say, whose very names force an avowal of their merit, there
are many others to which the most determined skepticism cannot for a moment refuse the tribute of praise and approbation.
*Temperance, sobriety, patience, constancy, perseverance, fore-
thought, considerateness, secrecy, order, insinuation, address,
presence of mind, quickness of conception, facility of expression*—these, and a thousand more of the same kind, no man
will ever deny to be excellences and perfections. As their merit
consists in their tendency to serve the person possessed of them,
without any magnificent claim to public and social desert, we
are the less jealous of their pretensions and readily admit them
into the catalogue of laudable qualities. We are not sensible
that, by this concession, we have paved the way for all the other
moral excellences, and cannot consistently hesitate any longer
with regard to disinterested benevolence, patriotism, and
humanity.

It seems, indeed, certain that first appearances are here, as
usual, extremely deceitful, and that it is more difficult, in a
speculative way, to resolve into self-love the merit which we
ascribe to the selfish virtues above mentioned, than that even of
the social virtues, justice and beneficence. For this latter pur-

---

[8] Ἀρετήν τινα, καὶ ἀσώματα, καὶ λήρους μεγάλῃ τῇ φωνῇ ξυνειρόντων.*
Again, Καὶ συναγαγόντες (οἱ φιλόσοφοι) εὖ ἐξαπάτητα μειράκια τήν τε
πολυθρύλητον ἀρετὴν τραγῳδοῦσι.† In another place, Ἦ ποῦ γάρ ἐστιν ἡ
πολυθρύλητος ἀρετή, καὶ φύσις, καὶ εἱμαρμένη, καὶ τύχη, ἀνυπόστατα καὶ
κενὰ πραγμάτων ὀνόματα.‡

* ["Who with a loud voice hold forth about some kind of 'virtue,' 'im-
material substances,' and all kinds of nonsense." Lucian, *Timon* 9.]

† ["And bringing together young people who are easily deceived, they
(*scil.* the philosophers) make tragic speeches about the hackneyed subject of virtue." *Icaromenippus.* 30.]

‡ ["Or where then is that hackneyed virtue, and nature, and fate, and
fortune, all of them empty names without substance"; (*Deorum con-
cilium,* i. 3).]

pose we need but say that whatever conduct promotes the good of the community is loved, praised, and esteemed by the community on account of that utility and interest of which everyone partakes; and though this affection and regard be, in reality, gratitude, not self-love, yet a distinction, even of this obvious nature, may not readily be made by superficial reasoners; and there is room at least to support the cavil and dispute for a moment. But as qualities which tend only to the utility of their possessor, without any reference to us or to the community, are yet esteemed and valued, by what theory or system can we account for this sentiment from self-love or deduce it from that favorite origin? There seems here a necessity for confessing that the happiness and misery of others are not spectacles entirely indifferent to us, but that the view of the former, whether in its causes or effects, like sunshine, or the prospect of well-cultivated plains (to carry our pretensions no higher), communicates a secret joy and satisfaction; the appearance of the latter, like a lowering cloud or barren landscape, throws a melancholy damp over the imagination. And this concession being once made, the difficulty is over, and a natural, unforced interpretation of the phenomena of human life will afterward, we hope, prevail among all speculative inquirers.

PART II [1]

It may not be improper, in this place, to examine the influence of bodily endowments, and of the goods of fortune, over our sentiments of regard and esteem and to consider whether these phenomena fortify or weaken the present theory. [2] It will naturally be expected that the beauty of the body, as is supposed by all ancient moralists, will be similar in some respects to that of the mind, and that every kind of esteem which is paid to a man will have something similar in its origin,

---

[1] [Part III in Editions G to N.]
[2] [This sentence was added in Edition N, which, however, stops at "origin."]

whether it arise from his mental endowments or from the situation of his exterior circumstances.

It is evident that one considerable source of *beauty* in all animals is the advantage which they reap from the particular structure of their limbs and members, suitably to the particular manner of life to which they are by nature destined. The just proportions of a horse described by Xenophon and Virgil are the same that are received at this day by our modern jockeys, because the foundation of them is the same—namely, experience of what is detrimental or useful in the animal.

Broad shoulders, a lank belly, firm joints, taper legs—all these are beautiful in our species, because signs of force and vigor. Ideas of utility and its contrary, though they do not entirely determine what is handsome or deformed, are evidently the source of a considerable part of approbation or dislike.

In ancient times bodily strength and dexterity, being of greater *use* and importance in war, was also much more esteemed and valued than at present. Not to insist on Homer and the poets, we may observe that historians scruple not to mention *force of body* among the other accomplishments even of Epaminondas, whom they acknowledge to be the greatest hero, statesman, and general of all the Greeks.[3] A like praise is given to Pompey, one of the greatest of the Romans.[4] This instance is similar to what we observed above with regard to memory.

---

[3] Diodorus Siculus, lib. xv, 88. It may not be improper to give the character of Epaminondas, as drawn by the historian, in order to show the ideas of perfect merit which prevailed in those ages. In other illustrious men, says he, you will observe that each possessed some one shining quality, which was the foundation of his fame: in Epaminondas all the *virtues* are found united: force of body, eloquence of expression, vigor of mind, contempt of riches, gentleness of disposition, and, *what is chiefly to be regarded,* courage and conduct in war.

[4] Cum alacribus, saltu; cum velocibus, cursu; cum validis recte certabat.* SALLUST apud VEGET. *De Re Mil.* 19.

* [He competed with the spirited in jumping, with the swift in racing, and with the strong in the proper manner. Sallust as cited by Vegetius.]

What derision and contempt, with both sexes, attend *impotence,* while the unhappy object is regarded as one deprived of so capital a pleasure in life, and at the same time as disabled from communicating it to others. *Barrenness* in women, being also a species of *inutility,* is a reproach, but not in the same degree; of which the reason is very obvious, according to the present theory.[5]

There is no rule in painting or statuary more indispensable than that of balancing the figures and placing them with the greatest exactness on their proper center of gravity. A figure which is not justly balanced is ugly, because it conveys the disagreeable ideas of fall, harm, and pain.[6]

A disposition or turn of mind which qualifies a man to rise in the world and advance his fortune is entitled to esteem and regard, as has already been explained. It may, therefore,

[5] [Edition G adds in a note: "To the same purpose, we may observe a Phenomenon, which might appear somewhat trivial and ludicrous; if anything could be trivial, which fortified conclusions of such importance; or ludicrous, which was employed in a philosophical reasoning. 'Tis a general remark, that those we call good *women's men,* who have either signalized themselves by their amorous exploits, or whose make of body or other symptoms promise any extraordinary vigor of that kind, are well received by the fair sex, and naturally engage the affections even of those whose virtue or situation prevents any design of ever giving employment to those talents. The imagination is pleased with these conceptions, and, entering with satisfaction into the ideas of so favorite an enjoyment, feels a complacency and good will toward the person. A like principle, operating more extensively, is the general source of more affection and approbation."]

[6] All men are equally liable to pain and disease, and sickness, and may again recover health and ease. These circumstances, as they make no distinction between one man and another, are no source of pride or humility, regard or contempt. But comparing our own species to superior ones, it is a very mortifying consideration that we should all be so liable to diseases and infirmities; and divines accordingly employ this topic in order to depress self-conceit and vanity. They would have more success if the common bent of our thoughts were not perpetually turned to compare ourselves with others. The infirmities of old age are mortifying, because a comparison with the young may take place. The king's evil is industriously concealed because it affects others, and is often transmitted to posterity. The case is nearly the same with such diseases as convey any nauseous or frightful images; the epilepsy, for instance, ulcers, sores, scabs, etc.

naturally be supposed that the actual possession of riches and authority will have a considerable influence over these sentiments.

Let us examine any hypothesis by which we can account for the regard paid to the rich and powerful: we shall find none satisfactory but that which derives it from the enjoyment communicated to the spectator by the images of prosperity, happiness, ease, plenty, authority, and the gratification of every appetite. Self-love, for instance, which some affect so much to consider as the source of every sentiment, is plainly insufficient for this purpose. Where no good will or friendship appears, it is difficult to conceive on what we can found our hope of advantage from the riches of others, though we naturally respect the rich, even before they discover any such favorable disposition toward us.

We are affected with the same sentiments when we lie so much out of the sphere of their activity that they cannot even be supposed to possess the power of serving us. A prisoner of war, in all civilized nations, is treated with a regard suited to his condition; and riches, it is evident, go far toward fixing the condition of any person. If birth and quality enter for a share, this still affords us an argument to our present purpose. For what is it we call a man of birth, but one who is descended from a long succession of rich and powerful ancestors, and who acquires our esteem by his connection with persons whom we esteem? His ancestors, therefore, though dead, are respected in some measure on account of their riches, and, consequently, without any kind of expectation.

But not to go so far as prisoners of war or the dead, to find instances of this disinterested regard for riches, we may only observe, with a little attention, those phenomena which occur in common life and conversation. A man who is himself, we shall suppose, of a competent fortune and of no profession, being introduced to a company of strangers, naturally treats them with different degrees of respect, as he is informed of their different fortunes and conditions, though it is impossible that he can so suddenly propose, and perhaps he would not accept

[handwritten marginal note: We are here in in early wrong western culture.]

of, any pecuniary advantage from them. A traveler is always admitted into company, and meets with civility, in proportion as his train and equipage speak him a man of great or moderate fortune. In short, the different ranks of men are, in a great measure, regulated by riches, and that with regard to superiors as well as inferiors, strangers as well as acquaintance.

What remains, therefore, but to conclude that as riches are desired for ourselves only as the means of gratifying our appetites, either at present or in some imaginary future period, they beget esteem in others merely from their having that influence. This indeed is their very nature or essence: they have a direct reference to the commodities, conveniences, and pleasures of life; the bill of a banker who is broke or gold in a desert island would otherwise be full as valuable. When we approach a man who is, as we say, at his ease, we are presented with the pleasing ideas of plenty, satisfaction, cleanliness, warmth; a cheerful house, elegant furniture, ready service, and whatever is desirable in meat, drink, or apparel. On the contrary, when a poor man appears, the disagreeable images of want, penury, hard labor, dirty furniture, coarse or ragged clothes, nauseous meat and distasteful liquor immediately strike our fancy. What else do we mean by saying that one is rich, the other poor? And as regard or contempt is the natural consequence of those different situations in life, it is easily seen what additional light and evidence this throws on our preceding theory with regard to all moral distinctions.[7]

[7] There is something extraordinary, and seemingly unaccountable, in the operation of our passions when we consider the fortune and situation of others. Very often another's advancement and prosperity produces envy, which has a strong mixture of hatred, and arises chiefly from the comparison of ourselves with the person. At the very same time, or at least in very short intervals, we may feel the passion of respect, which is a species of affection or good will, with a mixture of humility. On the other hand, the misfortunes of our fellows often cause pity, which has in it a strong mixture of good will. This sentiment of pity is nearly allied to contempt, which is a species of dislike, with a mixture of pride. I only point out these phenomena as a subject of speculation to such as are curious with regard to moral inquiries. It is sufficient for the present purpose to observe, in general, that

A man who has cured himself of all ridiculous prepossessions and is fully, sincerely, and steadily convinced, from experience as well as philosophy, that the difference of fortune makes less difference in happiness than is vulgarly imagined—such a one does not measure out degrees of esteem according to the rent-rolls of his acquaintance. He may, indeed, externally pay a superior deference to the great lord above the vassal, because riches are the most convenient, being the most fixed and determinate source of distinction; but his internal sentiments are more regulated by the personal characters of men than by the accidental and capricious favors of fortune.

In most countries of Europe, family, that is, hereditary riches, marked with titles and symbols from the sovereign, is the chief source of distinction. In England, more regard is paid to present opulence and plenty. Each practice has its advantages and disadvantages. Where birth is respected, unactive, spiritless minds remain in haughty indolence and dream of nothing but pedigrees and genealogies; the generous and ambitious seek honor and authority and reputation and favor. Where riches are the chief idol, corruption, venality, rapine prevail; arts, manufactures, commerce, agriculture flourish. The former prejudice, being favorable to military virtue, is more suited to monarchies. The latter, being the chief spur to industry, agrees better with a republican government. And we accordingly find that each of these forms of government, by varying the *utility* of those customs, has commonly a proportionable effect on the sentiments of mankind.

---

power and riches commonly cause respect, poverty and meanness contempt, though particular views and incidents may sometimes raise the passions of envy and of pity.

OF QUALITIES IMMEDIATELY AGREEABLE
TO OURSELVES

WHOEVER has passed an evening with serious, melancholy people and has observed how suddenly the conversation was animated and what sprightliness diffused itself over the countenance, discourse, and behavior of everyone on the accession of a good-humored, lively companion, such a one will easily allow that *cheerfulness* carries great merit with it and naturally conciliates the good will of mankind. No quality, indeed, more readily communicates itself to all around, because no one has a greater propensity to display itself in jovial talk and pleasant entertainment. The flame spreads through the whole circle, and the most sullen and morose are often caught by it. That the melancholy hate the merry, even though Horace says it, I have some difficulty to allow, because I have always observed that, where the jollity is moderate and decent, serious people are so much the more delighted as it dissipates the gloom with which they are commonly oppressed and gives them an unusual enjoyment.

From this influence of cheerfulness, both to communicate itself and to engage approbation, we may perceive that there is another set of mental qualities which, without any utility or any tendency to further good, either of the community or of the possessor, diffuse a satisfaction on the beholders and procure friendship and regard. Their immediate sensation to the person possessed of them is agreeable; others enter into the same humor and catch the sentiment by a contagion or natural sympathy; and as we cannot forbear loving whatever pleases, a kindly emotion arises toward the person who communicates so much satisfaction. He is a more animating spectacle: his presence diffuses over us more serene complacency and enjoyment; our imagination, entering into his feelings and disposition, is

affected in a more agreeable manner than if a melancholy,
dejected, sullen, anxious temper were presented to us. Hence
the affection and approbation which attend the former, the
aversion and disgust with which we regard the latter.[1]

Few men would envy the character which Caesar gives of
Cassius:

> He loves no play,
> As thou do'st, Anthony: He hears no music:
> Seldom he smiles; and smiles in such a sort,
> As if he mocked himself, and scorned his spirit
> That could be moved to smile at any thing.

Not only such men, as Caesar adds, are commonly *dangerous,*
but also, having little enjoyment within themselves, they can
never become agreeable to others or contribute to social entertainment. In all polite nations and ages, a relish for pleasure, if
accompanied with temperance and decency, is esteemed a considerable merit, even in the greatest men; and becomes still
more requisite in those of inferior rank and character. It is an
agreeable representation which a French writer gives of the
situation of his own mind in this particular: *Virtue I love,* says
he, *without austerity, pleasure without effeminacy, and life
without fearing its end.*[2]

Who is not struck with any signal instance of *greatness of
mind* or dignity of character; with elevation of sentiment, disdain of slavery, and with that noble pride and spirit which arises
from conscious virtue? The sublime, says Longinus, is often
nothing but the echo or image of magnanimity; and where this

---

[1] There is no man who, on particular occasions, is not affected with all the
disagreeable passions: fear, anger, dejection, grief, melancholy, anxiety, etc.
But these, so far as they are natural and universal, make no difference
between one man and another, and can never be the object of blame. It is
only when the disposition gives a *propensity* to any of these disagreeable
passions that they disfigure the character and, by giving uneasiness, convey
the sentiment of disapprobation to the spectator.

[2] "J'aime la vertu, sans rudesse;
  J'aime le plaisir, sans molesse;
  J'aime la vie, et n'en crains point la fin."
                              St. Evremond.

quality appears in anyone, even though a syllable be not uttered, it excites our applause and admiration, as may be observed of the famous silence of Ajax in the *Odyssey,* which expresses more noble disdain and resolute indignation than any language can convey.[3]

"Were I Alexander," said Parmenio, "I would accept of these offers made by Darius."—"So would I, too," replied Alexander, "were I Parmenio." This saying is admirable, says Longinus, from a like principle.[4]

"Go!" cries the same hero to his soldiers, when they refused to follow him to the Indies, "go, tell your countrymen that you left Alexander completing the conquest of the world."—"Alexander," said the Prince of Condé, who always admired this passage, "abandoned by his soldiers among barbarians not yet fully subdued, felt in himself such a dignity and right of empire that he could not believe it possible that anyone would refuse to obey him. Whether in Europe or in Asia, among Greeks or Persians, all was indifferent to him: wherever he found men, he fancied he should find subjects."

The confident [5] of Medea in the tragedy recommends caution and submission and, enumerating all the distresses of that unfortunate heroine, asks her what she has to support her against her numerous and implacable enemies? "Myself," replies she; "Myself, I say, and it is enough." Boileau justly recommends this passage as an instance of true sublime.[6]

When Phocion, the modest, the gentle Phocion, was led to execution, he turned to one of his fellow sufferers who was lamenting his own hard fate, "Is it not glory enough for you," says he, "that you die with Phocion?" [7]

Place in opposition the picture which Tacitus draws of Vitellius, fallen from empire, prolonging his ignominy from a wretched love of life, delivered over to the merciless rabble—tossed, buffeted, and kicked about; constrained, by their holding a poniard under his chin, to raise his head and expose him-

---

[3] Cap. 9.

[4] *Idem.*

[5] ["Confidant" in several editions.]

[6] *Réflexion* X. sur Longin.

[7] Plutarch in *Phoc.* 36.

self to every contumely. What abject infamy! What low humilia-
tion! Yet even here, says the historian, he discovered some
symptoms of a mind not wholly degenerate. To a tribune who
insulted him, he replied, "I am still your emperor." [8]

We never excuse the absolute want of spirit and dignity of
character, or a proper sense of what is due to one's self in
society and the common intercourse of life. This vice constitutes
what we properly call "meanness"—when a man can submit to
the basest slavery in order to gain his ends, fawn upon those
who abuse him, and degrade himself by intimacies and
familiarities with undeserving inferiors. A certain degree of
generous pride or self-value is so requisite that the absence of it
in the mind displeases, after the same manner as the want of a
nose, eye, or any of the most material features of the face or
members of the body.[9]

The utility of *courage,* both to the public and to the person
possessed of it, is an obvious foundation of merit; but to anyone
who duly considers of the matter it will appear that this quality
has a peculiar luster which it derives wholly from itself and
from that noble elevation inseparable from it. Its figure, drawn

---

[8] Tacit. *Hist.* lib. iii. 85. The author, entering upon the narration, says,
*Laniata veste, foedum spectaculum ducebatur, multis increpantibus, nullo
inlacrimante: deformitas exitus misericordiam abstulerat.** To enter
thoroughly into this method of thinking, we must make allowance for the
ancient maxims, that no one ought to prolong his life after it became dishonorable; but, as he had always a right to dispose of it, it then became a
duty to part with it.

* [Tacitus, *Histories.* iii. 85 . . . "With his robe torn, he was led along,
a filthy sight to see; many shouted at him, but none wept: the ugliness of
his end had removed any pity."]

[9] The absence of virtue may often be a vice, and that of the highest kind;
as in the instance of ingratitude, as well as meanness. Where we expect a
beauty, the disappointment gives an uneasy sensation, and produces a real
deformity. An abjectness of character, likewise, is disgustful and contemptible in another view. Where a man has no sense of value in himself, we are
not likely to have any higher esteem of him. And if the same person who
crouches to his superiors is insolent to his inferiors (as often happens), this
contrariety of behavior, instead of correcting the former vice, aggravates it
extremely by the addition of a vice still more odious. See Sect. VIII, "Of
Qualities immediately agreeable to others."

by painters and by poets, displays in each feature a sublimity and daring confidence which catches the eye, engages the affections, and diffuses by sympathy a like sublimity of sentiment over every spectator.

Under what shining colors does Demosthenes [10] represent Philip, where the orator apologizes for his own administration and justifies that pertinacious love of liberty with which he had inspired the Athenians! "I beheld Philip," says he, "he with whom was your contest, resolutely, while in pursuit of empire and dominion, exposing himself to every wound; his eye gored, his neck wrested, his arm, his thigh pierced; whatever part of his body fortune should seize on, that cheerfully relinquishing, provided that, with what remained, he might live in honor and renown. And shall it be said that he, born in Pella, a place heretofore mean and ignoble, should be inspired with so high an ambition and thirst of fame, while you, Athenians," etc. These praises excite the most lively admiration, but the views presented by the orator carry us not, we see, beyond the hero himself, nor ever regard the future advantageous consequences of his valor.

The martial temper of the Romans, inflamed by continual wars, had raised their esteem of courage so high that in their language it was called *virtue,* by way of excellence and of distinction from all other moral qualities. "*The Suevi,*" in the opinion of Tacitus,[11] "*dressed their hair with a laudable intent; not for the purpose of loving or being loved; they adorned themselves only for their enemies, and in order to appear more terrible*"—a sentiment of the historian which would sound a little oddly in other nations and other ages.

The Scythians, according to Herodotus,[12] after scalping their enemies, dressed the skin like leather and used it as a towel; and whoever had the most of those towels was most esteemed among them. So much had martial bravery, in that nation as well as in many others, destroyed the sentiments of humanity—a virtue surely much more useful and engaging.

[10] *Pro corona.* 247.   [11] *De moribus Germanorum* 38.
[12] Lib. iv. 64.

It is indeed observable that, among all uncultivated nations who have not, as yet, had full experience of the advantages attending beneficence, justice, and the social virtues, courage is the predominant excellence; what is most celebrated by poets, recommended by parents and instructors, and admired by the public in general. The ethics of Homer are, in this particular, very different from those of Fénelon, his elegant imitator, and such as were well suited to an age when one hero, as remarked by Thucydides,[13] could ask another, without offense, whether he were a robber or not. Such also, very lately, was the system of ethics which prevailed in many barbarous parts of Ireland, if we may credit Spencer in his judicious account of the state of that kingdom.[14]

Of the same class of virtues with courage is that undisturbed philosophical *tranquillity*, superior to pain, sorrow, anxiety, and each assault of adverse fortune. Conscious of his own virtue, say the philosophers, the sage elevates himself above every accident of life and, securely placed in the temple of wisdom, looks down on inferior mortals engaged in pursuit of honors, riches, reputation, and every frivolous enjoyment. These pretensions, no doubt, when stretched to the utmost, are by far too magnificent for human nature. They carry, however, a grandeur with them which seizes the spectator and strikes him with admiration. And the nearer we can approach in practice to this sublime tranquillity and indifference (for we must distinguish it from a stupid insensibility), the more secure enjoyment shall we attain within ourselves, and the more greatness of mind shall we discover to the world. The philosophical tranquillity may indeed be considered only as a branch of magnanimity.

Who admires not Socrates, his perpetual serenity and con-

---

[13] Lib. i. 5.

[14] It is a common use, says he, amongst their gentlemen's sons, that, as soon as they are able to use their weapons, they strait gather to themselves three or four stragglers or kern, with whom wandering a while up and down idly the country, taking only meat, he at last falleth into some bad occasion that shall be offered; which being once made known, he is thenceforth counted a man of worth, in whom there is courage.

tentment amidst the greatest poverty and domestic vexations, his resolute contempt of riches, and his magnanimous care of preserving liberty, while he refused all assistance from his friends and disciples, and avoided even the dependence of an obligation? Epictetus had not so much as a door to his little house or hovel, and therefore soon lost his iron lamp, the only furniture which he had worth taking. But resolving to disappoint all robbers for the future, he supplied its place with an earthen lamp, of which he very peaceably kept possession ever after.

Among the ancients, the heroes in philosophy as well as those in war and patriotism have a grandeur and force of sentiment which astonishes our narrow souls, and is rashly rejected as extravagant and supernatural. They, in their turn, I allow, would have had equal reason to consider as romantic and incredible the degree of humanity, clemency, order, tranquillity, and other social virtues to which, in the administration of government, we have attained in modern times had anyone been then able to have made a fair representation of them. Such is the compensation which nature, or rather education, has made in the distribution of excellences and virtues in those different ages.

The merit of *benevolence,* arising from its utility and its tendency to promote the good of mankind, has been already explained and is, no doubt, the source of a *considerable* part of that esteem which is so universally paid to it. But it will also be allowed that the very softness and tenderness of the sentiment, its engaging endearments, its fond expressions, its delicate attentions, and all that flow of mutual confidence and regard which enters into a warm attachment of love and friendship— it will be allowed, I say, that these feelings, being delightful in themselves, are necessarily communicated to the spectators and melt them into the same fondness and delicacy. The tear naturally starts in our eye on the apprehension of a warm sentiment of this nature; our breast heaves, our heart is agitated, and every humane, tender principle of our frame is set in motion and gives us the purest and most satisfactory enjoyment.

When poets form descriptions of Elysian fields, where the blessed inhabitants stand in no need of each other's assistance, they yet represent them as maintaining a constant intercourse of love and friendship, and soothe our fancy with the pleasing image of these soft and gentle passions. The idea of tender tranquillity in a pastoral Arcadia [15] is agreeable from a like principle, as has been observed above.[16]

Who would live amidst perpetual wrangling and scolding and mutual reproaches? The roughness and harshness of these emotions disturb and displease us; we suffer by contagion and sympathy, nor can we remain indifferent spectators, even though certain that no pernicious consequences would ever follow from such angry passions.

As a certain proof that the whole merit of benevolence is not derived from its usefulness, we may observe that, in a kind way of blame, we say "a person is *too good*," when he exceeds his part in society and carries his attention for others beyond the proper bounds. In like manner, we say "a man is *too high-spirited, too intrepid, too indifferent about fortune*"—reproaches which really at bottom imply more esteem than many panegyrics. Being accustomed to rate the merit and demerit of characters chiefly by their useful or pernicious tendencies, we cannot forbear applying the epithet of blame when we discover a sentiment which rises to a degree that is hurtful; but it may happen, at the same time, that its noble elevation, or its engaging tenderness, so seizes the heart as rather to increase our friendship and concern for the person.[17]

The amours and attachments of Harry IV of France, during the civil wars of the League, frequently hurt his interest and

[15] [Arcadia was a mountainous region inhabited by a simple pastoral people, which had little communication with the other parts of Greece. Arcadia, therefore, was spared involvement in the continuous wars among the Greeks, and its long peaceful existence made it a synonym for a region of simple life and pleasures.]

[16] Sect. V, Part 2, "Why Utility pleases."

[17] Cheerfulness could scarce admit of blame from its excess, were it not that dissolute mirth, without a proper cause or subject, is a sure symptom and characteristic of folly, and on that account disgustful.

his cause, but all the young, at least, and amorous who can sympathize with the tender passions will allow that this very weakness (for they will readily call it such) chiefly endears that hero and interests them in his fortunes.

The excessive bravery and resolute inflexibility of Charles XII ruined his own country and infested all his neighbors, but have such splendor and greatness in their appearance as strikes us with admiration, and they might in some degree be even approved of, if they betrayed not sometimes too evident symptoms of madness and disorder.

The Athenians pretended to the first invention of agriculture and of laws, and always valued themselves extremely on the benefit thereby procured to the whole race of mankind. They also boasted, and with reason, of their warlike enterprises, particularly against those innumerable fleets and armies of Persians which invaded Greece during the reigns of Darius and Xerxes. But though there be no comparison, in point of utility, between these peaceful and military honors, yet we find that the orators who have written such elaborate panegyrics on that famous city have chiefly triumphed in displaying the warlike achievements. Lysias, Thucydides, Plato, and Isocrates discover, all of them, the same partiality which, though condemned by calm reason and reflection, appears so natural in the mind of man.

It is observable that the great charm of poetry consists in lively pictures of the sublime passions, magnanimity, courage, disdain of fortune, or those of the tender affections, love, and friendship which warm the heart and diffuse over it similar sentiments and emotions. And though all kinds of passion, even the most disagreeable, such as grief and anger, are observed, when excited by poetry, to convey a satisfaction from a mechanism of nature not easy to be explained, yet those more elevated or softer affections have a peculiar influence and please from more than one cause or principle. Not to mention that they alone interest us in the fortune of the persons represented or communicate any esteem and affection for their character.

And can it possibly be doubted that this talent itself of poets to move the passions, this *pathetic* and *sublime* of sentiment is a very considerable merit, and, being enhanced by its extreme rarity, may exalt the person possessed of it above every character of the age in which he lives? The prudence, address, steadiness and benign government of Augustus, adorned with all the splendor of his noble birth and imperial crown, render him but an unequal competitor for fame with Virgil, who lays nothing into the opposite scale but the divine beauties of his poetical genius.

The very sensibility to these beauties, or a *delicacy* of taste, is itself a beauty in any character, as conveying the purest, the most durable, and most innocent of all enjoyments.

These are some instances of the several species of merit that are valued for the immediate pleasure which they communicate to the person possessed of them. No views of utility or of future beneficial consequences enter into this sentiment of approbation, yet is it of a kind similar to that other sentiment which arises from views of a public or private utility. The same social sympathy, we may observe, or fellow feeling with human happiness or misery, gives rise to both; and this analogy, in all the parts of the present theory, may justly be regarded as a confirmation of it.

SECTION VIII

OF QUALITIES IMMEDIATELY AGREEABLE TO OTHERS [1]

As the mutual shocks in *society*, and the oppositions of interest and self-love, have constrained mankind to establish the laws of *justice* in order to preserve the advantages of mutual

[1] It is the nature, and indeed the definition of virtue, that it is a quality of the mind agreeable to or approved of by everyone who considers or contemplates it. But some qualities produce pleasure because they are useful to society or useful or agreeable to the person himself; others produce it more immediately: which is the case with the class of virtues here considered.

assistance and protection, in like manner the eternal contrarieties in *company,* of men's pride and self-conceit, have introduced the rules of *good manners* or *politeness* in order to facilitate the intercourse of minds and an undisturbed commerce and conversation. Among well-bred people a mutual deference is affected; contempt of others disguised; authority concealed; attention given to each in his turn; and an easy stream of conversation maintained, without vehemence, without interruption, without eagerness for victory, and without any airs of superiority. These attentions and regards are immediately *agreeable* to others, abstracted from any consideration of utility or beneficial tendencies: they conciliate affection, promote esteem, and extremely enhance the merit of the person who regulates his behavior by them.

Many of the forms of breeding are arbitrary and casual; but the thing expressed by them is still the same. A Spaniard goes out of his own house before his guest, to signify that he leaves him master of all. In other countries the landlord walks out last, as a common mark of deference and regard.

But, in order to render a man perfect *good company,* he must have *wit* and *ingenuity* as well as good manners. What wit is it may not be easy to define, but it is easy surely to determine that it is a quality immediately *agreeable* to others and communicating, on its first appearance, a lively joy and satisfaction to everyone who has any comprehension of it. The most profound metaphysics, indeed, might be employed in explaining the various kinds and species of wit; and many classes of it, which are now received on the sole testimony of taste and sentiment, might perhaps be resolved into more general principles. But this is sufficient for our present purpose, that it does affect taste and sentiment; and bestowing an immediate enjoyment is a sure source of approbation and affection.

In countries where men pass most of their time in conversation and visits and assemblies, these *companionable* qualities, so to speak, are of high estimation and form a chief part of personal merit. In countries where men live a more domestic life and either are employed in business or amuse themselves in a narrower circle of acquaintance, the more solid qualities are chiefly regarded. Thus I have often observed that among the French the first questions with regard to a stranger are, *Is he polite? Has he wit?* In our own country, the chief praise bestowed is always that of a *good-natured, sensible fellow.*

In conversation, the lively spirit of dialogue is *agreeable,* even to those who desire not to have any share in the discourse; hence the teller of long stories, or the pompous declaimer, is very little approved of. But most men desire likewise their turn in the conversation and regard, with a very evil eye, that *loquacity* which deprives them of a right they are naturally so jealous of.

There is a sort of harmless *liars* frequently to be met with in company, who deal much in the marvelous. Their usual intention is to please and entertain; but as men are most delighted with what they conceive to be truth, these people mistake extremely the means of pleasing and incur universal blame. Some indulgence, however, to lying or fiction is given in *humorous* stories, because it is there really agreeable and entertaining, and truth is not of any importance.

Eloquence, genius of all kinds, even good sense and sound reasoning, when it rises to an eminent degree and is employed upon subjects of any considerable dignity and nice discernment—all these endowments seem immediately agreeable and have a merit distinct from their usefulness. Rarity, likewise, which so much enhances the price of everything, must set an additional value on these noble talents of the human mind.

Modesty may be understood in different senses, even abstracted from chastity, which has been already treated of. It sometimes means that tenderness and nicety of honor, that apprehension of blame, that dread of intrusion or injury toward others, that *pudor* which is the proper guardian of every kind of virtue and a sure preservative against vice and corruption. But its most usual meaning is when it is opposed to *impudence* and *arrogance,* and expresses a diffidence of our own judgment and a due attention and regard for others. In young men chiefly this quality is a sure sign of good sense, and is also the certain means of augmenting that endowment by preserving their ears open to instruction, and making them still grasp after new attainments. But it has a further charm to every spectator by flattering every man's vanity and presenting the appearance of a docile pupil who receives, with proper attention and respect, every word they utter.

Men have, in general, a much greater propensity to overvalue than undervalue themselves, notwithstanding the opinion of Aristotle.[2] This makes us more jealous of the excess on the former side and causes us to regard, with a peculiar indulgence, all tendency to modesty and self-diffidence as esteeming the danger less of falling into any vicious extreme of that nature. It is thus, in countries where men's bodies are apt to exceed in corpulency, personal beauty is placed in a much greater degree of slenderness than in countries where that is the most usual defect. Being so often struck with instances of one species of deformity, men think they can never keep at too great a distance from it, and wish always to have a leaning to the opposite side. In like manner, were the door opened to self-praise and were Montaigne's maxim observed, that one should say as frankly, *I have sense, I have learning, I have courage, beauty or wit,* as it is sure we often think so—were this the case, I say, everyone is sensible that such a flood of impertinence would break in upon us as would render society wholly intolerable. For this reason custom has established it as a rule in common societies that men should not indulge themselves in self-praise, or even speak much of themselves; and it is only among intimate friends, or people of very manly behavior, that one is allowed to do himself justice. Nobody finds fault with Maurice, Prince of Orange, for his reply to one who asked him whom he esteemed the first general of the age: *The Marquis of Spinola,* said he, *is the second.* Though it is observable that the self-praise implied is here better implied than if it had been directly expressed, without any cover or disguise.

He must be a very superficial thinker who imagines that all instances of mutual deferences are to be understood in earnest,

[2] *Ethic. ad Nicomachum.* iv. 3, 37.

and that a man would be more estimable for being ignorant of his own merits and accomplishments. A small bias toward modesty, even in the internal sentiment, is favorably regarded, especially in young people; and a strong bias is required in the outward behavior; but this excludes not a noble pride and spirit which may openly display itself in its full extent when one lies under calumny or oppression of any kind. The generous contumacy of Socrates, as Cicero calls it, has been highly celebrated in all ages, and, when joined to the usual modesty of his behavior, forms a shining character. Iphicrates, the Athenian, being accused of betraying the interests of his country, asked his accuser, *Would you,* says he, *have on a like occasion been guilty of that crime? By no means,* replied the other. *And can you then imagine,* cried the hero, *that Iphicrates would be guilty?* [3] In short, a generous spirit and self-value, well founded, decently disguised, and courageously supported under distress and calumny, is a great excellence and seems to derive its merit from the noble elevation of its sentiment or its immediate agreeableness to its possessor. In ordinary characters we approve of a bias toward modesty, which is a quality immediately agreeable to others. The vicious excess of the former virtue, namely, insolence or haughtiness, is immediately disagreeable to others; the excess of the latter is so to the possessor. Thus are the boundaries of these duties adjusted.

A desire of fame, reputation, or a character with others, is so far from being blamable that it seems inseparable from virtue, genius, capacity, and a generous or noble disposition. An attention even to trivial matters, in order to please, is also expected and demanded by society; and no one is surprised if he find a man in company to observe a greater elegance of dress and more pleasant flow of conversation than when he passes his time at home and with his own family. Wherein then consists *vanity* which is so justly regarded as a fault or imperfection? It seems to consist chiefly in such an intemperate display of our advantages, honors, and accomplishments, in such an importunate and open demand of praise and admiration as is offen-

[3] Quintil. lib. v. cap. 12.

sive to others and encroaches too far on *their* secret vanity and ambition. It is besides a sure symptom of the want of true dignity and elevation of mind, which is so great an ornament in any character. For why that impatient desire of applause, as if you were not justly entitled to it, and might not reasonably expect that it would forever attend you? Why so anxious to inform us of the great company which you have kept, the obliging things which were said to you, the honors, the distinctions which you met with, as if these were not things of course, and what we could readily, of ourselves, have imagined, without being told of them?

Decency, or a proper regard to age, sex, character, and station in the world, may be ranked among the qualities which are immediately agreeable to others, and which, by that means, acquire praise and approbation. An effeminate behavior in a man, a rough manner in a woman—these are ugly because unsuitable to each character, and different from the qualities which we expect in the sexes. It is as if a tragedy abounded in comic beauties, or a comedy in tragic. The disproportions hurt the eye and convey a disagreeable sentiment to the spectators, the source of blame and disapprobation. This is that *indecorum* which is explained so much at large by Cicero in his *Offices.*

Among the other virtues we may also give *cleanliness* a place, since it naturally renders us agreeable to others and is no inconsiderable source of love and affection. No one will deny that a negligence in this particular is a fault; and as faults are nothing but smaller vices, and this fault can have no other origin than the uneasy sensation which it excites in others, we may in this instance, seemingly so trivial, clearly discover the origin of moral distinctions about which the learned have involved themselves in such mazes of perplexity and error.

But besides all the *agreeable* qualities, the origin of whose beauty we can in some degree explain and account for, there still remains something mysterious and inexplicable, which conveys an immediate satisfaction to the spectator, but how, or why, or for what reason, he cannot pretend to determine. There is a *manner,* a grace, an ease, a genteelness, an I-know-not-what, which some men possess above others, which is very different from external beauty and comeliness, and which, however, catches our affection almost as suddenly and powerfully. And though this *manner* be chiefly talked of in the passion between the sexes, where the concealed magic is easily explained, yet surely much of it prevails in all our estimation of characters and forms no inconsiderable part of personal merit. This class of accomplishments, therefore, must be trusted entirely to the blind but sure testimony of taste and sentiment, and must be considered as a part of ethics left by nature to baffle all the pride of philosophy, and make her sensible of her narrow boundaries and slender acquisitions.

We approve of another because of his wit, politeness, modesty, decency, or any agreeable quality which he possesses, although he be not of our acquaintance, nor has ever given us any entertainment by means of these accomplishments. The idea which we form of their effect on his acquaintance has an agreeable influence on our imagination and gives us the sentiment of approbation. This principle enters into all the judgments which we form concerning manners and characters.

SECTION IX

CONCLUSION

PART I

IT may justly appear surprising that any man in so late an age should find it requisite to prove, by elaborate reasoning, [1] that *personal merit* consists altogether in the possession of mental qualities, *useful* or *agreeable* to the *person himself* or to *others.* It might be expected that this principle would have occurred even to the first, rude, unpracticed inquirers concerning

[1] [That virtue or personal merit: Editions G to N.]

the holy?

morals, and been received from its own evidence without any argument or disputation. Whatever is valuable in any kind, so naturally classes itself under the division of *useful* or *agreeable,* the *utile* or the *dulce,* that it is not easy to imagine why we should ever seek further, or consider the question as a matter of nice research or inquiry. And as everything useful or agreeable must possess these qualities with regard either to the *person himself* or to *others,* the complete delineation or description of merit seems to be performed as naturally as a shadow is cast by the sun, or an image is reflected upon water. If the ground on which the shadow is cast be not broken and uneven, nor the surface from which the image is reflected disturbed and confused, a just figure is immediately presented without any art or attention. And it seems a reasonable presumption that systems and hypotheses have perverted our natural understanding when a theory so simple and obvious could so long have escaped the most elaborate examination.

But however the case may have fared with philosophy, in common life these principles are still implicitly maintained; nor is any other topic of praise or blame ever recurred to when we employ any panegyric or satire, any applause or censure of human action and behavior. If we observe men in every intercourse of business or pleasure, in every discourse and conversation, we shall find them nowhere, except in the schools, at any loss upon this subject. What so natural, for instance, as the following dialogue? You are very happy, we shall suppose one to say, addressing himself to another, that you have given your daughter to Cleanthes. He is a man of honor and humanity. Everyone who has any intercourse with him is sure of *fair* and *kind* treatment.[2] I congratulate you, too, says another, on the promising expectations of this son-in-law, whose assiduous application to the study of the laws, whose quick penetration and early knowledge, both of men and business, prognosticate the greatest honors and advancement.[3] You surprise me, replies a third, when you talk of Cleanthes as a man of business and ap-

[2] Qualities useful to others.
[3] Qualities useful to the person himself. [Section VI.]

plication. I met him lately in a circle of the gayest company, and he was the very life and soul of our conversation: so much wit with good manners, so much gallantry without affectation, so much ingenious knowledge so genteelly delivered, I have never before observed in anyone.[4] You would admire him still more, says a fourth, if you knew him more familiarly. That cheerfulness which you might remark in him is not a sudden flash struck out by company; it runs through the whole tenor of his life, and preserves a perpetual serenity on his countenance and tranquillity in his soul. He has met with severe trials, misfortunes as well as dangers, and by his greatness of mind was still superior to all of them.[5] The image, gentlemen, which you have here delineated of Cleanthes, cried I, is that of accomplished merit. Each of you has given a stroke of the pencil to his figure; and you have unawares exceeded all the pictures drawn by Gratian or Castiglione. A philosopher might select this character as a model of perfect virtue.

And as every quality which is useful or agreeable to ourselves or others is, in common life, allowed to be a part of personal merit, so no other will ever be received where men judge of things by their natural, unprejudiced reason, without the delusive glosses of superstition and false religion. Celibacy, fasting, penance, mortification, self-denial, humility, silence, solitude, and the whole train of monkish virtues—for what reason are they everywhere rejected by men of sense but because they serve to no manner of purpose; neither advance a man's fortune in the world, nor render him a more valuable member of society; neither qualify him for the entertainment of company, nor increase his power of self-enjoyment? We observe, on the contrary, that they cross all these desirable ends, stupefy the understanding and harden the heart, obscure the fancy and sour the temper. We justly, therefore, transfer them to the opposite column and place them in the catalogue of vices; nor has any superstition force sufficient among men of the world to pervert entirely these natural sentiments. A gloomy, hair-

---

[4] Qualities immediately agreeable to others. [Section VIII.]
[5] Qualities immediately agreeable to the person himself. [Section VII.]

brained enthusiast, after his death, may have a place in the calendar, but will scarcely ever be admitted when alive into intimacy and society, except by those who are as delirious and dismal as himself.

It seems a happiness in the present theory that it enters not into that vulgar dispute concerning the *degrees* of benevolence or self-love which prevail in human nature—a dispute which is never likely to have any issue, both because men who have taken part are not easily convinced, and because the phenomena which can be produced on either side are so dispersed, so uncertain, and subject to so many interpretations that it is scarcely possible accurately to compare them or draw from them any determinate inference or conclusion. It is sufficient for our present purpose, if it be allowed, what surely, without the greatest absurdity, cannot be disputed, that there is some benevolence, however small, infused into our bosom; some spark of friendship for humankind; some particle of the dove kneaded into our frame, along with the elements of the wolf and serpent. Let these generous sentiments be supposed ever so weak, let them be insufficient to move even a hand or finger of our body, they must still direct the determinations of our mind and, where everything else is equal, produce a cool preference of what is useful and serviceable to mankind above what is pernicious and dangerous. A *moral distinction,* therefore, immediately arises; a general sentiment of blame and approbation; a tendency, however faint, to the objects of the one, and a proportionable aversion to those of the other. Nor will those reasoners who so earnestly maintain the predominant selfishness of humankind be anywise scandalized at hearing of the weak sentiments of virtue implanted in our nature. On the contrary, they are found as ready to maintain the one tenet as the other; and their spirit of satire (for such it appears, rather than of corruption) naturally gives rise to both opinions, which have, indeed, a great and almost an indissoluble connection together.

Avarice, ambition, vanity, and all passions vulgarly, though improperly, comprised under the denomination of *self-love* are here excluded from our theory concerning the origin of morals, not because they are too weak, but because they have not a proper direction for that purpose. The notion of morals implies some sentiment common to all mankind, which recommends the same object to general approbation and makes every man, or most men, agree in the same opinion or decision concerning it. It also implies some sentiment so universal and comprehensive as to extend to all mankind, and render the actions and conduct, even of the persons the most remote, an object of applause or censure, according as they agree or disagree with that rule of right which is established. These two requisite circumstances belong alone to the sentiment of humanity here insisted on. The other passions produce, in every breast, many strong sentiments of desire and aversion, affection and hatred, but these neither are felt so much in common nor are so comprehensive as to be the foundation of any general system and established theory of blame or approbation.

When a man denominates another his *enemy*, his *rival*, his *antagonist*, his *adversary*, he is understood to speak the language of self-love and to express sentiments peculiar to himself and arising from his particular circumstances and situation. But when he bestows on any man the epithets of *vicious* or *odious* or *depraved*, he then speaks another language and expresses sentiments in which he expects all his audience are to concur with him. He must here, therefore, depart from his private and particular situation and must choose a point of view common to him with others: he must move some universal principle of the human frame and touch a string to which all mankind have an accord and symphony. If he mean, therefore, to express that this man possesses qualities whose tendency is pernicious to society, he has chosen this common point of view and has touched the principle of humanity in which every man, in some degree, concurs. While the human heart is compounded of the same elements as at present, it will never be wholly indifferent to public good, nor entirely unaffected with the tendency of characters and manners. And though this affection of humanity may not generally be esteemed so strong as vanity or ambition, yet being common to all men, it can alone be the foundation of morals or of any general system of blame or praise. One man's ambition is not another's ambition, nor will the same event or object satisfy both; but the humanity of one man is the humanity of everyone; and the same object touches this passion in all human creatures.

But the sentiments which arise from humanity are not only the same in all human creatures and produce the same approbation or censure, but they also comprehend all human creatures; nor is there anyone whose conduct or character is not, by their means, an object, to everyone, of censure or approbation. On the contrary, those other passions, commonly denominated selfish, both produce different sentiments in each individual, according to his particular situation, and also contemplate the greater part of mankind with the utmost indifference and unconcern. Whoever has a high regard and esteem for me, flatters my vanity; whoever expresses contempt, mortifies and displeases me. But as my name is known but to a small part of mankind, there are few who come within the sphere of this passion, or excite, on its account, either my affection or disgust. But if you represent a tyrannical, insolent, or barbarous behavior, in any country or in any age of the world, I soon carry my eye to the pernicious tendency of such a conduct and feel the sentiment of repugnance and displeasure toward it. No character can be so remote as to be, in this light, wholly indifferent to me. What is beneficial to society or to the person himself must still be preferred. And every quality or action of every human being must by this means be ranked under some class or denomination expressive of general censure or applause.

What more, therefore, can we ask to distinguish the sentiments dependent on humanity from those connected with any other passion, or to satisfy us why the former are the origin of morals, not the latter? Whatever conduct gains my approbation, by touching my humanity, procures also the applause of all mankind by affecting the same principle in them; but what serves my avarice or ambition pleases these passions in me alone and affects not the avarice and ambition of the rest of mankind. There is no circumstance of conduct in any man, provided it have a beneficial tendency, that is not agreeable to my humanity, however remote the person; but every man, so far removed as neither to cross nor serve my avarice and ambition, is regarded as wholly indifferent by those passions. The distinction, therefore, between these species of sentiment being so great and evident, language must soon be molded upon it and must invent a peculiar set of terms in order to express those universal sentiments of censure or approbation which arise from humanity, or from views of general usefulness and its contrary. *Virtue* and *vice* become then known: morals are recognized; certain general ideas are framed of human conduct and behavior; such measures are expected from men in such situations: this action is determined to be conformable to our abstract rule; that other, contrary. And by such universal principles are the particular sentiments of self-love frequently controlled and limited.[6]

From instances of popular tumults, seditions, factions, panics, and of all passions which are shared with a multitude, we may learn the influence of society in exciting and supporting any emotion; while the most ungovernable disorders are raised, we find by that means, from the slightest and most frivolous oc-

---

[6] It seems certain, both from reason and experience, that a rude, untaught savage regulates chiefly his love and hatred by the ideas of private utility and injury, and has but faint conceptions of a general rule or system of behavior. The man who stands opposite to him in battle he hates heartily, not only for the present moment, which is almost unavoidable, but forever after; nor is he satisfied without the most extreme punishment and vengeance. But we, accustomed to society, and to more enlarged reflections, consider that this man is serving his own country and community; that any man, in the same situation, would do the same; that we ourselves, in like circumstances, observe a like conduct; that, in general, human society is best supported on such maxims. And by these suppositions and views, we correct, in some measure, our ruder and narrower passions. And though much of our friendship and enmity be still regulated by private considerations of benefit and harm, we pay at least this homage to general rules, which we are accustomed to respect, that we commonly pervert our adversary's conduct by imputing malice or injustice to him, in order to give vent to those passions which arise from self-love and private interest. When the heart is full of rage, it never wants pretenses of this nature, though sometimes as frivolous as those from which Horace, being almost crushed by the fall of a tree, affects to accuse of parricide the first planter of it.

casions. Solon was no very cruel, though perhaps an unjust, legislator, who punished neuters in civil wars; and few, I believe, would in such cases incur the penalty were their affection and discourse allowed sufficient to absolve them. No selfishness, and scarce any philosophy, have there force sufficient to support a total coolness and indifference; and he must be more or less than man, who kindles not in the common blaze. What wonder, then, that moral sentiments are found of such influence in life, though springing from principles which may appear at first sight somewhat small and delicate? But these principles, we must remark, are social and universal: they form, in a manner, the *party* of humankind against vice or disorder, its common enemy; and as the benevolent concern for others is diffused in a greater or less degree over all men, and is the same in all, it occurs more frequently in discourse, is cherished by society and conversation; and the blame and approbation consequent on it are thereby roused from that lethargy into which they are probably lulled in solitary and uncultivated nature. Other passions, though perhaps originally stronger, yet being selfish and private, are often overpowered by its force, and yield the dominion of our breast to those social and public principles.

Another spring of our constitution that brings a great addition of force to moral sentiment is the love of fame, which rules with such uncontrolled authority in all generous minds, and is often the grand object of all their designs and undertakings. By our continual and earnest pursuit of a character, a name, a reputation in the world, we bring our own deportment and conduct frequently in review and consider how they appear in the eyes of those who approach and regard us. This constant habit of surveying ourselves, as it were in reflection, keeps alive all the sentiments of right and wrong, and begets in noble natures a certain reverence for themselves as well as others, which is the surest guardian of every virtue. The animal conveniences and pleasures sink gradually in their value, while every inward beauty and moral grace is studiously acquired and the mind is accomplished in every perfection which can adorn or embellish a rational creature.

Here is the most perfect morality with which we are acquainted; here is displayed the force of many sympathies. Our moral sentiment is itself a feeling chiefly of that nature; and our regard to a character with others seems to arise only from a care of preserving a character with ourselves; and in order to attain this end, we find it necessary to prop our tottering judgment on the correspondent approbation of mankind.

But that we may accommodate matters and remove, if possible, every difficulty, let us allow all these reasonings to be false. Let us allow that, when we resolve the pleasure which arises from views of utility into the sentiments of humanity and sympathy, we have embraced a wrong hypothesis. Let us confess it necessary to find some other explication of that applause which is paid to objects, whether inanimate, animate, or rational, if they have a tendency to promote the welfare and advantage of mankind. However difficult it be to conceive that an object is approved of on account of its tendency to a certain end, while the end itself is totally indifferent, let us swallow this absurdity and consider what are the consequences. The preceding delineation or definition [7] of *personal merit* must still retain its evidence and authority: It must still be allowed that every quality of the mind which is *useful* or *agreeable* to the *person himself* or to *others* communicates a pleasure to the spectator, engages his esteem, and is admitted under the honorable denomination of virtue or merit. Are not justice, fidelity, honor, veracity, allegiance, chastity esteemed solely on account of their tendency to promote the good of society? Is not that tendency inseparable from humanity, benevolence, lenity, generosity, gratitude, moderation, tenderness, friendship, and all the other social virtues? Can it possibly be doubted that industry, discretion, frugality, secrecy, order, perseverance, forethought, judgment, and this whole class of virtues and accomplishments of which many pages would not contain the catalogue—can it be doubted, I say, that the tendency of these qualities to promote the interest and happiness of their possessor is the sole foundation of their merit? Who can dispute that a mind which supports a perpet-

[7] [of virtue: Editions G to N.]

ual serenity and cheerfulness, a noble dignity and undaunted spirit, a tender affection and good will to all around, as it has more enjoyment within itself, is also a more animating and rejoicing spectacle than if dejected with melancholy, tormented with anxiety, irritated with rage, or sunk into the most abject baseness and degeneracy? And as to the qualities immediately *agreeable to others,* they speak sufficiently for themselves; and he must be unhappy indeed, either in his own temper, or in his situation and company, who has never perceived the charms of a facetious wit or flowing affability, of a delicate modesty or decent genteelness of address and manner.

I am sensible that nothing can be more unphilosophical than to be positive or dogmatical on any subject, and that, even if *excessive* skepticism could be maintained, it would not be more destructive to all just reasoning and inquiry. I am convinced that where men are the most sure and arrogant, they are commonly the most mistaken, and have there given reins to passion without that proper deliberation and suspense which can alone secure them from the grossest absurdities. Yet I must confess that this enumeration puts the matter in so strong a light that I cannot, *at present,* be more assured of any truth which I learn from reasoning and argument, than that personal merit consists entirely in the usefulness or agreeableness of qualities to the person himself possessed of them, or to others who have any intercourse with him. But when I reflect that though the bulk and figure of the earth have been measured and delineated, though the motions of the tides have been accounted for, the order and economy of the heavenly bodies subjected to their proper laws, and *infinite* itself reduced to calculation, yet men still dispute concerning the foundation of their moral duties—when I reflect on this, I say, I fall back into diffidence and skepticism, and suspect that an hypothesis so obvious, had it been a true one, would long ere now have been received by the unanimous suffrage and consent of mankind.

PART II

HAVING explained the moral *approbation* attending merit or virtue,[1] there remains nothing but briefly to consider our interested *obligation* to it, and to inquire whether every man who has any regard to his own happiness and welfare will not best find his account in the practice of every moral duty. If this can be clearly ascertained from the foregoing theory, we shall have the satisfaction to reflect that we have advanced principles which not only, it is hoped, will stand the test of reasoning and inquiry, but may contribute to the amendment of men's lives and their improvement in morality and social virtue. And though the philosophical truth of any proposition by no means depends on its tendency to promote the interests of society, yet a man has but a bad grace who delivers a theory, however true, which he must confess leads to a practice dangerous and pernicious. Why rake into those corners of nature which spread a nuisance all around? Why dig up the pestilence from the pit in which it is buried? The ingenuity of your researches may be admired, but your systems will be detested, and mankind will agree, if they cannot refute them, to sink them at least in eternal silence and oblivion. Truths which are *pernicious* to society, if any such there be, will yield to errors which are salutary and *advantageous*.

But what philosophical truths can be more advantageous to society than those here delivered, which represent virtue in all her genuine and most engaging charms and make us approach her with ease, familiarity, and affection? The dismal dress falls off, with which many divines and some philosophers have covered her, and nothing appears but gentleness, humanity, beneficence, affability, nay, even at proper intervals, play, frolic, and gaiety. She talks not of useless austerities and rigors, suffering, and self-denial. She declares that her sole purpose is to make her votaries, and all mankind, during every instant of their ex-

---

[1] [Edition G omits the preceding clause.]

istence, if possible, cheerful and happy; nor does she ever willingly part with any pleasure but in hopes of ample compensation in some other period of their lives. The sole trouble which she demands is that of just calculation and a steady preference of the greater happiness. And if any austere pretenders approach her, enemies to joy and pleasure, she either rejects them as hypocrites and deceivers, or, if she admit them in her train, they are ranked, however, among the least favored of her votaries.

And, indeed, to drop all figurative expression, what hopes can we ever have of engaging mankind to a practice which we confess full of austerity and rigor? Or what theory of morals can ever serve any useful purpose unless it can show, by a particular detail, that all the duties which it recommends are also the true interest of each individual? The peculiar advantage of the foregoing system seems to be that it furnishes proper mediums for that purpose.

That the virtues which are immediately *useful* or *agreeable* to the person possessed of them are desirable in a view to self-interest, it would surely be superfluous to prove. Moralists, indeed, may spare themselves all the pains which they often take in recommending these duties. To what purpose collect arguments, to evince that temperance is advantageous and the excesses of pleasure hurtful? When it appears that these excesses are only denominated such because they are hurtful, and that if the unlimited use of strong liquors, for instance, no more impaired health or the faculties of mind and body, than the use of air or water, it would not be a whit more vicious or blamable.

It seems equally superfluous to prove that the *companionable* virtues of good manners and wit, decency and genteelness are more desirable than the contrary qualities. Vanity alone, without any other consideration, is a sufficient motive to make us wish for the possession of these accomplishments. No man was ever willingly deficient in this particular. All our failures here proceed from bad education, want of capacity, or a perverse and unpliable disposition. Would you have your company coveted, admired, followed rather than hated, despised, avoided? Can anyone seriously deliberate in the case? As no enjoyment is sincere without some reference to company and society, so no society can be agreeable, or even tolerable, where a man feels his presence unwelcome and discovers all around him symptoms of disgust and aversion.

But why, in the greater society or confederacy of mankind, should not the case be the same as in particular clubs and companies? Why is it more doubtful that the enlarged virtues of humanity, generosity, beneficence are desirable, with a view to happiness and self-interest, than the limited endowments of ingenuity and politeness? Are we apprehensive lest those social affections interfere in a greater and more immediate degree than any other pursuits with private utility, and cannot be gratified without some important sacrifice of honor and advantage? If so, we are but ill instructed in the nature of the human passions, and are more influenced by verbal distinctions than by real differences.

Whatever contradiction may vulgarly be supposed between the *selfish* and *social* sentiments or dispositions, they are really no more opposite than selfish and ambitious, selfish and revengeful, selfish and vain. It is requisite that there be an original propensity of some kind, in order to be a basis to self-love, by giving a relish to the objects of its pursuit; and none more fit for this purpose than benevolence or humanity. The goods of fortune are spent in one gratification or another: the miser who accumulates his annual income and lends it out at interest has really spent it in the gratification of his avarice. And it would be difficult to show why a man is more a loser by a generous action than by any other method of expense, since the utmost which he can attain by the most elaborate selfishness is the indulgence of some affection.

Now if life without passion must be altogether insipid and tiresome, let a man suppose that he has full power of modeling his own disposition, and let him deliberate what appetite or desire he would choose for the foundation of his happiness and enjoyment. Every affection, he would observe, when gratified by success, gives a satisfaction proportioned to its force and violence; but besides this advantage, common to all, the immediate feeling of benevolence and friendship, humanity and kindness is sweet, smooth, tender, and agreeable, independent of all fortune and accidents. These virtues are, besides, attended with a pleasing consciousness or remembrance and keep us in humor with ourselves as well as others, while we retain the agreeable reflection of having done our part toward mankind and society. And though all men show a jealousy of our success in the pursuits of avarice and ambition, yet are we almost sure of their good will and good wishes so long as we persevere in the paths of virtue and employ ourselves in the execution of generous plans and purposes. What other passion is there where we shall find so many advantages united: an agreeable sentiment, a pleasing consciousness, a good reputation? But of these truths, we may observe, men are of themselves pretty much convinced; nor are they deficient in their duty to society because they would not wish to be generous, friendly, and humane, but because they do not feel themselves such.

Treating vice with the greatest candor and making it all possible concessions, we must acknowledge that there is not, in any instance, the smallest pretext for giving it the preference above virtue with a view to self-interest, except, perhaps, in the case of justice, where a man, taking things in a certain light, may often seem to be a loser by his integrity. And though it is allowed that, without a regard to property, no society could subsist, yet, according to the imperfect way in which human affairs are conducted, a sensible knave, in particular incidents, may think that an act of iniquity or infidelity will make a considerable addition to his fortune without causing any considerable breach in the social union and confederacy. That *honesty is the best policy* may be a good general rule, but is liable to many exceptions. And he, it may perhaps be thought, conducts himself with most wisdom who observes the general rule and takes advantage of all the exceptions.

I must confess that if a man think that this reasoning much requires an answer, it will be a little difficult to find any which will to him appear satisfactory and convincing. If his heart rebel not against such pernicious maxims, if he feel no reluctance to the thoughts of villany or baseness, he has indeed lost a considerable motive to virtue; and we may expect that his practice will be answerable to his speculation. But in all ingenuous natures the antipathy to treachery and roguery is too strong to be counterbalanced by any views of profit or pecuniary advantage. Inward peace of mind, consciousness of integrity, a satisfactory review of our own conduct—these are circumstances very requisite to happiness and will be cherished and cultivated by every honest man who feels the importance of them.

Such a one has, besides, the frequent satisfaction of seeing knaves, with all their pretended cunning and abilities, betrayed by their own maxims; and while they purpose to cheat with moderation and secrecy, a tempting incident occurs—nature is frail—and they give in to the snare, whence they can never extricate themselves without a total loss of reputation and the forfeiture of all future trust and confidence with mankind.

But were they ever so secret and successful, the honest man, if he has any tincture of philosophy, or even common observation and reflection, will discover that they themselves are, in the end, the greatest dupes, and have sacrificed the invaluable enjoyment of a character, with themselves at least, for the acquisition of worthless toys and gewgaws. How little is requisite to supply the *necessities* of nature? And in a view to *pleasure*, what comparison between the unbought satisfaction of conversation, society, study, even health and the common beauties of nature, but above all, the peaceful reflection on one's own conduct? What comparison, I say, between these and the feverish, empty amusements of luxury and expense? These natural pleasures, indeed, are really without price, both because they are below all price in their attainment and above it in their enjoyment.

APPENDIX I

CONCERNING MORAL SENTIMENT

If the foregoing hypothesis be received, it will now be easy for us to determine the question first started,[1] concerning the general principles of morals; and though we postponed the decision of that question lest it should then involve us in intricate speculations which are unfit for moral discourses, we may resume it at present and examine how far either *reason* or *sentiment* enters into all decisions of praise or censure.

One principal foundation of moral praise being supposed to lie in the usefulness of any quality or action, it is evident that *reason* must enter for a considerable share in all decisions of this kind, since nothing but that faculty can instruct us in the tendency of qualities and actions and point out their beneficial consequences to society and to their possessor. In many cases, this is an affair liable to great controversy: doubts may arise; opposite interests may occur; and a preference must be given to one side, from very nice views and a small overbalance of utility. This is particularly remarkable in questions with regard to justice, as is, indeed, natural to suppose from that species of utility which attends this virtue.[2] Were every single instance of justice, like that of benevolence, useful to society, this would be a more simple state of the case and seldom liable to great controversy. But as single instances of justice are often pernicious in their first and immediate tendency, and as the advantage to society results only from the observance of the general rule and from the concurrence and combination of several persons in the same equitable conduct, the case here becomes more intricate and involved. The various circumstances of society, the

---

1 [Sect. I, "Of the General Principles of Morals."]
2 [See Appendix III, "Some further Considerations with regard to Justice."]

various consequences of any practice, the various interests which may be proposed—these, on many occasions, are doubtful and subject to great discussion and inquiry. The object of municipal laws is to fix all the questions with regard to justice: the debates of civilians, the reflections of politicians, the precedents of history and public records are all directed to the same purpose. And a very accurate *reason* or *judgment* is often requisite to give the true determination amidst such intricate doubts arising from obscure or opposite utilities.

But though reason, when fully assisted and improved, be sufficient to instruct us in the pernicious or useful tendency of qualities and actions, it is not alone sufficient to produce any moral blame or approbation. Utility is only a tendency to a certain end; and were the end totally indifferent to us, we should feel the same indifference toward the means. It is requisite a *sentiment* should here display itself in order to give a preference to the useful above the pernicious tendencies. This sentiment can be no other than a feeling for the happiness of mankind, and a resentment of their misery, since these are the different ends which virtue and vice have a tendency to promote. Here, therefore, *reason* instructs us in the several tendencies of actions, and *humanity* makes a distinction in favor of those which are useful and beneficial.

This partition between the faculties of understanding and sentiment, in all moral decisions, seems clear from the preceding hypothesis; but I shall suppose that hypothesis false. It will then be requisite to look out for some other theory that may be satisfactory; and I dare venture to affirm that none such will ever be found so long as we suppose reason to be the sole source of morals. To prove this, it will be proper to weigh the five following considerations:

I. It is easy for a false hypothesis to maintain some appearance of truth, while it keeps wholly in generals, makes use of undefined terms, and employs comparisons instead of instances. This is particularly remarkable in that philosophy which ascribes the discernment of all moral distinctions to reason alone, without the concurrence of sentiment. It is impossible that, in any particular instance, this hypothesis can so much as be rendered intelligible, whatever specious figure it may make in general declamations and discourses. Examine the crime of *ingratitude*, for instance, which has place wherever we observe good will, expressed and known, together with good offices performed on the one side, and a return of ill will or indifference, with ill offices or neglect, on the other; anatomize all these circumstances and examine, by your reason alone, in what consists the demerit or blame: you never will come to any issue or conclusion.

Reason judges either of *matter of fact* or of *relations*. Inquire then, first, where is that matter of fact which we here call *crime;* point it out; determine the time of its existence; describe its essence or nature; explain the sense or faculty to which it discovers itself. It resides in the mind of the person who is ungrateful. He must, therefore, feel it, and be conscious of it. But nothing is there except the passion of ill will or absolute indifference. You cannot say that these of themselves always, and in all circumstances, are crimes. No; they are only crimes when directed toward persons who have before expressed and displayed good will toward us. Consequently, we may infer that the crime of ingratitude is not any particular individual *fact,* but arises from a complication of circumstances which, being presented to the spectator, excites the *sentiment* of blame by the particular structure and fabric of his mind.

This representation, you say, is false. Crime, indeed, consists not in a particular *fact* of whose reality we are assured by *reason,* but it consists in certain *moral relations* discovered by reason, in the same manner as we discover by reason the truths of geometry or algebra. But what are the relations, I ask, of which you here talk? In the case stated above I see, first, good will and good offices in one person; then, ill will and ill offices in the other. Between these there is the relation of *contrariety*. Does the crime consist in that relation? But suppose a person bore me ill will or did me ill offices, and I, in return, were indifferent toward him, or did him good offices—here is the same relation of *contrariety;* and yet my conduct is often highly laudable. Twist and turn this matter as much as you will, you can never rest the morality on relation, but must have recourse to the decisions of sentiment.

When it is affirmed that two and three are equal to the half of ten, this relation of equality I understand perfectly. I conceive that if ten be divided into two parts, of which one has as many units as the other, and if any of these parts be compared to two added to three, it will contain as many units as that compound number. But when you draw thence a comparison to moral relations, I own that I am altogether at a loss to understand you. A moral action, a crime, such as ingratitude, is a complicated object. Does the morality consist in the relation of its parts to each other? How? After what manner? Specify the relation: be more particular and explicit in your propositions, and you will easily see their falsehood.

No, say you, the morality consists in the relation of actions to the rule of right; and they are denominated good or ill, according as they agree or disagree with it. What then is this rule of right? In what does it consist? How is it determined? By reason, you say, which examines the moral relations of actions. So that moral relations are determined by the comparison of actions to a rule. And that rule is determined by considering the moral relations of objects. Is not this fine reasoning?

All this is metaphysics, you cry. That is enough; there needs nothing more to give a strong presumption of falsehood. Yes, replied I, here are metaphysics, surely; but they are all on your side, who advance an abstruse hypothesis which can never be made intelligible, nor quadrate with any particular instance or illustration. The hypothesis which we embrace is plain. It maintains that morality is determined by sentiment. It defines virtue to be *whatever mental action or quality gives to a spectator the pleasing sentiment of approbation;* and vice the contrary. We then proceed to examine a plain matter of fact—to wit, what actions have this influence: we consider all the circumstances in which these actions agree; and thence endeavor to extract some general observations with regard to these sentiments. If you call this metaphysics and find anything abstruse here, you need only conclude that your turn of mind is not suited to the moral sciences.

II. When a man at any time deliberates concerning his own conduct (as, whether he had better, in a particular emergency, assist a brother or a benefactor), he must consider these separate relations, with all the circumstances and situations of the persons, in order to determine the superior duty and obligation. And in order to determine the proportion of lines in any triangle, it is necessary to examine the nature of that figure, and the relations which its several parts bear to each other. But notwithstanding this appearing similarity in the two cases, there is at bottom an extreme difference between them. A speculative reasoner concerning triangles or circles considers the several known and given relations of the parts of these figures, and thence infers some unknown relation which is dependent on the former. But in moral deliberations we must be acquainted, beforehand, with all the objects and all their relations to each other; and from a comparison of the whole fix our choice or approbation. No new fact to be ascertained, no new relation to be discovered. All the circumstances of the case are supposed to be laid before us ere we can fix any sentence of blame or approbation. If any material circumstance be yet unknown or doubtful, we must first employ our inquiry or intellectual faculties to assure us of it, and must suspend for a time all moral decision or sentiment. While we are ignorant whether a man were aggressor or not, how can we determine whether the person who killed him be criminal or innocent? But after every circumstance, every relation is known, the understanding has no further room to operate, nor any object on which it could employ itself. The approbation or blame which then ensues cannot be the work of the judgment but of the heart; and it is not a speculative proposition or affirmation, but an active feeling or sentiment. In the disquisitions of the understanding, from known circumstances and relations we infer some new and unknown. In moral decisions, all the circumstances and relations must be previously known; and the mind, from the contemplation of the whole, feels some new impression of affection or disgust, esteem or contempt, approbation or blame.

Hence the great difference between a mistake of *fact* and one of *right;* and hence the reason why the one is commonly criminal and not the other. When Oedipus killed Laius, he was ignorant of the relation, and from circumstances, innocent and involuntary, formed erroneous opinions concerning the action which he committed. But when Nero killed Agrippina,[3] all the relations between himself and the person, and all the circumstances of the fact, were previously known to him; but the motive of revenge or fear or interest prevailed in his savage heart over the sentiments of duty and humanity. And when we express that detestation against him to which he himself in a little time became insensible, it is not that we see any relations of which he was ignorant, but that, from the rectitude of our disposition, we feel sentiments against which he was hardened, from flattery and a long perseverance in the most enormous crimes. In these sentiments then, not in a discovery of relations of any kind, do all moral determinations consist. Before we can pretend to form any decision of this kind, everything must be known and ascertained on the side of the object or action. Nothing remains but to feel, on our part, some sentiment of blame or approbation, whence we pronounce the action criminal or virtuous.

III. This doctrine will become still more evident if we compare moral beauty with natural, to which in many particulars it bears so near a resemblance. It is on the proportion, relation, and position of parts that all natural beauty depends, but it would be absurd thence to infer that the perception of beauty, like that of truth in geometrical problems, consists wholly in the perception of relations and was performed entirely by the understanding or intellectual faculties. In all the sciences our mind, from the known relations, investigates the unknown; but in all decisions of taste or external beauty, all the relations are

---

[3] [According to the Greek legend, Oedipus killed his father, Laius, whom he had not seen since early childhood, whereas Nero hired a freedman to kill his mother, Agrippina.]

beforehand obvious to the eye; and we thence proceed to feel a sentiment of complacency or disgust, according to the nature of the object and disposition of our organs.

Euclid has fully explained all the qualities of the circle, but has not, in any proposition, said a word of its beauty. The reason is evident. The beauty is not a quality of the circle. It lies not in any part of the line whose parts are equally distant from a common center. It is only the effect which that figure produces upon the mind, whose peculiar fabric or structure renders it susceptible of such sentiments. In vain would you look for it in the circle or seek it, either by your senses or by mathematical reasonings, in all the properties of that figure.

Attend to Palladio and Perrault while they explain all the parts and proportions of a pillar: they talk of the cornice and frieze, and base and entablature, and shaft and architrave; and give the description and position of each of these members. But should you ask the description and position of its beauty, they would readily reply that the beauty is not in any of the parts or members of a pillar but results from the whole when that complicated figure is presented to an intelligent mind susceptible to those finer sensations. Till such a spectator appear, there is nothing but a figure of such particular dimensions and proportions—from his sentiments alone arise its elegance and beauty.

Again, attend to Cicero while he paints the crimes of a Verres or a Catiline; you must acknowledge that the moral turpitude results, in the same manner, from the contemplation of the whole when presented to a being whose organs have such a particular structure and formation. The orator may paint rage, insolence, barbarity, on the one side; meekness, suffering, sorrow, innocence, on the other. But if you feel no indignation or compassion arise in you from this complication of circumstances, you would in vain ask him in what consists the crime or villainy which he so vehemently exclaims against; at what time or on what subject it first began to exist; and what has a few months afterwards become of it, when every disposition and thought of all the actors is totally altered or annihilated. No satisfactory answer can be given to any of these questions upon the abstract hypothesis of morals; and we must at last acknowledge that the crime or immorality is no particular fact or relation which can be the object of the understanding, but arises entirely from the sentiment of disapprobation which, by the structure of human nature, we unavoidably feel on the apprehension of barbarity or treachery.

IV. Inanimate objects may bear to each other all the same relations which we observe in moral agents, though the former can never be the object of love or hatred, nor are consequently susceptible of merit or iniquity. A young tree which overtops and destroys its parent [4] stands in all the same relations with Nero when he murdered Agrippina, and if morality consisted merely in relations would, no doubt, be equally criminal.

V. It appears evident that the ultimate ends of human actions can never, in any case, be accounted for by *reason*, but recommend themselves entirely to the sentiments and affections of mankind without any dependence on the intellectual faculties. Ask a man *why he uses exercise;* he will answer, *because he desires to keep his health.* If you then inquire *why he desires health,* he will readily reply, *because sickness is painful.* If you push your inquiries further and desire a reason *why he hates pain,* it is impossible he can ever give any. This is an ultimate end, and is never referred to any other object.

Perhaps to your second question, *why he desires health,* he may also reply that *it is necessary for the exercise of his calling.* If you ask *why he is anxious on that head,* he will answer, *because he desires to get money.* If you demand, *Why? It is the instrument of pleasure,* says he. And beyond this, it is an absurdity to ask for a reason. It is impossible there can be a progress *in infinitum,* and that one thing can always be a reason why another is desired. Something must be desirable on its own account, and because of its immediate accord or agreement with human sentiment and affection.

Now, as virtue is an end and is desirable on its own account, without fee or reward, merely for the immediate satisfaction which it conveys, it is requisite that there should be some senti-

---

4 [from whose seed it sprung: Editions G and K.]

ment which it touches—some internal taste or feeling, or whatever you please to call it, which distinguishes moral good and evil, and which embraces the one and rejects the other.

Thus the distinct boundaries and offices of *reason* and of *taste* are easily ascertained. The former conveys the knowledge of truth and falsehood; the latter gives the sentiment of beauty and deformity, vice and virtue. The one discovers objects as they really stand in nature, without addition or diminution; the other has a productive faculty; and gilding or staining all natural objects with the colors borrowed from internal sentiment raises, in a manner, a new creation. Reason, being cool and disengaged, is no motive to action, and directs only the impulse received from appetite or inclination by showing us the means of attaining happiness or avoiding misery. Taste, as it gives pleasure or pain, and thereby constitutes happiness or misery, becomes a motive to action and is the first spring or impulse to desire and volition. From circumstances and relations, known or supposed, the former leads us to the discovery of the concealed and unknown. After all circumstances and relations are laid before us, the latter makes us feel from the whole a new sentiment of blame or approbation. The standard of the one, being founded on the nature of things, is eternal and inflexible, even by the will of the Supreme Being; the standard of the other, arising from the internal frame and constitution of animals, is ultimately derived from that Supreme Will which bestowed on each being its peculiar nature and arranged the several classes and orders of existence.

APPENDIX II

OF SELF-LOVE [1]

THERE is a principle, supposed to prevail among many, which is utterly incompatible with all virtue or moral sentiment; and as it can proceed from nothing but the most depraved disposition, so in its turn it tends still further to encourage that depravity. This principle is that all *benevolence* is mere hypocrisy, friendship a cheat, public spirit a farce, fidelity a snare to procure trust and confidence; and that, while all of us, at bottom, pursue only our private interest, we wear these fair disguises in order to put others off their guard and expose them the more to our wiles and machinations. What heart one must be possessed of who professes such principles, and who feels no internal sentiment that belies so pernicious a theory, it is easy to imagine; and also, what degree of affection and benevolence he can bear to a species whom he represents under such odious colors and supposes so little susceptible of gratitude or any return of affection. Or, if we should not ascribe these principles wholly to a corrupted heart, we must at least account for them from the most careless and precipitate examination. Superficial reasoners, indeed, observing many false pretenses among mankind, and feeling, perhaps, no very strong restraint in their own disposition, might draw a general and a hasty conclusion that all is equally corrupted, and that men, different from all other animals, and indeed from all other species of existence, admit of no degrees of good or bad, but are, in every instance, the same creatures under different disguises and appearances.

There is another principle, somewhat resembling the former, which has been much insisted on by philosophers, and has been the foundation of many a system—that, whatever affection one may feel, or imagine he feels for others, no passion is, or can be,

---

[1] [In editions G to Q this appeared as Part I of Section II, "Of Benevolence."]

disinterested; that the most generous friendship, however sincere, is a modification of self-love; and that, even unknown to ourselves, we seek only our own gratification while we appear the most deeply engaged in schemes for the liberty and happiness of mankind. By a turn of imagination, by a refinement of reflection, by an enthusiasm of passion, we seem to take part in the interests of others and imagine ourselves divested of all selfish considerations. But, at bottom, the most generous patriot, and most niggardly miser, the bravest hero, and most abject coward have, in every action, an equal regard to their own happiness and welfare.

Whoever concludes from the seeming tendency of this opinion that those who make profession of it cannot possibly feel the true sentiments of benevolence, or have any regard for genuine virtue, will often find himself, in practice, very much mistaken. Probity and honor were no strangers to Epicurus and his sect. Atticus and Horace seem to have enjoyed from nature, and cultivated by reflection, as generous and friendly dispositions as any disciple of the austerer schools; and among the modern, Hobbes and Locke, who maintained the selfish system of morals, lived irreproachable lives, though the former lay not under any restraint of religion which might supply the defects of his philosophy. An Epicurean or a Hobbist readily allows that there is such a thing as friendship in the world without hypocrisy or disguise, though he may attempt, by a philosophical chemistry, to resolve the elements of this passion, if I may so speak, into those of another and explain every affection to be self-love twisted and molded by a particular turn of imagination into a variety of appearances. But as the same turn of imagination prevails not in every man, nor gives the same direction to the original passion, this is sufficient, even according to the selfish system, to make the widest difference in human characters and denominate one man virtuous and humane, another vicious and meanly interested. I esteem the man whose self-love, by whatever means, is so directed as to give him a concern for others and render him serviceable to society, as I hate or despise him who has no regard to anything beyond his own gratifications and enjoyments. In vain would you suggest that these characters, though seemingly opposite, are at bottom the same, and that a very inconsiderable turn of thought forms the whole difference between them. Each character, notwithstanding these inconsiderable differences, appears to me, in practice, pretty durable and untransmutable; and I find not in this more than in other subjects that the natural sentiments, arising from the general appearances of things, are easily destroyed by subtle reflections concerning the minute origin of these appearances. Does not the lively, cheerful color of a countenance inspire me with complacency and pleasure, even though I learn from philosophy that all difference of complexion arises from the most minute differences of thickness in the most minute parts of the skin, by means of which a superficies is qualified to reflect one of the original colors of light, and absorb the others?

But though the question concerning the universal or partial selfishness of man be not so material, as is usually imagined, to morality and practice, it is certainly of consequence in the speculative science of human nature, and is a proper object of curiosity and inquiry. It may not, therefore, be unsuitable, in this place, to bestow a few reflections upon it.[2]

The most obvious objection to the selfish hypothesis is that as it is contrary to common feeling and our most unprejudiced notions, there is required the highest stretch of philosophy to establish so extraordinary a paradox. To the most careless observer there appear to be such dispositions as benevolence and

[2] Benevolence naturally divides into two kinds, the *general* and the *particular*. The first is where we have no friendship, or connection, or esteem for the person, but feel only a general sympathy with him, or a compassion for his pains, and a congratulation with his pleasures. The other species of benevolence is founded on an opinion of virtue, on services done us, or on some particular connections. Both these sentiments must be allowed real in human nature; but whether they will resolve into some nice considerations of self-love is a question more curious than important. The former sentiment, to wit, that of general benevolence, or humanity, or sympathy, we shall have occasion frequently to treat of in the course of this inquiry; and I assume it as real from general experience, without any other proof.

generosity, such affections as love, friendship, compassion, gratitude. These sentiments have their causes, effects, objects, and operations marked by common language and observation, and plainly distinguished from those of the selfish passions. And as this is the obvious appearance of things, it must be admitted till some hypothesis be discovered which, by penetrating deeper into human nature, may prove the former affections to be nothing but modifications of the latter. All attempts of this kind have hitherto proved fruitless, and seem to have proceeded entirely from that love of *simplicity* which has been the source of much false reasoning in philosophy. I shall not here enter into any detail on the present subject. Many able philosophers have shown the insufficiency of these systems; and I shall take for granted what, I believe, the smallest reflection will make evident to every impartial inquirer.

But the nature of the subject furnishes the strongest presumption that no better system will ever, for the future, be invented in order to account for the origin of the benevolent from the selfish affections, and reduce all the various emotions of the human mind to a perfect simplicity. The case is not the same in this species of philosophy as in physics. Many a hypothesis in nature, contrary to first appearances, has been found on more accurate scrutiny solid and satisfactory. Instances of this kind are so frequent that a judicious as well as witty philosopher [3] has ventured to affirm, if there be more than one way in which any phenomenon may be produced, that there is a general presumption for its arising from the causes which are the least obvious and familiar. But the presumption always lies on the other side in all inquiries concerning the origin of our passions and of the internal operations of the human mind. The simplest and most obvious cause which can there be assigned for any phenomenon is probably the true one. When a philosopher, in the explication of his system, is obliged to have recourse to some very intricate and refined reflections, and to suppose them essential to the production of any passion or emotion, we have reason to be extremely on our guard against so fallacious a

[3] Mons. Fontenelle.

hypothesis. The affections are not susceptible of any impression from the refinements of reason or imagination; and it is always found that a vigorous exertion of the latter faculties, necessarily from the narrow capacity of the human mind, destroys all activity in the former. Our predominant motive or intention is, indeed, frequently concealed from ourselves when it is mingled and confounded with other motives which the mind, from vanity or self-conceit, is desirous of supposing more prevalent. But there is no instance that a concealment of this nature has ever arisen from the abstruseness and intricacy of the motive. A man that has lost a friend and patron may flatter himself that all his grief arises from generous sentiments, without any mixture of narrow or interested considerations; but a man that grieves for a valuable friend who needed his patronage and protection—how can we suppose that his passionate tenderness arises from some metaphysical regards to a self-interest which has no foundation or reality? We may as well imagine that minute wheels and springs, like those of a watch, give motion to a loaded wagon, as account for the origin of passion from such abstruse reflections.

Animals are found susceptible of kindness, both to their own species and to ours; nor is there, in this case, the least suspicion of disguise or artifice. Shall we account for all *their* sentiments, too, from refined deductions of self-interest? Or if we admit a disinterested benevolence in the inferior species, by what rule of analogy can we refuse it in the superior?

Love between the sexes begets a complacency and good will very distinct from the gratification of an appetite. Tenderness to their offspring, in all sensible beings, is commonly able alone to counterbalance the strongest motives of self-love, and has no manner of dependence on that affection. What interest can a fond mother have in view who loses her health by assiduous attendance on her sick child, and afterwards languishes and dies of grief when freed, by its death, from the slavery of that attendance?

Is gratitude no affection of the human breast, or is that a word merely without any meaning or reality? Have we no satisfaction in one man's company above another's, and no desire of the welfare of our friend, even though absence or death should prevent us from all participation in it? Or what is it commonly that gives us any participation in it, even while alive and present, but our affection and regard to him?

These and a thousand other instances are marks of a general benevolence in human nature, where no *real* interest binds us to the object. And how an *imaginary* interest, known and avowed for such, can be the origin of any passion or emotion seems difficult to explain. No satisfactory hypothesis of this kind has yet been discovered, nor is there the smallest probability that the future industry of men will ever be attended with more favorable success.

But further, if we consider rightly of the matter, we shall find that the hypothesis which allows of a disinterested benevolence, distinct from self-love, has really more *simplicity* in it and is more conformable to the analogy of nature than that which pretends to resolve all friendship and humanity into this latter principle. There are bodily wants or appetites acknowledged by everyone, which necessarily precede all sensual enjoyment and carry us directly to seek possession of the object. Thus hunger and thirst have eating and drinking for their end; and from the gratification of these primary appetites arises a pleasure which may become the object of another species of desire or inclination that is secondary and interested. In the same manner, there are mental passions by which we are impelled immediately to seek particular objects, such as fame, or power, or vengeance, without any regard to interest; and when these objects are attained, a pleasing enjoyment ensues as the consequence of our indulged affections. Nature must, by the internal frame and constitution of the mind, give an original propensity to fame ere we can reap any pleasure from that acquisition or pursue it from motives of self-love and a desire of happiness. If I have no vanity, I take no delight in praise; if I be void of ambition, power gives me no enjoyment; if I be not angry, the punishment of an adversary is totally indifferent to me. In all these cases there is a passion which points immediately to the object and constitutes it our good or happiness, as there are other secondary passions which afterwards arise and pursue it as a part of our happiness when once it is constituted such by our original affections. Were there no appetite of any kind antecedent to self-love, that propensity could scarcely ever exert itself, because we should, in that case, have felt few and slender pains or pleasures, and have little misery or happiness to avoid or to pursue.

Now, where is the difficulty in conceiving that this may likewise be the case with benevolence and friendship, and that, from the original frame of our temper, we may feel a desire of another's happiness or good, which, by means of that affection, becomes our own good and is afterwards pursued from the combined motives of benevolence and self-enjoyment? Who sees not that vengeance, from the force alone of passion, may be so eagerly pursued as to make us knowingly neglect every consideration of ease, interest, or safety, and, like some vindictive animals, infuse our very souls into the wounds we give an enemy? [4] And what a malignant philosophy must it be that will not allow to humanity and friendship the same privileges which are indisputably granted to the darker passions of enmity and resentment? Such a philosophy is more like a satire than a true delineation or description of human nature, and may be a good foundation for paradoxical wit and raillery, but is a very bad one for any serious argument or reasoning.

---

[4] *Animasque in vulnere ponunt.** Virg. *Geor.* 4, 238.
Dum alteri noceat, sui negligens,† says Seneca of anger. *De ira.* i. 1.

  * ["And in the wound they put their souls!" Virgil, *Georgics* 4, 238.]
  † ["It disregards itself while it inflicts harm upon another!" Seneca, *On Anger.* i. 1.]

APPENDIX III [1]

SOME FURTHER CONSIDERATIONS WITH REGARD TO JUSTICE

THE intention of this Appendix is to give some more particular explication of the origin and nature of Justice, and to mark some differences between it and the other virtues.

The social virtues of humanity and benevolence exert their influence immediately by a direct tendency or instinct, which chiefly keeps in view the simple object, moving the affections, and comprehends not any scheme or system, nor the consequences resulting from the concurrence, imitation, or example of others. A parent flies to the relief of his child, transported by that natural sympathy which actuates him and which affords no leisure to reflect on the sentiments or conduct of the rest of mankind in like circumstances. A generous man cheerfully embraces an opportunity of serving his friend, because he then feels himself under the dominion of the beneficent affections; nor is he concerned whether any other person in the universe were ever before actuated by such noble motives or will ever afterwards prove their influence. In all these cases the social passions have in view a single individual object and pursue the safety or happiness alone of the person loved and esteemed. With this they are satisfied; in this they acquiesce. And as the good resulting from their benign influence is in itself complete and entire, it also excites the moral sentiment of approbation without any reflection on further consequences, and without any more enlarged views of the concurrence or imitation of the other members of society. On the contrary, were the generous friend or disinterested patriot to stand alone in the practice of beneficence, this would rather enhance his value in our eyes and join the praise of rarity and novelty to his other, more exalted merits.

[1] [Appendix II in Editions G to Q.]

The case is not the same with the social virtues of justice and fidelity. They are highly useful or, indeed, absolutely necessary to the well-being of mankind. But the benefit resulting from them is not the consequence of every individual single act, but arises from the whole scheme or system concurred in by the whole or the greater part of the society. General peace and order are the attendants of justice, or a general abstinence from the possessions of others; but a particular regard to the particular right of one individual citizen may frequently, considered in itself, be productive of pernicious consequences. The result of the individual acts is here, in many instances, directly opposite to that of the whole system of actions; and the former may be extremely hurtful, while the latter is, to the highest degree, advantageous. Riches inherited from a parent are in a bad man's hand the instrument of mischief. The right of succession may, in one instance, be hurtful. Its benefit arises only from the observance of the general rule; and it is sufficient if compensation be thereby made for all the ills and inconveniences which flow from particular characters and situations.

Cyrus, young and inexperienced, considered only the individual case before him and reflected on a limited fitness and convenience when he assigned the long coat to the tall boy, and the short coat to the other of smaller size. His governor instructed him better, while he pointed out more enlarged views and consequences, and informed his pupil of the general, inflexible rules necessary to support general peace and order in society.

The happiness and prosperity of mankind arising from the social virtue of benevolence and its subdivisions may be compared to a wall built by many hands— which still rises by each stone that is heaped upon it and receives increase proportional to the diligence and care of each workman. The same happiness, raised by the social virtue of justice and its subdivisions, may be compared to the building of a vault where each individual stone would, of itself, fall to the ground; nor is the whole fabric supported but by the mutual assistance and combination of its corresponding parts.

All the laws of nature which regulate property as well as all civil laws are general and regard alone some essential circumstances of the case, without taking into consideration the characters, situations, and connections of the person concerned or any particular consequences which may result from the determination of these laws in any particular case which offers. They deprive, without scruple, a beneficent man of all his possessions if acquired by mistake, without a good title, in order to bestow them on a selfish miser who has already heaped up immense stores of superfluous riches. Public utility requires that property should be regulated by general inflexible rules; and though such rules are adopted as best serve the same end of public utility, it is impossible for them to prevent all particular hardships or make beneficial consequences result from every individual case. It is sufficient if the whole plan or scheme be necessary to the support of civil society and if the balance of good, in the main, do thereby preponderate much above that of evil. Even the general laws of the universe, though planned by Infinite Wisdom, cannot exclude all evil or inconvenience in every particular operation.

It has been asserted by some that justice arises from *human conventions* and proceeds from the voluntary choice, consent, or combination of mankind. If by *convention* be here meant a *promise* (which is the most usual sense of the word), nothing can be more absurd than this position. The observance of promises is itself one of the most considerable parts of justice; and we are not surely bound to keep our word because we have given our word to keep it. But if by convention be meant a sense of common interest, which sense each man feels in his own breast, which he remarks in his fellows, and which carries him, in concurrence with others, into a general plan or system of actions which tends to public utility, it must be owned that in this sense justice arises from human conventions. For if it be allowed (what is indeed evident) that the particular consequences of a particular act of justice may be hurtful to the public as well as to individuals, it follows that every man, in embracing that virtue, must have an eye to the whole plan or system and must expect the concurrence of his fellows in the same conduct and behavior. Did all his views terminate in the consequences of each act of his own, his benevolence and humanity, as well as his self-love, might often prescribe to him measures of conduct very different from those which are agreeable to the strict rules of right and justice.

Thus two men pull the oars of a boat by common convention, for common interest, without any promise or contract; thus gold and silver are made the measures of exchange; thus speech, and words, and language are fixed by human convention and agreement. Whatever is advantageous to two or more persons if all perform their part, but what loses all advantage if only one perform, can arise from no other principle. There would otherwise be no motive for any one of them to enter into that scheme of conduct.[2]

[2] This theory concerning the origin of property and consequently of justice is in the main the same with that hinted at and adopted by Grotius. "Hinc discimus, quae fuerit causa, ob quam a primaeva communione rerum primo mobilium, deinde et immobilium discessum est: nimirum quod cum non contenti homines vesci sponte natis, antra habitare, corpore aut nudo agere, aut corticibus arborum ferarumve pellibus vestito, vitae genus exquisitus, delegissent, industria opus fuit, quàm singuli rebus singulis adhiberent: quo minus autem fructus in commune conferrentur, primum obstitit locorum, in quae homines discesserunt, distantia, deinde justitiae et amoris defectus, per quem fiebat, ut nec in labore, nec in consumptione fructuum quae debebat, aequalitas servaretur. Simul discimus, quomodo res in proprietatem iverint; non animi actu solo, neque enim scire alii poterant, quid alii suum esse vellent, ut eo abstinerent, et idem velle plures poterant; sed pacto quodam aut expresso, ut per divisionem, aut tacito, ut per occupationem." *De jure belli et pacis*, lib. ii. cap. 2 § 2. art. 4–5.*

* ["From this we learn the reason why primitive common ownership, first of movable, and then also of immovable, property was abandoned: no wonder, for when men were no longer content to eat food in its natural state, to live in caves, to go about nude or clad in the bark of trees or in the skins of wild animals, and when they had chosen a more refined way of life, industry was required which each individual had to apply to a different pursuit. The first obstacle to garnering a common stock of produce was the distance between the places to which men had scattered, and secondly, a decline of justice and love, as a result of which equality was preserved neither in work nor in the necessary consumption of the produce. At the same time we learn how property developed into private property: it was not through a single act of the mind, for people could not possibly know what others wanted as their own and consequently

The word *natural* is commonly taken in so many senses, and is of so loose a signification, that it seems vain to dispute whether justice be natural or not. If self-love, if benevolence be natural to man, if reason and forethought be also natural, then may the same epithet be applied to justice, order, fidelity, property, society. Men's inclination, their necessities, lead them to combine, their understanding and experience tell them that this combination is impossible where each governs himself by no rule and pays no regard to the possessions of others. And from these passions and reflections conjoined, as soon as we observe like passions and reflections in others, the sentiment of justice, throughout all ages, has infallibly and certainly had place, to some degree or other, in every individual of the human species. In so sagacious an animal, what necessarily arises from the exertion of his intellectual faculties may justly be esteemed natural.[3]

Among all civilized nations it has been the constant endeavor to remove everything arbitrary and partial from the decision of property and to fix the sentence of judges by such general views and considerations as may be equal to every member of the society. For besides that nothing could be more dangerous than to accustom the bench, even in the smallest instance, to regard private friendship or enmity, it is certain that men, where they imagine that there was no other reason for the preference of their adversary but personal favor, are apt to entertain the strongest ill-will against the magistrates and

---

keep away from it, and it was possible that several people wanted the same thing; it was rather by some kind of agreement either explicit, as by a division, or tacit, as by seizure." *On the Law of War and Peace.* ii. 2, 2, 4 and 5.]

3 Natural may be opposed either to what is *unusual, miraculous,* or *artificial.* In the two former senses, justice and property are undoubtedly natural. But as they suppose reason, forethought, design, and a social union and confederacy among men, perhaps that epithet cannot strictly, in the last sense, be applied to them. Had men lived without society, property had never been known, and neither justice nor injustice had ever existed. But society among human creatures had been impossible without reason and forethought. Inferior animals that unite are guided by instinct, which supplies the place of reason. But all these disputes are merely verbal.

judges. When natural reason, therefore, points out no fixed view of public utility by which a controversy of property can be decided, positive laws are often framed to supply its place and direct the procedure of all courts of judicature. Where these two fail, as often happens, precedents are called for; and a former decision, though given itself without any sufficient reason, justly becomes a sufficient reason for a new decision. If direct laws and precedents be wanting, imperfect and indirect ones are brought in aid, and the controverted case is ranged under them by analogical reasonings, and comparisons, and similitudes, and correspondences which are often more fanciful than real. In general, it may safely be affirmed that jurisprudence is, in this respect, different from all the sciences, and that in many of its nicer questions there cannot properly be said to be truth or falsehood on either side. If one pleader bring the case under any former law or precedent by a refined analogy or comparison, the opposite pleader is not at a loss to find an opposite analogy or comparison; and the preference given by the judge is often founded more on taste and imagination than on any solid argument. Public utility is the general object of all courts of judicature; and this utility, too, requires a stable rule in all controversies; but where several rules, nearly equal and indifferent, present themselves, it is a very slight turn of thought which fixes the decision in favor of either party.[4]

4 That there be a separation or distinction of possessions, and that this separation be steady and constant, this is absolutely required by the interests of society, and hence the origin of justice and property. What possessions are assigned to particular persons, this is, generally speaking, pretty indifferent, and is often determined by very frivolous views and considerations. We shall mention a few particulars.

Were a society formed among several independent members, the most obvious rule which could be agreed on would be to annex property to *present* possession, and leave everyone a right to what he at present enjoys. The relation of possession, which takes place between the person and the object, naturally draws on the relation of property.

For a like reason, occupation or first possession becomes the foundation of property.

Where a man bestows labor and industry upon any object which before belonged to nobody, as in cutting down and shaping a tree, in cultivating

⁵ We may just observe, before we conclude this subject, that, after the laws of justice are fixed by views of general utility, the injury, the hardship, the harm which result to any individual from a violation of them enter very much into consideration

---

a field, etc., the alteration which he produces causes a relation between him and the object, and naturally engages us to annex it to him by the new relation of property. This cause here concurs with the public utility, which consists in the encouragement given to industry and labor.

Perhaps, too, private humanity toward the possessor concurs, in this instance, with the other motives, and engages us to leave with him what he has acquired by his sweat and labor, and what he has flattered himself in the constant enjoyment of. For though private humanity can by no means be the origin of justice, since the latter virtue so often contradicts the former, yet when the rule of separate and constant possession is once formed by the indispensable necessities of society, private humanity, and an aversion to the doing a hardship to another may, in a particular instance, give rise to a particular rule of property.

I am much inclined to think that the right of succession or inheritance much depends on those connections of the imagination, and that the relation to a former proprietor begetting a relation to the object is the cause why the property is transferred to a man after the death of his kinsman. It is true, industry is more encouraged by the transference of possession to children or near relations; but this consideration will only have place in a cultivated society, whereas the right of succession is regarded even among the greatest barbarians.

Acquisition of property, by *accession,* can be explained noway but by having recourse to the relations and connections of the imagination.

The property of rivers, by the laws of most nations, and by the natural turn of our thought, is attributed to the proprietors of their banks, excepting such vast rivers as the Rhine or the Danube, which seem too large to follow as an accession to the property of the neighboring fields. Yet even these rivers are considered as the property of that nation through whose dominions they run, the idea of a nation being of a suitable bulk to correspond with them and bear them such a relation in the fancy.

The accessions which are made to land bordering upon rivers follow the land, say the Civilians, provided it be made by what they call *alluvion,* that is, insensibly and imperceptibly; which are circumstances that assist the imagination in the conjunction.

Where there is any considerable portion torn at once from one bank and added to another, it becomes not *his* property whose land it falls on till it unite with the land, and till the trees and plants have spread their roots into both. Before that, the thought does not sufficiently join them.

In short, we must ever distinguish between the necessity of a separation

and are a great source of that universal blame which attends every wrong or iniquity. By the laws of society, this coat, this horse is mine and *ought* to remain perpetually in my possession; I reckon on the secure enjoyment of it; by depriving me of it, you disappoint my expectations and doubly displease me and offend every bystander. It is a public wrong so far as the rules of equity are violated; it is a private harm so far as an individual is injured. And though the second consideration could have no place were not the former previously established—for otherwise the distinction of *mine* and *thine* would be unknown in society—yet there is no question but the regard to general good is much enforced by the respect to particular. What injures the community without hurting any individual is often more lightly thought of; but where the greatest public wrong is also conjoined with a considerable private one, no wonder the highest disapprobation attends so iniquitous a behavior.

APPENDIX IV [1]

OF SOME VERBAL DISPUTES

NOTHING is more usual than for philosophers to encroach upon the province of grammarians and to engage in disputes of words, while they imagine that they are handling contro-

and constancy in men's possession, and the rules which assign particular objects to particular persons. The first necessity is obvious, strong, and invincible; the latter may depend on a public utility more light and frivolous, on the sentiment of private humanity and aversion to private hardship, on positive laws, on precedents, analogies, and very fine connections and turns of the imagination. [This note was added in Edition K.]

[5] [Some copies of Edition G do not contain this paragraph. In others, the page having been torn out, a new page was inserted containing the paragraph.]

[1] [This appears as Part I of Section VI, "Of Qualities useful to Ourselves," in Editions G to N.]

versies of the deepest importance and concern. [2][It was in order to avoid altercations, so frivolous and endless, that I endeavored to state with the utmost caution the object of our present inquiry and proposed simply to collect, on the one hand, a list of those mental qualities which are the object of love or esteem and form a part of personal merit, and, on the other hand, a catalogue of those qualities which are the object of censure or reproach, and which detract from the character of the person possessed of them, subjoining some reflections concerning the origin of these sentiments of praise or blame. On all occasions where there might arise the least hesitation, I avoided the terms *virtue* and *vice;* because some of those qualities which I classed among the objects of praise receive in the English language the appellation of *talents* rather than of virtues, as some of the blamable or censurable qualities are often called *defects* rather than vices. It may now perhaps be expected that, before we conclude this moral inquiry, we should exactly separate the one from the other, should mark the precise boundaries of virtues and talents, vices and defects, and should explain the reason and origin of that distinction. But in order to excuse myself from this undertaking, which would at last prove only a grammatical inquiry, I shall subjoin the four following reflections

2 [The bracketed passage: "It was in order . . . estimation of them" (p. 130) was omitted in editions G to M, which contained the following paragraph instead:

"Thus, were we here to assert or to deny *that all laudable qualities of the mind were to be considered as virtues or moral attributes,* many would imagine that we had entered upon one of the profoundest speculations of ethics; though it is probable, all the while, that the greatest part of the dispute would be found entirely verbal. To avoid, therefore, all frivolous subtleties and altercations, as much as possible, we shall content ourselves with observing, *first,* that, in common life, the sentiments of censure or approbation produced by mental qualities of every kind are very similar; and *secondly,* that all ancient moralists (the best models), in treating of them, make little or no difference among them."

Edition N omits as far as "Were we to say," etc., (p. 129), and substitutes as follows: "Thus were we to seek an exact definition or description of those mental qualities which are denominated *virtues,* we might be somewhat at a loss and might find ourselves at first involved in inextricable difficulties."]

which shall contain all that I intend to say on the present subject.

First, I do not find that in the English, or any other modern tongue, the boundaries are exactly fixed between virtues and talents, vices and defects; or that a precise definition can be given of the one as contradistinguished from the other. Were we to say, for instance, that the esteemable qualities alone which are voluntary are entitled to the appellation of virtues, we should soon recollect the qualities of courage, equanimity, patience, self-command, with many others, which almost every language classes under this appellation, though they depend little or not at all on our choice. Should we affirm that the qualities alone which prompt us to act our part in society are entitled to that honorable distinction, it must immediately occur that these are indeed the most valuable qualities, and are commonly denominated the *social* virtues; but that this very epithet supposes that there are also virtues of another species.[3] Should we lay hold of the distinction between *intellectual* and *moral* endowments and affirm the last alone to be the real and genuine virtues, because they alone lead to action, we should find that many of those qualities usually called intellectual virtues, such as prudence, penetration, discernment, discretion, had also a considerable influence on conduct. The distinction between the *heart* and the *head* may also be adopted: the qualities of the first may be defined such as, in their immediate exertion, are accompanied with a feeling or sentiment, and these alone may be called the genuine virtues; but industry, frugality, temperance, secrecy, perseverance, and many other laudable powers or habits, generally styled virtues, are exerted without any immediate sentiment in the person possessed of them, and are only known to him by their effects. It is fortunate,

[3] [Edition N appends the following note:

"It seems to me, that in our language there are always said to be virtues of many different kinds; but when a man is said to be *virtuous* or is denominated a man of virtue, we chiefly regard his social qualities, which are indeed the most valuable. They are called the *virtues* by way of excellence."]

amidst all this seeming perplexity, that the question, being merely verbal, cannot possibly be of any importance. A moral, philosophical discourse needs not enter into all those caprices of language which are so variable in different dialects and in different ages of the same dialect.[4] But, on the whole, it seems to me that though it is always allowed that there are virtues of many different kinds, yet, when a man is called *virtuous*, or is denominated a man of virtue, we chiefly regard his social qualities, which are indeed the most valuable. It is at the same time certain that any remarkable defect in courage, temperance, economy, industry, understanding, dignity of mind would bereave even a very good-natured, honest man of this honorable appellation. Who did ever say, except by way of irony, that such a one was a man of great virtue, but an egregious blockhead?

But, *secondly*, it is no wonder that languages should not be very precise in marking the boundaries between virtues and talents, vices and defects, since there is so little distinction made in our internal estimation of them.] It seems, indeed, certain that the *sentiment* of conscious worth, the self-satisfaction proceeding from a review of a man's own conduct and character—it seems certain, I say, that this sentiment which, though the most common of all others, has no proper name in our language,[5]

---

4 [For the next four sentences Edition N substitutes as follows:

"It may happen that, in treating of ethics, we may sometimes mention laudable qualities which the English tongue does not always rank under the appellation of virtue; but we do it only because we are at a loss how to draw the exact line between the one and the other; or at least because we consider the question as merely grammatical. And the more fully to justify our practice in this particular, we shall endeavor to make it appear, *first*, that in common life the sentiments of censure or approbation produced by mental qualities of every kind are nearly similar; and *secondly*, that all ancient moralists (the best models), in treating of them, make little or no difference among them."]

5 The term pride is commonly taken in a bad sense; but this sentiment seems indifferent, and may be either good or bad, according as it is well or ill founded, and according to the other circumstances which accompany it. The French express this sentiment by the term *amour propre;* but as they also express self-love as well as vanity by the same term, there arises thence a great confusion in Rochefoucauld and many of their moral writers.

arises from the endowments of courage and capacity, industry and ingenuity, as well as from any other mental excellences. Who, on the other hand, is not deeply mortified with reflecting on his own folly and dissoluteness and feels not a secret sting or compunction whenever his memory presents any past occurrence where he behaved with stupidity or ill manners? No time can efface the cruel ideas of a man's own foolish conduct, or of affronts which cowardice or imprudence has brought upon him. They still haunt his solitary hours, damp his most aspiring thoughts, and show him, even to himself, in the most contemptible and most odious colors imaginable.

What is there, too, we are more anxious to conceal from others than such blunders, infirmities, and meannesses, or more dread to have exposed by raillery and satire? And is not the chief object of vanity: our bravery or learning, our wit or breeding, our eloquence or address, our taste or abilities? These we display with care, if not with ostentation; and we commonly show more ambition of excelling in them than even in the social virtues themselves, which are in reality of such superior excellence. Good nature and honesty, especially the latter, are so indispensably required that, though the greatest censure attends any violation of these duties, no eminent praise follows such common instances of them as seem essential to the support of human society. And hence the reason, in my opinion, why, though men often extol so liberally the qualities of their heart, they are shy in commending the endowments of their head; because the latter virtues, being supposed more rare and extraordinary, are observed to be the more usual objects of pride and self-conceit; and when boasted of, beget a strong suspicion of these sentiments.

It is hard to tell whether you hurt a man's character most by calling him a knave or a coward, and whether a beastly glutton or drunkard be not as odious and contemptible as a selfish, ungenerous miser. Give me my choice, and I would rather, for my own happiness and self-enjoyment, have a friendly, humane heart than possess all the other virtues of Demosthenes and Philip united. But I would rather pass with the world for one endowed with extensive genius and intrepid courage, and should thence expect stronger instances of general applause and admiration. The figure which a man makes in life, the reception which he meets with in company, the esteem paid him by his acquaintance—all these advantages depend as much upon his good sense and judgment as upon any other part of his character. Had a man the best intentions in the world and were the farthest removed from all injustice and violence, he would never be able to make himself be much regarded without a moderate share at least of parts and understanding.

What is it then we can here dispute about? If sense and courage, temperance and industry, wisdom and knowledge confessedly form a considerable part of *personal merit,* if a man possessed of these qualities is both better satisfied with himself and better entitled to the good will, esteem, and services of others than one entirely destitute of them—if, in short, the *sentiments* are similar which arise from these endowments and from the social virtues, is there any reason for being so extremely scrupulous about a *word,* or disputing whether they be entitled to the denomination of virtues? [6] It may, indeed, be pretended that the sentiment of approbation, which those accomplishments produce, besides its being *inferior,* is also somewhat *different* from that which attends the virtues of justice and humanity. But this seems not a sufficient reason for ranking them entirely under different classes and appellations. The character of Caesar and that af Cato, as drawn by Sallust, are

[6] [Editions G to M add in a note:

"It seems to me that in our language courage, temperance, industry, frugality, etc., according to popular style, are called *virtues;* but when a man is said to be *virtuous,* or is denominated a man of virtue, we chiefly regard his social qualities. It is needless for a moral, philosophical discourse to enter into all these caprices of language, which are so variable in different dialects, and in different ages of the same dialect. The *sentiments* of men, being more uniform as well as more important, are a fitter subject of speculation; though at the same time we may just observe that wherever the social virtues are talked of, it is plainly implied by this distinction that there are also other virtues of a different nature."]

both of them virtuous, in the strictest and most limited sense of the word, but in a different way; nor are the sentiments entirely the same which arise from them. The one produces love, the other esteem; the one is amiable, the other awful. We should wish to meet the one character in a friend, the other we should be ambitious of in ourselves. In like manner, the approbation which attends temperance, or industry, or frugality may be somewhat different from that which is paid to the social virtues, without making them entirely of a different species. And, indeed, we may observe that these endowments, more than the other virtues, produce not, all of them, the same kind of approbation. Good sense and genius beget esteem and regard; wit and humor excite love and affection.[7]

Most people, I believe, will naturally, without premeditation, assent to the definition of the elegant and judicious poet!

> Virtue (for mere good nature is a fool)
> Is sense and spirit with humanity.[8]

[7] LOVE and esteem are nearly the same passion, and arise from similar causes. The qualities which produce both are such as communicate pleasure. But where this pleasure is severe and serious; or where its object is great, and makes a strong impression; or where it produces any degree of humility and awe: in all these cases, the passion which arises from the pleasure is more properly denominated esteem than love. Benevolence attends both; but is connected with love in a more eminent degree. There seems to be still a stronger mixture of pride in contempt than of humility in esteem; and the reason would not be difficult to one who studied accurately the passions. All these various mixtures, and compositions, and appearances of sentiment form a very curious subject of speculation, but are wide of our present purpose. Throughout this inquiry, we always consider, in general, what qualities are a subject of praise or of censure, without entering into all the minute differences of sentiment which they excite. It is evident that whatever is contemned is also disliked, as well as what is hated; and we here endeavor to take objects according to their most simple views and appearances. These sciences are but too apt to appear abstract to common readers, even with all the precautions which we can take to clear them from superfluous speculations and bring them down to every capacity.

[8] [Armstrong:] *The Art of Preserving Health.* Book IV.

What pretensions has a man to our generous assistance or good offices who has dissipated his wealth in profuse expenses, idle vanities, chimerical projects, dissolute pleasures, or extravagant gaming? These vices (for we scruple not to call them such) bring misery unpitied and contempt on everyone addicted to them.

Achaeus, a wise and prudent prince, fell into a fatal snare which cost him his crown and life, after having used every reasonable precaution to guard himself against it. On that account, says the historian, he is a just object of regard and compassion; his betrayers alone of hatred and contempt.[9]

The precipitate flight and improvident negligence of Pompey, at the beginning of the civil wars, appeared such notorious blunders to Cicero as quite palled his friendship toward that great man. *In the same manner,* says he, *as want of cleanliness, decency, or discretion in a mistress are found to alienate our affections.* For so he expresses himself where he talks, not in the character of a philosopher, but in that of a statesman and man of the world, to his friend Atticus.[10]

But the same Cicero, in imitation of all the ancient moralists, when he reasons as a philosopher, enlarges very much his ideas of virtue and comprehends every laudable quality or endowment of the mind under that honorable appellation. [11] This leads to the *third* reflection which we proposed to make, to wit, that the ancient moralists, the best models, made no material distinction among the different species of mental endowments and defects, but treated all alike under the appellation of virtues and vices, and made them indiscriminately the object of their moral reasonings. The *prudence* explained in Cicero's *Offices* [12] is that sagacity which leads to the discovery of truth and preserves us from error and mistake. *Magnanimity, temperance, decency* are there also at large discoursed of. And as

9 Polybius, lib. viii. cap. 2, 8, and 9.
10 Lib. ix. epist. 10, 2.
11 [The following sentence was added in Edition O.]
12 Lib. i. cap. 6.

that eloquent moralist followed the common received division
of the four cardinal virtues, our social duties form but one
head in the general distribution of his subject.[13]

We need only peruse the titles of chapters in Aristotle's
Ethics to be convinced that he ranks courage, temperance,

[13] The following passage of Cicero is worth quoting, as being the most
clear and express to our purpose that anything can be imagined, and, in a
dispute which is chiefly verbal must, on account of the author, carry an
authority from which there can be no appeal.

"Virtus autem, quae est per se ipsa laudabilis, et sine qua nihil laudari
potest, tamen habet plures partes, quarum alia est aliâ ad laudationem
aptior. Sunt enim aliae virtutes, quae videntur in moribus hominum, et
quadam comitate ac beneficentia positae: aliae quae in ingenii aliqua fa-
cultate, aut animi magnitudine ac robore. Nam clementia, justitia, benig-
nitas, fides, fortitudo in periculis communibus, jucunda est auditu in lauda-
tionibus. Omnes enim hae virtutes non tam ipsis, qui eas in se habent,
quam generi hominum fructuosae putantur. Sapientia et magnitudo animi,
qua omnes res humanae, tenues et pro nihilo putantur; et in cogitando
vis quaedam ingenii, et ipsa eloquentia admirationis habet non minus,
jucunditatis minus. Ipsos enim magis videtur, quos laudamus, quam illos,
apud quos laudamus, ornare ac tueri: sed tamen in laudando jungenda
sunt etiam haec genera virtutum. Ferunt enim aures hominum, cum illa
quae jucunda et grata, tum etiam illa quae mirabilia sunt in virtute,
laudari." * *De orat.* lib. ii. cap. 84.

I suppose, if Cicero were now alive, it would be found difficult to fetter
his moral sentiments by narrow systems; or persuade him that no qualities
were to be admitted as *virtues,* or acknowledged to be a part of *personal
merit,* but what were recommended by *The Whole Duty of Man.* [This
note was added in Edition Q.]

* ["But virtue, which is worth praising for its own sake and without
which nothing can be praised, still does have several parts, some of which
are more suitable for praise than others. Some virtues seem to reside in
the manners men have, i.e., in some sort of friendliness and kindness;
others lie in some mental faculty, such as magnanimity and strength of
mind. For when praise is given, it is enjoyable to hear of mercy, justice,
kindness, loyalty, and courage in common dangers. For all these virtues
are regarded as advantageous not so much for those who have them but
for mankind. Wisdom and magnanimity, in whose light all human affairs
are considered trifling and worthless—and also a certain intellectual
power of thought and eloquence itself—are more admirable than enjoyable. For they seem to adorn and contemplate those whom we praise
rather than those before whom we praise them: however, these kinds of
virtue must also be brought in when praise is given. For human ears can
stand not only the praise of what is enjoyable and pleasant, but also of
what is admirable in virtue." *De oratore (Of the Orator).* ii. 84.]

magnificence, magnanimity, modesty, prudence, and a manly openness among the virtues, as well as justice and friendship.

To *sustain* and to *abstain,* that is, to be patient and continent, appeared to some of the ancients a summary comprehension of all morals.

Epictetus has scarcely ever mentioned the sentiment of humanity and compassion but in order to put his disciples on their guard against it. The virtue of the *Stoics* seems to consist chiefly in a firm temper and a sound understanding. With them, as with Solomon and the Eastern moralists, folly and wisdom are equivalent to vice and virtue.

Men will praise thee, says David,[14] when thou dost well unto thyself. I hate a wise man, says the Greek poet, who is not wise to himself.[15]

Plutarch is no more cramped by systems in his philosophy than in his history. Where he compares the great men of Greece and Rome, he fairly sets in opposition all their blemishes and accomplishments of whatever kind, and omits nothing considerable which can either depress or exalt their characters. His moral discourses contain the same free and natural censure of men and manners.

The character of Hannibal, as drawn by Livy,[16] is esteemed partial, but allows him many eminent virtues. Never was there a genius, says the historian, more equally fitted for those opposite offices of commanding and obeying; and it were, therefore, difficult to determine whether he rendered himself *dearer* to the general or to the army. To none would Hasdrubal entrust more willingly the conduct of any dangerous enterprise; under none did the soldiers discover more courage and confidence; great boldness in facing danger, great prudence in the

---

14 Psalm 49.

15 Μισῶ σοφιστὴν ὅστις σὐδ' αὐτῷ σοφός. Euripides [Fragment 905. Edition G gives as the reference: *Incert. apud Lucianum, apologia pro mercede conductis.* Edition K does the same in the text, but makes the correction in the Errata.]

16 Lib. xxi. cap. 4.

midst of it. No labor could fatigue his body or subdue his mind. Cold and heat were indifferent to him. Meat and drink he sought as supplies to the necessities of nature, not as gratifications of his voluptuous appetites. Waking or rest he used indiscriminately, by night or by day. These great *virtues* were balanced by great *vices:* inhuman cruelty; perfidy more than *punic:* no truth, no faith, no regard to oaths, promises or religion.

The character of Alexander the Sixth, to be found in Guicciardin,[17] is pretty similar, but juster, and is a proof that even the moderns, where they speak naturally, hold the same language with the ancients. In this pope, says he, there was a singular capacity and judgment: admirable prudence, a wonderful talent of persuasion, and in all momentous enterprises a diligence and dexterity incredible. But these *virtues* were infinitely overbalanced by his *vices:* no faith, no religion, insatiable avarice, exorbitant ambition, and a more than barbarous cruelty.

Polybius,[18] reprehending Timaeus for his partiality against Agathocles, whom he himself allows to be the most cruel and impious of all tyrants, says, If he took refuge in Syracuse, as asserted by that historian, flying the dirt and smoke and toil of his former profession of a potter; and if, proceeding from such slender beginnings, he became master in a little time of all Sicily, brought the Carthaginian state into the utmost danger, and at last died in old age and in possession of sovereign dignity —must he not be allowed something prodigious and extraordinary, and to have possessed great talents and capacity for business and action? His historian, therefore, ought not to have alone related what tended to his reproach and infamy, but also what might redound to his *praise* and *honor*.

In general, we may observe that the distinction of voluntary or involuntary was little regarded by the ancients in their moral reasonings, where they frequently treated the question

17 Lib. i.
18 Lib. xii. 15.

as very doubtful *whether virtue could be taught or not?* [19] They justly considered that cowardice, meanness, levity, anxiety, impatience, folly, and many other qualities of the mind might appear ridiculous and deformed, contemptible and odious, though independent of the will. Nor could it be supposed at all times in every man's power to attain every kind of mental more than of exterior beauty.

[20] And here there occurs the *fourth* reflection which I purposed to make, in suggesting the reason why modern philosophers have often followed a course in their moral inquiries so different from that of the ancients. In later times, philosophy of all kinds, especially ethics, have been more closely united with theology than ever they were observed to be among the heathens; and as this latter science admits of no terms of composition, but bends every branch of knowledge to its own purpose without much regard to the phenomena of nature, or to the unbiased sentiments of the mind, hence reasoning, and even language, have been warped from their natural course, and distinctions have been endeavored to be established where the difference of the objects was, in a manner, imperceptible. Philosophers, or rather divines under that disguise, treating all morals as on a like footing with civil laws guarded by the sanctions of reward and punishment, were necessarily led to render this circumstance of *voluntary* or *involuntary* the foundation of their whole theory. Everyone may employ *terms* in what sense he pleases; but this, in the meantime, must be allowed, that *sentiments* are every day experienced of blame and praise which have objects beyond the dominion of the will or choice, and of

[19] *Vid.* Plato in *Menone,* Seneca in *de otio sap.* cap. 31.* So also Horace, *Virtutem doctrina paret, naturane donet.*† *Epist.* lib. i. ep. 18, 100. Aeschines Socraticus, *Dial.* i. [The reference to Aes. Soc. was added in Edition O.]

   * [See Plato in *Meno;* Seneca in *De otio sapientis* ("On the Leisure of the Wise Man") 31.]

   † [("Whether learning paves the way for virtue or nature bestows it." *Epistles.* i. 18, 100.) Aeschines Socraticus, *Dialogue* I.]

[20] [This sentence and the next do not occur in Editions G to N, which resume: "But modern philosophers, treating," etc.]

which it behooves us, if not as moralists, as speculative philosophers at least, to give some satisfactory theory and explication.

A blemish, a fault, a vice, a crime—these expressions seem to denote different degrees of censure and disapprobation, which are, however, all of them, at the bottom pretty nearly of the same kind or species. The explication of one will easily lead us into a just conception of the others; [21] and it is of greater consequence to attend to things than to verbal appellations. That we owe a duty to ourselves is confessed even in the most vulgar system of morals; and it must be of consequence to examine that duty in order to see whether it bears any affinity to that which we owe to society. It is probable that the approbation attending the observance of both is of a similar nature and arises from similar principles, whatever appellation we may give to either of these excellences.

[21] [The remainder of the paragraph was added in Edition N.]

A DIALOGUE [1]

My friend Palamedes, who is as great a rambler in his principles as in his person, and who has run over, by study and travel, almost every region of the intellectual and material world, surprised me lately with an account of a nation with whom, he told me, he had passed a considerable part of his life, and whom he found, in the main, a people extremely civilized and intelligent.

There is a country, said he, in the world called Fourli, no matter for its longitude or latitude, whose inhabitants have ways of thinking in many things, particularly in morals, diametrically opposite to ours. When I came among them, I found that I must submit to double pains: first, to learn the meaning of the terms in their language, and, then, to know the import of those terms and the praise or blame attached to them. After a word had been explained to me, and a character which it expressed had been described, I concluded that such an epithet must necessarily be the greatest reproach in the world, and was extremely surprised to find one in a public company apply it to a person with whom he lived in the strictest intimacy and friendship. *You fancy,* said I one day to an acquaintance, *that Changuis is your mortal enemy: I love to extinguish quarrels; and I must therefore tell you that I heard him talk of you in the most obliging manner.* But to my great astonishment, when I repeated Changuis's words, though I had both remembered and understood them perfectly, I found that they were taken for the most mortal affront, and that I had very innocently rendered the breach between these persons altogether irreparable.

[1] [The author's sentiments underlying this essay are expressed in an exchange of letters between the author and Gilbert Elliot. See Burton, *Life and Correspondence of David Hume,* Vol. I, 12. Part of this correspondence is reprinted in the Green and Grose edition of *Essays Moral, Political, and Literary,* Vol. I, 52ff. (See also the Editor's Introduction, p. xvif.]

As it was my fortune to come among this people on a very advantageous footing, I was immediately introduced to the best company; and being desired by Alcheic to live with him, I readily accepted of his invitation, as I found him universally esteemed for his personal merit, and indeed regarded by everyone in Fourli as a perfect character.

One evening he invited me, as an amusement, to bear him company in a serenade which he intended to give to Gulki, with whom, he told me, he was extremely enamored; and I soon found that his taste was not singular; for we met many of his rivals who had come on the same errand. I very naturally concluded that this mistress [2] of his must be one of the finest women in town, and I already felt a secret inclination to see her and be acquainted with her. But as the moon began to rise, I was much surprised to find that we were in the midst of the university where Gulki studied; and I was somewhat ashamed for having attended my friend on such an errand.

I was afterwards told that Alcheic's choice of Gulki was very much approved of by all the good company in town, and that it was expected, while he gratified his own passion, he would perform to that young man the same good office which he had himself owed to Elcouf. It seems Alcheic had been very handsome in his youth, had been courted by many lovers, but had bestowed his favors chiefly on the sage Elcouf, to whom he was supposed to owe, in a great measure, the astonishing progress which he had made in philosophy and virtue.

It gave me some surprise that Alcheic's wife (who by-the-by happened also to be his sister) was nowise scandalized at this species of infidelity.

Much about the same time I discovered (for it was not attempted to be kept a secret from me or anybody) that Alcheic was a murderer and a parricide, and had put to death an innocent person, the most nearly connected with him, and whom he was bound to protect and defend by all the ties of nature and humanity. When I asked, with all the caution and defer-

[2] ["Flame of his" in editions G and K.]

ence imaginable, what was his motive for this action, he replied coolly that he was not then so much at ease in his circumstances as he is at present, and that he had acted, in that particular, by the advice of all his friends.

Having heard Alcheic's virtue so extremely celebrated, I pretended to join in the general voice of acclamation, and only asked, by way of curiosity, as a stranger, which of all his noble actions was most highly applauded; and I soon found that all sentiments were united in giving the preference to the assassination of Usbek. This Usbek had been to the last moment Alcheic's intimate friend, had laid many high obligations upon him, had even saved his life on a certain occasion, and had, by his will, which was found after the murder, made him heir to a considerable part of his fortune. Alcheic, it seems, conspired with about twenty or thirty more, most of them also Usbek's friends; and falling all together on that unhappy man when he was not aware, they had torn him with a hundred wounds and given him that reward for all his past favors and obligations. Usbek, said the general voice of the people, had many great and good qualities: his very vices were shining, magnificent, and generous; but this action of Alcheic's sets him far above Usbek in the eyes of all judges of merit, and is one of the noblest that ever perhaps the sun shone upon.

Another part of Alcheic's conduct, which I also found highly applauded, was his behavior toward Calish, with whom he was joined in a project or undertaking of some importance. Calish, being a passionate man, gave Alcheic one day a sound drubbing, which he took very patiently, waited the return of Calish's good humor, kept still a fair correspondence with him, and by that means brought the affair in which they were joined to a happy issue and gained to himself immortal honor by his remarkable temper and moderation.

I have lately received a letter from a correspondent in Fourli by which I learn that, since my departure, Alcheic, falling into a bad state of health, has fairly hanged himself and has died, universally regretted and applauded in that country. So virtuous and noble a life, says each Fourlian, could not be better crowned than by so noble an end; and Alcheic has proved by this, as well as by all his other actions, what was his constant principle during his life, and what he boasted of near his last moments, that a wise man is scarcely inferior to the great god Vitzli. This is the name of the supreme deity among the Fourlians.

The notions of this people, continued Palamedes, are as extraordinary with regard to good manners and sociableness as with regard to morals. My friend Alcheic formed once a party for my entertainment composed of all the prime wits and philosophers of Fourli, and each of us brought his mess along with him to the place where we assembled. I observed one of them to be worse provided than the rest and offered him a share of my mess, which happened to be a roasted pullet; and I could not but remark that he and all the rest of the company smiled at my simplicity. I was told that Alcheic had once so much interest with his club as to prevail with them to eat in common, and that he had made use of an artifice for that purpose. He persuaded those whom he observed to be *worst* provided to offer their mess to the company; after which the others, who had brought more delicate fare, were ashamed not to make the same offer. This is regarded as so extraordinary an event that it has since, as I learn, been recorded in the history of Alcheic's life, composed by one of the greatest geniuses of Fourli.

Pray, said I, Palamedes, when you were at Fourli, did you also learn the art of turning your friends into ridicule by telling them strange stories and then laughing at them if they believed you? I assure you, replied he, had I been disposed to learn such a lesson, there was no place in the world more proper. My friend, so often mentioned, did nothing from morning to night but sneer, and banter, and rally; and you could scarcely ever distinguish whether he were in jest or earnest. But you think, then, that my story is improbable, and that I have used, or rather abused, the privilege of a traveler. To be sure, said I, you were but in jest. Such barbarous and savage manners are not only incompatible with a civilized, intelligent people, such as you said these were, but are scarcely compatible with human nature. They exceed all we ever read of among the Mingrelians and Topinamboues.

Have a care, cried he, have a care! You are not aware that you are speaking blasphemy and are abusing your favorites, the Greeks, especially the Athenians, whom I have couched, all along, under these bizarre names I employed. If you consider aright, there is not one stroke of the foregoing character which might not be found in the man of highest merit at Athens, without diminishing in the least from the brightness of his character. The amours of the Greeks, their marriages,[3] and the exposing of their children cannot but strike you immediately. The death of Usbek is an exact counterpart to that of Caesar.

All to a trifle, said I, interrupting him; you did not mention that Usbek was a usurper.

I did not, replied he, lest you should discover the parallel I aimed at. But even adding this circumstance, we should make no scruple, according to our sentiments of morals, to denominate Brutus and Cassius ungrateful traitors and assassins, though you know that they are, perhaps, the highest characters of all antiquity; and the Athenians erected statues to them, which they placed near those of Harmodius and Aristogiton, their own deliverers. And if you think this circumstance which you mention so material to absolve these patriots, I shall compensate it by another, not mentioned, which will equally aggravate their crime. A few days before the execution of their fatal purpose, they all swore fealty to Caesar; and protesting to hold his person ever sacred, they touched the altar with those hands which they had already armed for his destruction.[4]

I need not remind you of the famous and applauded story of Themistocles, and of his patience toward Eurybiades the Spar-

---

[3] The laws of Athens allowed a man to marry his sister by the father. Solon's law forbids pederasty to slaves, as being an act of too great dignity for such mean persons.

[4] Appian. *Bell. civ.* lib. iii. Suetonius in *Vita Caesaris* 84.

tan, his commanding officer who, heated by debate, lifted his cane to him in a council of war (the same thing as if he had cudgeled him). *Strike!* cries the Athenian, *strike! but hear me.*

You are too good a scholar not to discover the ironical Socrates and his Athenian club in my last story; and you will certainly observe that it is exactly copied from Xenophon, with a variation only of the names; [5] and I think I have fairly made it appear that an Athenian man of merit might be such a one as with us would pass for incestuous, a parricide, an assassin, an ungrateful, perjured traitor, and something else too abominable to be named, not to mention his rusticity and ill-manners; and having lived in this manner, his death might be entirely suitable. He might conclude the scene by a desperate act of self-murder, and die with the most absurd blasphemies in his mouth. And notwithstanding all this, he shall have statues if not altars erected to his memory; poems and orations shall be composed in his praise; great sects shall be proud of calling themselves by his name; and the most distant posterity shall blindly continue their admiration, though, were such a one to arise among themselves, they would justly regard him with horror and execration.

I might have been aware, replied I, of your artifice. You seem to take pleasure in this topic and are, indeed, the only man I ever knew who was well acquainted with the ancients and did not extremely admire them. But instead of attacking their philosophy, their eloquence, or poetry, the usual subjects of controversy between us, you now seem to impeach their morals and accuse them of ignorance in a science which is the only one, in my opinion, in which they are not surpassed by the moderns. Geometry, physics, astronomy, anatomy, botany, geography, navigation—in these we justly claim the superiority; but what have we to oppose to their moralists? Your representation of things is fallacious. You have no indulgence for the manners and customs of different ages. Would you try a Greek or Roman by the common law of England? Hear him defend himself by his own maxims, and then pronounce.

[5] *Mem. Soc.* lib. iii. 14, 1.

There are no manners so innocent or reasonable but may be rendered odious or ridiculous if measured by a standard unknown to the persons, especially if you employ a little art or eloquence in aggravating some circumstances and extenuating others, as best suits the purpose of your discourse. All these artifices may easily be retorted on you. Could I inform the Athenians, for instance, that there was a nation in which adultery, both active and passive, so to speak, was in the highest vogue and esteem, in which every man of education chose for his mistress a married woman, the wife, perhaps, of his friend and companion, and valued himself upon these infamous conquests as much as if he had been several times a conqueror in boxing or wrestling at the Olympic games; in which every man also took a pride in his tameness and facility with regard to his own wife and was glad to make friends or gain interest by allowing her to prostitute her charms, and even, without any such motive, gave her full liberty and indulgence—I ask what sentiments the Athenians would entertain of such a people, they who never mentioned the crime of adultery but in conjunction with robbery and poisoning? Which would they admire most, the villainy or the meanness of such a conduct?

Should I add that the same people were as proud of their slavery and dependence as the Athenians of their liberty; and though a man among them were oppressed, disgraced, impoverished, insulted, or imprisoned by the tyrant, he would still regard it as the highest merit to love, serve, and obey him, and even to die for his smallest glory or satisfaction. These noble Greeks would probably ask me whether I spoke of a human society or of some inferior servile species.

It was then I might inform my Athenian audience that these people, however, wanted not spirit and bravery. If a man, say I, though their intimate friend, should throw out, in a private company, a raillery against them, nearly approaching any of those with which your generals and demagogues every day regale each other in the face of the whole city, they never can forgive him; but in order to revenge themselves, they oblige him immediately to run them through the body, or be himself murdered. And if a man who is an absolute stranger to them should desire them, at the peril of their own life, to cut the throat of their bosom companion, they immediately obey and think themselves highly obliged and honored by the commission. These are their maxims of honor; this is their favorite morality.

But though so ready to draw their sword against their friends and countrymen, no disgrace, no infamy, no pain, no poverty will ever engage these people to turn the point of it against their own breast. A man of rank would row in the galleys, would beg his bread, would languish in prison, would suffer any tortures, and still preserve his wretched life. Rather than escape his enemies by a generous contempt of death, he would infamously receive the same death from his enemies, aggravated by their triumphant insults, and by the most exquisite sufferings.

It is very usual too, continue I, among this people, to erect jails where every art of plaguing and tormenting the unhappy prisoners is carefully studied and practiced. And in these jails it is usual for a parent voluntarily to shut up several of his children in order that another child whom he owns to have no greater or rather less merit than the rest may enjoy his whole fortune and wallow in every kind of voluptuousness and pleasure. Nothing so virtuous in their opinion as this barbarous partiality.

But what is more singular in this whimsical nation, say I to the Athenians, is that a frolic of yours during the Saturnalia,[6] when the slaves are served by their masters, is seriously continued by them throughout the whole year, and throughout the whole course of their lives, accompanied, too, with some circumstances which still further augment the absurdity and ridicule. Your sport only elevates for a few days those whom fortune has thrown down, and whom she, too, in sport, may really elevate forever above you; but this nation gravely exalts those whom nature has subjected to them, and whose inferiority and infirmities are absolutely incurable. The women,

[6] The Greeks kept the feast of Saturn or Cronus, as well as the Romans. See Lucian. *Epist. Saturn.*

though without virtue, are their masters and sovereigns: these they reverence, praise, and magnify; to these they pay the highest deference and respect; and in all places and all times, the superiority of the females is readily acknowledged and submitted to by everyone who has the least pretensions to education and politeness. Scarce any crime would be so universally detested as an infraction of this rule.

You need go no farther, replied Palamedes; I can easily conjecture the people whom you aim at. The strokes with which you have painted them are pretty just, and yet you must acknowledge that scarce any people are to be found, either in ancient or modern times, whose national character is, upon the whole, less liable to exception. But I give you thanks for helping me out with my argument. I had no intention of exalting the moderns at the expense of the ancients. I only meant to represent the uncertainty of all these judgments concerning characters, and to convince you that fashion, vogue, custom, and law were the chief foundation of all moral determinations. The Athenians, surely, were a civilized, intelligent people, if ever there were one; and yet their man of merit might, in this age, be held in horror and execration. The French are also, without doubt, a very civilized, intelligent people; and yet their man of merit might, with the Athenians, be an object of the highest contempt and ridicule, and even hatred. And what renders the matter more extraordinary: these two people are supposed to be the most similar in their national character of any in ancient and modern times; and while the English flatter themselves that they resemble the Romans, their neighbors on the Continent draw the parallel between themselves and those polite Greeks. What wide difference, therefore, in the sentiments of morals must be found between civilized nations and barbarians, or between nations whose characters have little in common? How shall we pretend to fix a standard for judgments of this nature?

By tracing matters, replied I, a little higher and examining the first principles which each nation establishes of blame or censure. The Rhine flows north, the Rhone south; yet both spring from the *same* mountain, and are also actuated, in their opposite directions, by the *same* principle of gravity. The different inclinations of the ground on which they run cause all the difference of their courses.

In how many circumstances would an Athenian and a Frenchman of merit certainly resemble each other? Good sense, knowledge, wit, eloquence, humanity, fidelity, truth, justice, courage, temperance, constancy, dignity of mind—these you have all omitted in order to insist only on the points in which they may by accident differ. Very well; I am willing to comply with you and shall endeavor to account for these differences from the most universal, established principles of morals.

The Greek loves I care not to examine more particularly. I shall only observe that, however blamable, they arose from a very innocent cause, the frequency of the gymnastic exercises among that people, and were recommended, though absurdly, as the source of friendship, sympathy, mutual attachment, and fidelity [7]—qualities esteemed in all nations and all ages.

The marriage of half brothers and sisters seems no great difficulty. Love between the nearer relations is contrary to reason and public utility; but the precise point where we are to stop can scarcely be determined by natural reason, and is therefore a very proper subject for municipal law or custom. If the Athenians went a little too far on the one side, the canon law has surely pushed matters a great way into the other extreme.[8]

Had you asked a parent at Athens why he bereaved his child of that life which he had so lately given it, It is because I love it, he would reply, and regard the poverty which it must inherit from me as a greater evil than death, which it is not capable of dreading, feeling, or resenting.[9]

How is public liberty, the most valuable of all blessings, to be recovered from the hands of a usurper or tyrant if his power shields him from public rebellion and our scruples from

---

[7] Plat. *Symp.* p. 182. Ex edit. Seranir.

[8] See *Inquiry*, Sect. IV, "Of Political Society."

[9] Plut. *De amore prolis, sub fine.*

private vengeance? That his crime is capital by law, you acknowledge; and must the highest aggravation of his crime, the putting of himself above law, form his full security? You can reply nothing but by showing the great inconveniences of assassination; which, could anyone have proved clearly to the ancients, he had reformed their sentiments in this particular.

Again, to cast your eye on the picture which I have drawn of modern manners, there is almost as great difficulty, I acknowledge, to justify French as Greek gallantry, except only that the former is much more natural and agreeable than the latter. But our neighbors, it seems, have resolved to sacrifice some of the domestic to the social pleasures and to prefer ease, freedom, and an open commerce to a strict fidelity and constancy. These ends are both good, and are somewhat difficult to reconcile; nor need we be surprised if the customs of nations incline too much, sometimes to the one side, sometimes to the other.

The most inviolable attachment to the laws of our country is everywhere acknowledged a capital virtue; and where the people are not so happy as to have any legislature but a single person, the strictest loyalty is, in that case, the truest patriotism.

Nothing surely can be more absurd and barbarous than the practice of dueling; but those who justify it say that it begets civility and good manners. And a duelist, you may observe, always values himself upon his courage, his sense of honor, his fidelity and friendship—qualities which are here indeed very oddly directed, but which have been esteemed universally since the foundation of the world.

Have the gods forbidden self-murder? An Athenian allows that it ought to be forborne. Has the Deity permitted it? A Frenchman allows that death is preferable to pain and infamy.

You see then, continued I, that the principles upon which men reason in morals are always the same, though the conclusions which they draw are often very different. That they all reason aright with regard to this subject, more than with regard to any other, it is not incumbent on any moralist to show. It is sufficient that the original principles of censure or blame are uniform, and that erroneous conclusions can be corrected by sounder reasoning and larger experience. Though many ages have elapsed since the fall of Greece and Rome, though many changes have arrived in religion, language, laws, and customs, none of these revolutions has ever produced any considerable innovation in the primary sentiments of morals more than in those of external beauty. Some minute differences, perhaps, may be observed in both. Horace [10] celebrates a low forehead, and Anacreon joined eyebrows; [11] but the Apollo and the Venus of antiquity are still our models for male and female beauty; in like manner as the character of Scipio continues our standard for the glory of heroes, and that of Cornelia for the honor of matrons.

It appears that there never was any quality recommended by anyone, as a virtue or moral excellence, but on account of its being *useful* or *agreeable* to a man *himself* or to *others*. For what other reason can ever be assigned for praise or approbation? Or where would be the sense of extolling a *good* character or action which, at the same time, is allowed to be *good for nothing?* All the differences, therefore, in morals may be reduced to this one general foundation and may be accounted for by the different views which people take of these circumstances.

Sometimes men differ in their judgment about the usefulness of any habit or action; sometimes also the peculiar circumstances of things render one moral quality more useful than others and give it a peculiar preference.

It is not surprising that during a period of war and disorder the military virtues should be more celebrated than the pacific and attract more the admiration and attention of mankind.

How usual is it (says Tully [Cicero]) to find Cimbrians, Celtiberians, and other barbarians, who bear with inflexible constancy all the fatigues and dangers of the field, but are immediately dispirited under the pain and hazard of a languishing distemper; while, on the other hand, the Greeks

---

10 *Epist*. lib. i. epist. 7, 26. Also lib. i. ode 3.
11 Ode 28. Petronius (cap. 86) joins both these circumstances as beauties.

patiently endure the slow approaches of death, when armed with sickness and disease, but timorously fly his presence when he attacks them violently with swords and falchions! [12]

So different is even the same virtue of courage among warlike or peaceful nations! And indeed we may observe that, as the difference between war and peace is the greatest that arises among nations and public societies, it produces also the greatest variations in moral sentiment and diversifies the most our ideas of virtue and personal merit.

Sometimes, too, magnanimity, greatness of mind, disdain of slavery, inflexible rigor and integrity may better suit the circumstances of one age than those of another, and have a more kindly influence, both on public affairs and on a man's own safety and advancement. Our idea of merit, therefore, will also vary a little with these variations; and Labeo, perhaps, be censured for the same qualities which procured Cato the highest approbation.

A degree of luxury may be ruinous and pernicious in a native of Switzerland, which only fosters the arts, and encourages industry in a Frenchman or Englishman. We are not, therefore, to expect either the same sentiments or the same laws in Berne which prevail in London or Paris.

Different customs have also some influence as well as different utilities, and by giving an early bias to the mind may produce a superior propensity either to the useful or the agreeable qualities, to those which regard self or those which extend to society. These four sources of moral sentiment still subsist, but particular accidents may, at one time, make any one of them flow with greater abundance than at another.

The customs of some nations shut up the women from all social commerce. Those of others make them so essential a part of society and conversation that, except where business is transacted, the male sex alone are supposed almost wholly incapable of mutual discourse and entertainment. As this difference is the most material that can happen in private life, it must also produce the greatest variation in our moral sentiments.

[12] *Tusc. Quaest.* lib. ii, 27.

Of all nations in the world where polygamy was not allowed, the Greeks seem to have been the most reserved in their commerce with the fair sex, and to have imposed on them the strictest laws of modesty and decency. We have a strong instance of this in an oration of Lysias.[13] A widow, injured, ruined, undone, calls a meeting of a few of her nearest friends and relations; and though never before accustomed, says the orator, to speak in the presence of men, the distress of her circumstances constrained her to lay the case before them. The very opening of her mouth in such company required, it seems, an apology.

When Demosthenes prosecuted his tutors to make them refund his patrimony, it became necessary for him, in the course of the lawsuit, to prove that the marriage of Aphobus's sister with Onetor was entirely fraudulent, and that, notwithstanding her sham marriage, she had lived with her brother at Athens for two years past, ever since her divorce from her former husband. And it is remarkable that though these were people of the first fortune and distinction in the city, the orator could prove this fact noway but by calling for her female slaves to be put to the question, and by the evidence of one physician who had seen her in her brother's house during her illness.[14] So reserved were Greek manners.

We may be assured that an extreme purity of manners was the consequence of this reserve. Accordingly we find that, except the fabulous stories of a Helen and a Clytemnestra, there scarcely is an instance of any event in the Greek history which proceeded from the intrigues of women. On the other hand, in modern times, particularly in a neighboring nation, the females enter into all transactions and all management of church and state; and no man can expect success who takes not care to obtain their good graces. Harry the Third, by incurring the displeasure of the fair endangered his crown and lost his life as much as by his indulgence to heresy.

13 *Orat.* 33.
14 In *Onetorem,* [873-4].

It is needless to dissemble: the consequence of a very free commerce between the sexes, and of their living much together, will often terminate in intrigues and gallantry. We must sacrifice somewhat of the *useful* if we be very anxious to obtain all the *agreeable* qualities, and cannot pretend to reach alike every kind of advantage. Instances of license, daily multiplying, will weaken the scandal with the one sex and teach the other, by degrees, to adopt the famous maxim of La Fontaine with regard to female infidelity, *that if one knows it, it is but a small matter: if one knows it not, it is nothing.*[15]

Some people are inclined to think that the best way of adjusting all differences and of keeping the proper medium between the *agreeable* and the *useful* qualities of the sex is to live with them after the manner of the Romans and the English (for the customs of these two nations seem similar in this respect)[16]—that is, without gallantry[17] and without jealousy. By a parity of reason, the customs of the Spaniards and of the Italians of an age ago (for the present are very different) must be the worst of any because they favor both gallantry and jealousy.

Nor will these different customs of nations affect the one sex only; their idea of personal merit in the males must also be somewhat different with regard at least to conversation, address, and humor. The one nation where the men live much apart will naturally more approve of prudence, the other of gaiety. With the one, simplicity of manners will be in the highest esteem; with the other, politeness. The one will distinguish

---

[15] Quand on le sçait c'est peu de chose;
Quand on l'ignore, ce n'est rien.

[16] During the time of the emperors, the Romans seem to have been more given to intrigues and gallantry than the English are at present: and the women of condition, in order to retain their lovers, endeavored to fix a name of reproach on those who were addicted to wenching and low amours. They were called *Ancillarioli.* See Seneca *de beneficiis,* lib. i. cap. 9. See also Martial. lib. xii. epig. 58.

[17] The gallantry here meant is that of amours and attachments, not that of complaisance, which is as much paid to the fair sex in England as in any other country.

themselves by good sense and judgment, the other by taste and delicacy. The eloquence of the former will shine most in the senate, that of the other on the theater.

These, I say, are the *natural* effects of such customs. For it must be confessed that chance has a great influence on national manners; and many events happen in society which are not to be accounted for by general rules. Who could imagine, for instance, that the Romans, who lived freely with their women, should be very indifferent about music and esteem dancing infamous, while the Greeks, who never almost saw a woman but in their own houses, were continually piping, singing, and dancing?

The differences of moral sentiment which naturally arise from a republican or monarchical government are also very obvious, as well as those which proceed from general riches or poverty, union or faction, ignorance or learning. I shall conclude this long discourse with observing that different customs and situations vary not the original ideas of merit (however they may some consequences) in any very essential point, and prevail chiefly with regard to young men, who can aspire to the agreeable qualities and may attempt to please. The *manner,* the *ornaments,* the *graces* which succeed in this shape are more arbitrary and casual; but the merit of riper years is almost everywhere the same and consists chiefly in integrity, humanity, ability, knowledge, and the other more solid and useful qualities of the human mind.

What you insist on, replied Palamedes, may have some foundation when you adhere to the maxims of common life and ordinary conduct. Experience and the practice of the world readily correct any great extravagance on either side. But what say you to *artificial* lives and manners? How do you reconcile the maxims on which, in different ages and nations, these are founded?

What do you understand by *artificial* lives and manners? said I. I explain myself, replied he. You know that religion had, in ancient times, very little influence on common life, and that, after men had performed their duty in sacrifices and prayers at the temple, they thought that the gods left the rest of their conduct to themselves and were little pleased or offended with those virtues or vices which only affected the peace and happiness of human society. In those ages, it was the business of philosophy alone to regulate men's ordinary behavior and deportment; and, accordingly, we may observe that this being the sole principle by which a man could elevate himself above his fellows, it acquired a mighty ascendant over many and produced great singularities of maxims and of conduct. At present, when philosophy has lost the allurement of novelty, it has no such extensive influence, but seems to confine itself mostly to speculations in the closet, in the same manner as the ancient religion was limited to sacrifices in the temple. Its place is now supplied by the modern religion, which inspects our whole conduct and prescribes a universal rule to our actions, to our words, to our very thoughts and inclinations—a rule so much the more austere as it is guarded by infinite, though distant, rewards and punishments, and no infraction of it can ever be concealed or disguised.

Diogenes is the most celebrated model of extravagant philosophy. Let us seek a parallel to him in modern times. We shall not disgrace any philosophic name by a comparison with the Dominics or Loyolas, or any canonized monk or friar. Let us compare him to Pascal, a man of parts and genius, as well as Diogenes himself, and perhaps, too, a man of virtue had he allowed his virtuous inclinations to have exerted and displayed themselves.

The foundation of Diogenes' conduct was an endeavor to render himself an independent being as much as possible, and to confine all his wants and desires and pleasures within himself and his own mind. The aim of Pascal was to keep a perpetual sense of his dependence before his eyes, and never to forget his numberless wants and infirmities. The ancient supported himself by magnanimity, ostentation, pride, and the idea of his own superiority above his fellow creatures. The modern made constant profession of humility and abasement, of the contempt and hatred of himself, and endeavored to attain these supposed virtues as far as they are attainable. The austerities of the Greek were in order to inure himself to hardships and prevent his ever suffering; those of the Frenchman were embraced merely for their own sake, and in order to suffer as much as possible. The philosopher indulged himself in the most beastly pleasures, even in public; the saint refused himself the most innocent, even in private. The former thought it his duty to love his friends, and to rail at them, and reprove them, and scold them; the latter endeavored to be absolutely indifferent toward his nearest relations and to love and speak well of his enemies. The great object of Diogenes' wit was every kind of superstition, that is, every kind of religion known in his time. The mortality of the soul was his standard principle; and even his sentiments of a Divine Providence seem to have been licentious. The most ridiculous superstitions directed Pascal's faith and practice; and an extreme contempt of this life, in comparison of the future, was the chief foundation of his conduct.

In such a remarkable contrast do these two men stand, yet both of them have met with general admiration in their different ages, and have been proposed as models of imitation. Where, then, is the universal standard of morals which you talk of? And what rule shall we establish for the many different, nay, contrary sentiments of mankind?

An experiment, said I, which succeeds in the air will not always succeed in a vacuum. When men depart from the maxims of common reason and affect these *artificial* lives, as you call them, no one can answer for what will please or displease them. They are in a different element from the rest of mankind, and the natural principles of their mind play not with the same regularity as if left to themselves, free from the illusions of religious superstition or philosophical enthusiasm.